Wisdom With
Understanding
is Better
Than Rubies

Lurine Karon Greenberg
Fine Arts Collection

The Lhasa Atlas

The Lhasa Atlas

Traditional Tibetan Architecture and Townscape

Knud Larsen and
Amund Sinding–Larsen

Shambhala

Boston

2001

Shambhala Publications, Inc.
Horticultural Hall
300 Massachusetts Avenue
Boston, Massachusetts 02115
www.shambhala.com

Published in association with
Serindia Publications, UK

9 8 7 6 5 4 3 2 1

First Shambhala Edition

Printed and bound in Florence, Italy, by Conti Tipocolor
This edition is printed on acid-free paper that meets the
American National Standards Institute z39.48 Standard.

Distributed in the United States by Random House, Inc.,
and in Canada by Random House of Canada Ltd

Library of Congress Cataloging-in-Publication Data

Sinding-Larsen, Amund
    The Lhasa atlas: traditional Tibetan architecture and townscape / Amund Sinding-Larsen and Knud
Larsen
        p. cm.
    Includes bibliographical references and index.
    ISBN 1–57062–867–X (cloth: alk. paper)
        1. Vernacular architecture — China — Lhasa. 2. Historic buildings — China — Lhasa. 3. Lhasa
(China) — Buildings, structures, etc. 4. Lhasa (China) — Maps. I. Larsen, Knud. II. Title

NA1547.L45 S56 2001
720'.951'5'—dc21   2001031142
                                                                                                                     CIP

*Page 2: The most important monuments
of 18th-century Central Tibet. Thangka
painting, Musée Guimet, Paris. Photo
RMN – Jean Schormans.*

Contents

Illustration Sources

PHOTOGRAPHS

All photographs are by Knud Larsen, except the following, for which permission has kindly been granted:

The British Library: p. 22, 26 top.

Trustees of The British Museum: pp. 16–17, 27, 86 left, 87 right, 143 centre.

LHCA project (1995–97): pp. 60E, 61H, 61I, 99, 111 bottom, 112 bottom left, 112 bottom right, 119, 125, 127 bottom, 135 bottom right, 135 top, 136 top left, 136 bottom right, 137 all, 142 both, 144 all, 146 bottom right.

Erik Bjerketvedt Nordbye (2000): p. 155.

NTNU Student Group (1994): pp. 130 both, 131, 133 top.

The Pitt Rivers Museum, University of Oxford: p. 26 bottom, photo no. BL.H.274; p. 32 top, photo no. SC.T.2.292; p. 36, photo no. SC.T.2.224, p. 53 bottom, photo no. BL.H.137, p. 122, photo no. SC.T.2.271.

The Royal Geographical Society: pp. 32 bottom, 90 right, 146 left.

SATELLITE PHOTOGRAPHS

The satellite photographs are from the first generation U.S. photo-reconnaissance program – CORONA – which operated from June 1959 to May 1972. Images presented in this book to a special scale have been digitally enhanced.

MAPS

All maps not publicly available have been produced specially for this book by the LHCA project, except the following:

Courtesy of Dr. Martin Brauen, University of Zürich: pp. 28 top, 29.

The British Library: pp. 8, 20–21.

Courtesy of Professor Emeritus Chie Nakane, University of Tokyo: pp. 30, 31.

PAINTINGS

The paintings are reproduced by permission of the following:

Musée des arts asiatiques-Guimet, Paris (Jean Schormans): cover and p. 2.

Courtesy of the Kanwal Krishna heirs: pp. 19 both, 95 top, 101, 107 top left, 149 bottom.

Tsewang Tashi: p. 18.

LINE DRAWINGS

All line drawings are made specially for this book by the authors from LHCA surveys and the following sources:

Archaeological Studies on Monasteries of the Tibetan Buddhism. 1996: pp. 113, 148 left.

Chinese Ancient Constructions, Potala Palace in Tibet. 1996: pp. 49, 102, 104–105, 109, 111.

Demeures des Hommes, Sanctuaires des Dieux. 1987: p. 50.

The History of the Cultural Relics of Lhasa. 1985: pp. 88 bottom, 110, 122, 138, 139, 140, 141, 146.

The Jokhang Temple. 1985: pp. 46 top right, 48, 114, 115.

Minyag Chökyi Gyaltsen (1995–97): pp. 46 top left both, 47, 51, 52, 120, 121, 126, 127 bottom left, 128 bottom, 129 bottom.

NTNU Student Group (1994): 130, 131.

Tibet Heritage Fund (1997–99): pp. 114 bottom, 118, 125, 127 top both, 128 top, 129 top, 132, 134, 135, 136, 137.

List of Maps

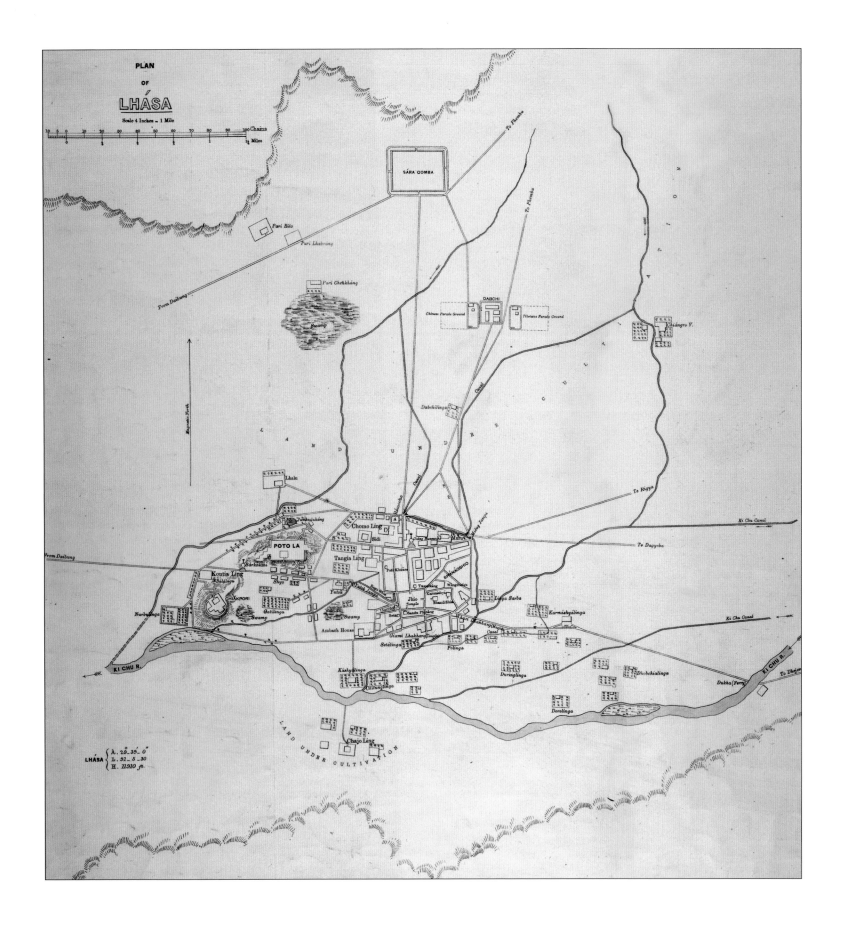

Preface and Acknowledgements

In the summer of 1994, the authors of this book conceived of an idea for a research project called the 'Lhasa Historical City Atlas' (LHCA). The idea evolved from discussions in Lhasa that established the Network for University Cooperation Tibet-Norway, a network[1] which allows academic institutions in Tibet and Norway to exchange scholars and students and conduct joint research.

After seven years of effort, a result is *The Lhasa Atlas*, a book that documents Lhasa old town in a manner and with an accuracy surpassing anything published before, with new digital maps of the historical urban area and new architectural knowledge, especially of Lhasa's traditional secular buildings.

This book aims to describe the architectural and spatial features that give the old town its particular character, as well as the special topological and historical relationships that make Lhasa unique. Through text and maps, the book also presents important aspects relating to the conservation of individual buildings and townscape. In order to put our recent documentation of old Lhasa in a larger perspective, we include earlier surveys and maps, and introduce traditional methods of decoration and building in Tibetan architecture.

To understand the background to *The Lhasa Atlas*, it is useful to review the many elements of the 'Lhasa Historical City Atlas' project. The LHCA project focused on the traditional townscape area inside the Lingkor, the 7.5-kilometres pilgrim route surrounding old Lhasa. The study area, bordered by the four streets of Lingkor Chang Lam (north), Jingdrol Shar Lam (south), Lingkor Nub Lam (west) and Lingkor Shar Lam (east), is approximately 4 square kilometres, though the old town itself makes up only a quarter of this.

Project members surveyed and documented buildings within the Lingkor boundary. At the start of fieldwork in 1995, in all 330 secular and religious old buildings were registered; this number was reduced to around 200 buildings at the end of fieldwork in 1999. Because of this destruction, the LHCA material gathered is now partly historical.

The LHCA project objectives were:

- to register and document all historical buildings constructed before 1950 and still existing when the survey started in 1995. We include a few buildings from the 1950s. Also, to document the historical townscape by securing as much information as possible about the old town, its history and its architectural components. This is particularly important because traditional knowledge, not just traditional buildings, is disappearing fast;

- to establish a practical dialogue with relevant authorities in Lhasa;

- to establish cooperation with experts in order to contribute to the exchange of knowledge.

The historical buildings and townscape of old Lhasa have never been recorded in such detail as undertaken by the LHCA project. The project is but one aspect of increasing public activity concerned with safeguarding Lhasa's unique cultural heritage, a process that must be balanced with the needs of a contemporary urban environment.

Fieldwork started in 1995; main registration and photographic work took place in 1996–98; and in 1998–99 all remaining historical buildings were again visited and reviewed. During our visits to Lhasa – at least once and usually twice each year – we presented our project work and carried on extensive and fruitful discussions with our Lhasa partners and local authorities.

The method of documentation focused on a level of registration and analysis similar to that used in 'emergency archaeology', with baseline information established for all historical structures and the townscape. Specific documentation used in the LHCA project followed in general the Survey of Architectural Values in the Environment (SAVE) method[2] developed by the Danish Ministry of Environment.

The survey focused on the general arrangement – plan and layout of volumes and storeys – and a visual and photographic registration of each building.[3] Every building was inspected and described using a standard information format, established specifically for this project. Individual townscape components were described and analysed in graphics and in text. All building plans sketched and checked on site were then incorporated into our upgraded versions of Lhasa municipal maps.

The material is collected in an integrated database using advanced database software that allows easy access to information on all buildings, building elements and townscape components. Our overall and radical revision of the available municipal maps has resulted in the detailed maps published here for the first time. A future digital version of *The Lhasa Atlas* anticipates the inclusion of interactive maps for direct use of database material.

Opposite: 'Plan of Lhasa', 1884. Not to scale. The first Western-style map of Lhasa is probably this one, published in 1884 by the Survey of India in Dehra Dun. The overall shape and relative location of map features are largely correct, but with so many inaccuracies that the author has probably not been to Lhasa. It is thus supposed not to be based on an actual survey in Lhasa, but produced from verbal accounts and on-site sketches made by others. These men were probably 'pundits', British-trained spies of Indian origin who, from the mid-1860s, entered Tibet disguised as holy men or traders. This map is interesting for its exaggerations and those elements regarded as important. It was copied in the publications by Rockhill (1891), Graham Sandberg (1901) and Chandra Das (1902).

We hope the Lhasa authorities may be among the prime users of information contained in the LHCA database, which provides ready access to existing old buildings inside the Lingkor. This aspect of the project may be of direct value, on a daily basis, in their conservation planning and urban development policy.

Preserving the authenticity of traditional structures and townscape has become a major concern of authorities and interest groups worldwide. International efforts to save physical heritage are now frequently as involved with protecting the larger environments that surround buildings as the individual structures themselves. This gradual shift in attitude has rescued many invaluable townscape environments from damage and destruction.

In the face of grave threats to the traditional secular parts of Lhasa, the People's Government of Lhasa City is today showing an increasingly active commitment towards safeguarding the historical town and its unique heritage. The Potala Palace, admitted to the UNESCO World Heritage List[4] in 1994, was joined in 2000 by the Jokhang Temple and surrounding Barkor area.

We wish to contribute to the knowledge of traditional buildings in Lhasa. With their disappearance, so too goes a link to the past and the loss of irreplaceable knowledge of importance to present and future generations.

We, Knud Larsen and Amund Sinding-Larsen, are responsible for the research project and authorship of *The Lhasa Atlas*. Other researchers in Asia and Europe have helped us greatly, particularly during fieldwork conducted in Lhasa; we acknowledge their views and contributions at appropriate places in the book.

We wish to express our gratitude to the many institutions and individuals who helped us along the way, especially the Network for University Cooperation Tibet–Norway, Norwegian Research Council, the Norwegian Agency for Development Cooperation (NORAD) and the Ministry of Foreign Affairs, Norway for generous grants that supported the project work and our research trips to Lhasa and Central Tibet. NUFU[5] kindly funded a study trip to Norway for two of our Lhasa partners. The Department of Architectural Design at the Norwegian Institute of Science and Technology, NTNU, hosted the project.

Without the support of our colleagues in Lhasa, we could not have completed the project. Lhasa City officials gave us permission to visit and survey both public and private buildings. Residents and building owners alike actively supported us in our work. Partners and interpreters at the Tibet Academy of Social Sciences (TASS) and the Lhasa Urban Construction Committee (LUCC) provided steady assistance and the friendly, essential links between authorities, local residents and our team.

At the Network for University Cooperation Tibet–Norway, the following people provided continuous help: Chairman Jens Braarvig, Sissel Thorsdalen, Ingvild Hestad and Rinzin Thargyal.

We wish further to thank Heather Stoddard for her encouragement, erudition and aid as a mediator; André Alexander for coordinating the building survey fieldwork and for research on building typology; Erik Ruud for the first new Geographical Information Systems (GIS)-based maps for the project; Olav Roger Jensen for establishing the project's initial GIS model; Stian Haugli for invaluable assistance on digitized maps and satellite photos; Minyag Chokyi Gyaltsen for detailed building surveys and historical information; Per Kværne for encouragement and advice; Guo Zhan of the State Administration of Cultural Heritage for advice and corrections throughout the project; Wang Jinghui of the China Academy of Urban Planning and Design for help and discussions; Minja Yang, deputy director of UNESCO World Heritage Centre, Paris, for continuous support and encouragement; and Anthony Aris, publisher, for indispensable assistance.

Architects, artists, other professionals and students[6] participated in the Lhasa surveys and deserve special mention, especially Pimpim de Azevedo, Maans P. Davidson, Hilde Hanson, Veronique Martin, Moritz Wermelskirch and Odd Oeverdahl.

Thanks also to Gregers Algreen-Ussing and Kurt Boye Jensen, members of the Danish SAVE project, who shared their experiences and encouraged us to use the registration method; and to Ane Oedegaard Kjoede for digitized maps; and Arna Mathiesen for photo archives.

In Lhasa, we relied on the knowledge of several residents, academics and others to understand the history and development of the old town. Our heartfelt thanks go to them.

For translation, support and wonderful company in Lhasa, we warmly thank Dolma, Diki Drogar, Puchung Tsering and Kalsang Yeshe.

Paddy Booz and Toby Matthews saw the book through its intensive editing and complex production processes.

Finally, special thanks for encouragement to Dotar, Barbro Engesveen, Ashish Krishna, Chie Nakane, the late Hugh Richardson, Tsering Shakya, Shitra Sharma, Tsewang Tashi and Mridula Vichitra.

The authors are architects, not historians, anthropologists or Tibetologists. We neither speak nor read Tibetan. We have approached the challenge of this project as experts in observing and analysing physical structures and environments, and thus this study has a primary focus on what can be seen and touched. We ask for tolerance if we have been too quick in drawing conclusions based on insufficient knowledge of matters outside our field.

Knud Larsen and Amund Sinding-Larsen
Oslo, May 2001

Introduction

Lhasa is in legends glorified as the 'place of the gods'. Numerous Western authors have developed this and related themes in their work, and the authors of *The Lhasa Atlas* would gladly take part in that glorification, but as architects we have not been primarily concerned with such subjects. We have concentrated on what Old Lhasa looks like today and our work is first of all about maps. The subtitle of the book, 'Traditional Tibetan Architecture and Townscape', could add the word 'Observed' because observation on-site has been our working method.

Research over the past years has revealed to us that Lhasa old town, in spite of its unique traditional architecture, has up to now failed to receive the study and documentation that it warrants. As the ancient capital of Tibet, it is by far the most impressive of the few surviving traditional Tibetan towns, with an overlaying historical streetscape of exceptional quality. Among its splendid buildings are the Potala Palace, seat of the Dalai Lamas, and the Jokhang Temple, most sacred building of Tibetan Buddhism. Many religious chapels, monasteries, shrines and memorials complement the outstanding secular structures that still stand. In short, Tibetan architecture as a whole truly deserves a place among the great building cultures of the world.

In this book, references to Tibet generally mean the Tibet Autonomous Region (TAR), an administrative unit which was instituted in 1965, and made up of the former provinces of U and Tsang. This area covers 1.2 million sq km, a region approximately 1600 kilometres long by 800 kilometres wide, roughly as large as France, Spain and Germany combined, or more than four times the size of California.

Cultural Tibet, however, is far larger and takes in the whole of the Tibetan Plateau and its border zones. This 'Greater Tibet' includes Sikkim, northern Nepal and Ladakh in northernmost India. Bhutan, a unified and independent country since the 17th century, also has close historical and cultural ties with Tibet. Significant parts of China's Gansu, Qinghai, Sichuan, and Yunnan provinces are ethnically Tibetan as well. Groups indelibly influenced by Tibetan culture are the Sherpas of Nepal,

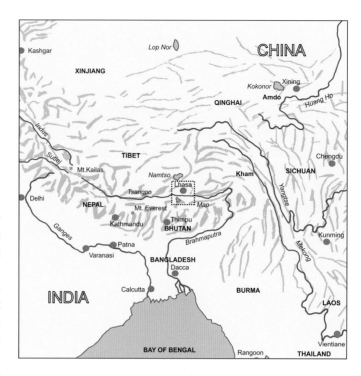

Lhasa and surrounding Asian regions. Scale 1 : 30 million. This map is approximately 2700 km on each side. In a direct line, Lhasa lies just 800 km from the Bay of Bengal and is relatively close to several Asian cities, but it has always been remote because of the barrier of the Himalaya range.

the Drukpas of Bhutan, and the Ladakhis of north India; dozens of smaller groups speaking diverse dialects contribute to the complex Tibetan world.

This Tibetan homeland, a vast plateau cut off to the south by the world's highest mountains, the Himalaya, contains perhaps six million Tibetans. The TAR has around 2.5 million of these, with close to three million living in the above mentioned Chinese provinces.

Many of Asia's mightiest rivers have their sources on the Tibetan Plateau: the Yangtze, Mekong, Huang He (Yellow), Salween, Indus and Brahmaputra. This last, know in Tibet as the Tsangpo, is the land's largest river, which, with its tributaries, has always been the main settled area.

Tibetan culture developed in this relatively watered southern part of the country, where raising barley and other crops proved possible in fertile valleys. The dry, relatively steady climate of Central Tibet has a warm summer, long spring and autumn, and only during the winter (December to March) does cold harshness come to dominate. Snow rarely settles for long below 5000 metres, so the occasional snowstorm does not leave its mark for long. Lhasa, warmer than one would think, enjoys about 3,000 hours of sunlight per year, an average of more than eight hours of sun every day.

Beyond this region lies a colder, higher zone of rolling mountainous grassland, severe but inhabitable. Here tough nomads living in black tents tend livestock, primarily yak, the ubiquitous Tibetan animal. Finally, the great northern plains

Central Tibet and Lhasa.
Scale 1 : 1 million. This modern digital map, made by the authors from different sources in February 2001, shows the Tsangpo (Brahmaputra), Yarlung and Kyichu valleys, with Lhasa. It covers an area roughly 180 by 180 km. Main features: the Yarlung valley, original seat of the Yarlung dynasty (7th–9th centuries), to the south-east; Yamdrok Tso, the large, multi-fingered lake south of the Tsangpo river. It has no natural outlet. The Tsangpo river, here called Yarlung Tsangpo, runs from west to east along Tibet's southern edge, just north of the main Himalaya range. In eastern Tibet it turns in a dramatic bend to cut through the Himalayas, and thereafter becomes known as the Brahmaputra. It finally enters the Bay of Bengal after passing through Assam and Bangladesh; Lhasa airport at Gongkar, on the south bank of the Tsangpo; Samye, Tibet's oldest monastery (late 8th century), just north of the Tsangpo; the Kyichu river, a tributary of the Tsangpo, which runs through the Lhasa valley. It enters the great river just west of Gongkar.

of the Changtang, making up nearly half of the Tibetan Plateau, suffer from extremes of altitude, wind and cold. Almost devoid of people, this is the realm of the wild yak, snow leopard, wolf, kiang and antelope.

Central Tibet's Tsangpo, Yarlung and Kyichu river valleys – all within an area roughly 300 kilometres east–west by 250 kilometres north–south – are the starting point of Tibetan history. In the 7th century Buddhism was probably first introduced from China and Central Asia, soon followed by the arrival of Buddhist missionaries from India. Songtsen Gampo of the Yarlung dynasty, a successful warrior king, moved the capital to Lhasa and is reputed to have built an early palace on Marpori hill, site of the Potala. He transferred his court here from the Yarlung region and, taking hold of the Lhasa valley's agricultural potential and strategic location for trade, built the foundations for the future town.

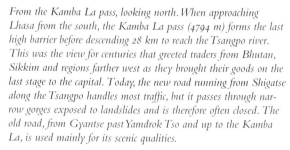

From the Kamba La pass, looking north. When approaching Lhasa from the south, the Kamba La pass (4794 m) forms the last high barrier before descending 28 km to reach the Tsangpo river. This was the view for centuries that greeted traders from Bhutan, Sikkim and regions farther west as they brought their goods on the last stage to the capital. Today, the new road running from Shigatse along the Tsangpo handles most traffic, but it passes through narrow gorges exposed to landslides and is therefore often closed. The old road, from Gyantse past Yamdrok Tso and up to the Kamba La, is used mainly for its scenic qualities.

From the Kamba La pass, looking south. The Kamba La pass straddles a narrow ridge and is marked by clusters of brightly coloured prayer flags whipping in the wind. If one turns from north to south, leaving behind the Tsangpo valley, the new view down and across Yamdrok Tso lake and the distant mountains is breathtaking. Beyond the glittering turquoise lake, considered sacred by Tibetans, stands the pointed snow summit of Nojin Kangtsang (7191 m), and at the farthest limit the Himalayan border with Bhutan.

Above: Kyichu valley with Lhasa. Satellite photograph, 1965. United States Corona intelligence satellite photos were taken from 1960 to 1972. Released for public use a few years ago, they are available from the Internet. The photo used here (18 January 1965) shows the Kyichu valley (3600–3700 m), located in the southern part of Central Tibet at about the same latitude as Cairo and New Orleans. Impressive peaks up to 2000 m above the valley floor line the central valley, which extends for another 100 km north-east of Lhasa. The focus of the Kyichu valley remains Lhasa, where the river runs along the town's southern edge. Elsewhere, the Kyichu generally divides the land of the valley quite evenly on each side, but around Lhasa the developed and available land is almost exclusively located north of the river. This satellite image, a contact copy from a filmstrip, covers an area of about 18 by 55 km. The afternoon sun, coming in from the lower left side, makes the mountains stand out clearly (it is easier to grasp the three-dimensional quality of the picture if you turn the book upside down). The almost uniform slopes of relatively soft rock have been weathered by water and environmental erosion. Soil runoff is considerable and the valley bottoms are wide and flat. Visible features in Lhasa are the two hills of Marpori, with the Potala Palace, and Chakpori; a water channel coming from the area of Sera monastery that runs west of the Potala; and the large marshy area (dark) between the Potala and Drepung monastery. Also visible is a thin line running east from Lhasa on the south bank of the river; this dirt road leads towards Ganden monastery, eastern Tibet and Sichuan province. As the crow flies, the distance from central Lhasa to Drepung is 8.5 km, to Sera 4.5 km, to Yerpa 16 km and to Ganden 35 km. To the west, the Kyichu river makes a turn to join the Tsangpo river some 50 km further south. The area called the 'Lhasa valley', roughly defined in white outline, is today filling up with the expanding urban structure of Lhasa.

Over time, spiritual and secular institutions blended together, touching all aspects of life and culminating in the creation of the country's thousands of monateries, temples and retreats. Although Tibetan Buddhism has many schools, the main Gelukpa sect dominated after the 17th century, with the Dalai Lamas at the apex of Tibet's theocracy. Buddhism fostered learning and philosophy that survives to this day, albeit in limited form. Many buildings of special architectural interest go back two or three

Greater Lhasa. Satellite photograph, 1970. Scale 1 : 60 000. This Corona satellite view (21 November 1970), composed and digitally enhanced by the authors, shows the same area as the Greater Lhasa 1985 map (p. 15) and allows one to study fifteen years of growth. Very prominent is the diversion channel (here dry and white) from the Sera area running southward and westward past the Potala, where it disappears. Today this channel is underground. Most prominent of all is the large marshy area north-west of the old town.

Its characteristic form helps locate Lhasa on satellite film strips, and this photo shows that the marsh originally extended all the way from the north-west to the east of the old town, and even into it.

The Jokhang and Barkor seem to have been located on the slightly elevated part of the landscape. The town, expanding slowly until the present generation, spread across waterlogged areas, making consolidation of the ground necessary.

hundred years, with a very few exhibiting parts or remnants from the earliest period (7th century onward).

Central Tibet and Lhasa have always been connected to the larger world by tracks regularly exposed to landslides, flooding, snow and ice. This is still the case today. Roads now emanate from Lhasa in all directions: westward to Gyantse and Shigatse, then on to West Tibet or the Tibet–Nepal border; southward via Gyantse through the Chumbi valley to Sikkim and Bhutan (though these borders are largely closed); northward to Golmud in Qinghai province, then on to north and central China; and eastward and south-eastward, leading eventually to Chengdu (capital of Sichuan province) and Kunming (capital of Yunnan province). Tibet's only major airport is located at Gongkar, about 90 kilometres south of Lhasa near the mouth of the Kyichu river. The entire Tibetan region is crisscrossed by age-old pilgrimage and trade routes, many of which

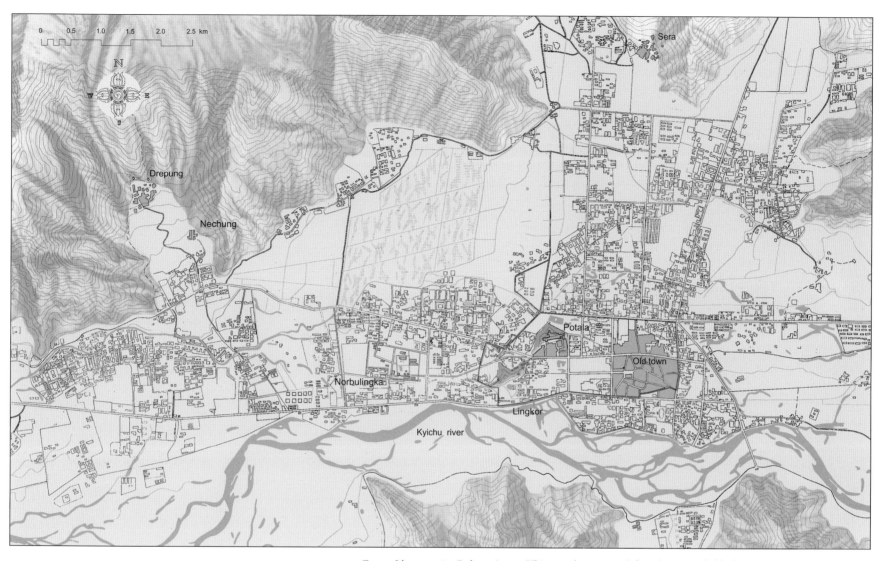

are still travelled by pilgrims bound for the myriad holy places that dot the countryside.

Lhasa, the historic focus of Tibetans, has been a magnet like other great religious cities, such as Rome, Mecca, Varanasi and Jerusalem. Its spectacular setting among majestic mountains has been enhanced by historic isolation and remoteness. Until recently, all goods were brought in by pack animals over enormous distances. Lhasa in the 1950s was a town of moderate size with a population of 30,000. Today it has grown into a regional capital, covering almost the entire floor of the Lhasa valley, with a population ten times that number. Traditional sections are threatened by many of the problems facing old historic towns; in a short span of years the city has grown into a modern urban environment. Recent developments have radically changed a so-called medieval townscape, with increasing demolition of old buildings, to replace them with modern

Greater Lhasa, c.1985. Scale 1 : 60 000. This map shows the approximate physical extent of present-day Lhasa. All plots shown as empty along the river to the west and towards Sera monastery to the north are today filled with construction. The same is true for most areas east of the old town and between the town and the marshes to the northwest. The Lingkor, the 7.5-km-long pilgrim path that defines the extent of old Lhasa, is indicated with a red line. Outside the Lingkor, about 2 km west of the Potala, is Norbulingka, a public park that was once the Summer Palace of the Dalai Lamas. Mountains are shown with contours at 40 m. The valley plain has a gentle slope of 1 : 100 from the foot of the mountains towards the Kyichu river.

Panorama of Lhasa from the south. F. Spencer Chapman, 1936. This photograph exposes with great clarity the main features of both town and landscape. The flat valley bottom, with the Kyichu river running from east to west (towards left in the photo), reveals Marpori and Chakpori, the hills upon which stand the Potala and the Medical College (Mentsikhang). The precise form of the old town appears vividly at a good distance east-south-east from Marpori. *To the north and south are mountains above 5,500 m, a rise of 2,000 m from the valley floor. A number of noble families have moved out of town and built mansions along the bank of the river; otherwise, very few buildings stand outside the Lingkor. The flood diversion channel is seen in white behind the hills, and in the northern foothills one glimpses Sera monastery and Pabongka, the ancient monastery built atop a massive rock. Frederick Spencer* *Chapman, the photographer, went to Lhasa in the summer of 1936 as private secretary to Basil Gould, leader of a British mission intended to counter Chinese involvement in Tibet's affairs. In Lhasa until February 1937, Spencer Chapman had ample time to make friends and photograph extensively.*

construction, much of it inappropriate, that is filling up open or vacant areas inside the traditional town.

In the mid-1980s, most religious and secular buildings remained intact, but today the number of such standing structures has been reduced by more than a third, to approximately 200. With limited open land for expansion, the future safeguarding of Lhasa's historical core has become critical. And yet there is a growing recognition, very late in the day, of the importance of this cultural heritage.

The buildings under survey in this book, though not all necessarily very old, represent a continuous tradition of outstanding spiritual and material culture. Even buildings constructed up to the 1970s adhere to centuries-old methods, and the townhouses and urban fabric of Lhasa old town provide unique links between the past and the present, between long-established ways of life and the living reality of families and individuals today.

The old town, covering just one sq km, once had simple roads and paths that led through fields and meadows, via the odd farmstead, to all points of outlying Lhasa. But this compact, traditional centre of the historical capital is today of reduced importance. Although the old town still sees intensive commerce and small-scale trade, the real commercial centre of Lhasa has moved to new urban blocks north and west of it. North and west of these again grow the main new housing areas of Lhasa, some developed with three- or four-storey blocks of flats, others providing private courtyard houses of one or two storeys.

This growth is reflected in administrative organization. Seven rural districts and one urban municipal area, covering 554 sq km, make up Lhasa Prefecture. Lhasa City as a defined territory covers almost 80 sq km, and the central part of Lhasa, once so tiny, now covers approximately 40 sq km. In 1998 the population of Lhasa City was officially 382,000, with 50,000 living in the inner city, largely in the old town, though these numbers should probably be higher.

Until contemporary urban development, the traditional town plan – and townscape – concentrated on the chief religious, cultural and public buildings and the routes used for processional and daily domestic purposes. Within the townscape itself, many streets, structures and spaces had their own natural qualities and development, and were taken for granted as merely incidental.

The town plan developed from the 1960s onward provided considerable space for major urban functions, allocating them to separated plots of land in an emerging urban landscape. In the last two decades, however, schools, public institutions government buildings and hospitals have increasingly competed with government housing for space in the central urban areas, once provided so generously with land in the 1960s and 70s. All around Lhasa, and in numerous pockets inside its increasingly urban fabric, new activities are based mostly on industrial production. The townscape is undergoing tremendous change.

Areas south and south-west of the old town are fast developing as extensions to the new commercial and administrative

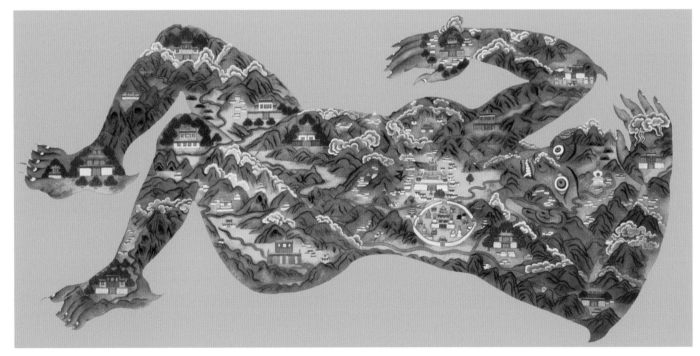

The Demoness. Modern painting by Tsewang Tashi. The artist presents here a traditional legend. Myths and beliefs from the time of King Songtsen Gampo (7th century) describe a pre-Buddhist 'demoness' hostile to Buddhism. She is lying on her back covering all of Tibet. Songtsen Gampo is said to have started building 108 temples throughout the country, from Lhasa to the frontiers of his empire, to pin down vital body parts – shoulders, hips, elbows, knees, hands, feet – in order to tame the demoness. The strategically placed temples emanated outwards from the centre in a series of concentric zones; the Jokhang was the central temple, placed above her heart. The first 'maps' of Tibet were possibly of this geomantic type.

zones, while industrial development is located primarily to the west. Military camps now stand on all sides of the city, particularly to the south-west, and parts of the Kyichu river south of the Potala have been filled in and built upon with residential-commercial compounds. Only one bridge now crosses the river, east of the old town, but future plans envisage several new bridges, railway stations and a burst of urban development south of river. Industrial pollution and traffic starkly influence the overall environment and give Lhasa, despite its altitude and unequalled natural surroundings, the appearance of just any other modern city.

All of these rapid, irrevocable changes make one long for a continuity and link to things gone by. Luckily, we have been able to make this connection to the past, and to add invaluable perspective to our survey work, through historically significant maps, photographs and paintings. This material comes from wonderfully diverse sources, and even the modern materials tell their own fascinating stories.

The earliest is a magnificent 18th-century thangka (scroll painting; see frontispiece, p. 2), which presents sacred monuments in a similar manner to those seen on many Tibetan murals. The perspective, a bird's-eye view, displays the monuments in a constructed landscape and includes Tibet's most important religious sites. The size of each object seems to indicate its importance, with the Jokhang being first, followed by Samye, oldest monastery in Tibet, and then the Potala. The sun and moon look down on trees all hung with jewels; the painting perhaps intends to describe the celestial counterpart to Lhasa and its surroundings.

A delightful map-painting from around 1860, commissioned by a British official and painted by a Tibetan artist, is in fact a series of large watercolours of buildings, panoramas and cultural activities from sites throughout Tibet. Given that the subjects he paints are spread over so vast a geographical area, the piecing together of this series of picture maps is a testament to the astonishing skill of the artist.

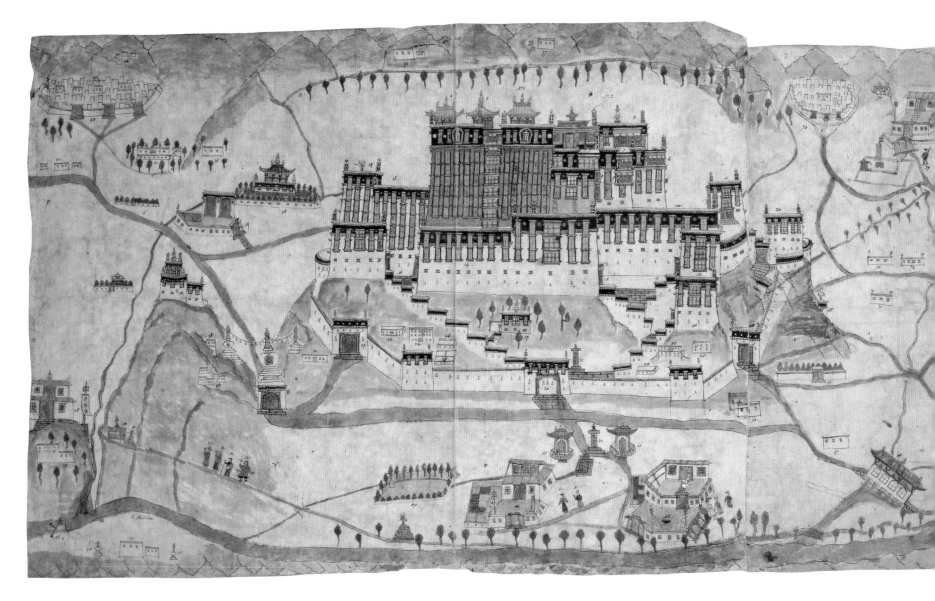

Lhasa with the Potala and Jokhang, from the 'Wise Collection' of Tibetan picture-maps and drawings, c.1860. British Library accession number: Add Or. 3031 (1 and 2). This unique collection of large panoramic picture-maps, stretching from Ladakh and Zangskar in the west through Central Tibet to eastern Tibet and south to Bhutan, contains 25 related drawings and presents an authentically Tibetan world view. The collection was commissioned by an as-yet unidentified British official and later acquired by Thomas Wise (1802–89), a Scottish polymath and collector. The artist, probably a monk or lay priest from the Nyingmapa school from Lahul, painted the watercolours on paper in a refreshingly free manner, with great detail, information and charm. This image is 65 by 150 cm and presents the main features of the Potala Palace and the Jokhang Temple, seen from the south, placed within the entire width of the Lhasa valley with the southern mountaintops in the foreground along the Kyichu river and the northern mountains at the top of the painting. From the west, at the base of the northern mountains, are shown Drepung and Nechung monasteries and in the middle is Sera monastery. The Potala, with the village of Shöl

within its perimeter wall, is the central object. Except for parts of this wall, it is drawn in a pure frontal view, without conventional perspective. Two dominant features of today's scene are missing: the Barkhang Chenmo (printing house) built in 1926 and the section of the Potala Red Palace that houses the 13th Dalai Lama's funerary chapel, built in the mid-1930s. The Jokhang Temple is drawn from a bird's-eye perspective in an attempt to look inside this low, complex building, in opposition to the Potala, whose main aspect is the monumental front. The difference in artistic interpretation of these two structures underlines in a strikingly natural way the great contrasts between them. The Barkor market street that surrounds the Jokhang complex is marked by two huge prayer masts (darchen), a walk-through stupa and the historical stele and willow tree in front of the Jokhang's main entrance. Ramoche Temple, shown just above the Jokhang, is turned on its side to emphasize its relation to the old road of Ramoche Lam. The roofed Yuthok Zampa Bridge is turned 45 degrees to show its position in the landscape. On the plain in front of Shöl are the two pavilions with steles and the free-standing stele known as Doring

Chima. Just below these to the right is perhaps the Chinese official residence and yamen. The Lingkor circumambulation path around Lhasa, used by pilgrims through the centuries, is flanked to the east and along the river with rows of trees. On the river is a ferry. Just below the Potala on the riverside, the Lingkor turns around a heap of stones that honours a Mongolian regent who was killed here in the late 17th century. The same or a similar heap of stones is seen on the Aufschnaiter map (p. 28). The stones were still there in 1997 but have now been removed. The Lingkor is shown to turn sharply around Chakpori hill, with the Medical College at its summit. Between Chakpori and Marpori one can see the three stupas of the West Gate (Bargo Kani), and to the left of Chakpori appears the much smaller Bhamari hill with its Chinese-style temple, Gesar Lhakhang (late 18th century). From Bhamari, the Lingkor next passes the Elephant House (Langkhang), recognizable by its two high doors, and finally, just beyond, the Lukhang chapel sitting on an island in an artificial pond.

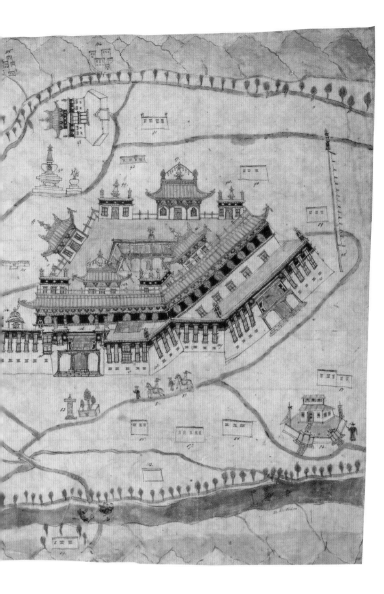

members of an invading army, carried out what is probably the first true survey of Lhasa.

After a very long pause in such surveying, some unexpected visitors arrived. Two Austrians, Heinrich Harrer and Peter Aufschnaiter, escaped from a British prisoner-of-war camp in north India in April 1944 and made their way to Tibet. Harrer is best known for his book *Seven Years in Tibet* and Aufschnaiter for his wonderful maps from Tibet and Nepal. Aufschnaiter, an engineer, was involved in many projects in Lhasa, including the design and construction of new anti-flood dykes along the Kyichu river and the creation of an irrigation channel. In planning a sewer system for Lhasa, Aufschnaiter and Harrer needed good maps, so they spent months painstakingly creating them, using 60-year-old surveying equipment. The Aufschnaiter maps, mostly from 1947 and 1948, are astonishingly accurate and correct. His main map of Lhasa formed the basis and starting point for our survey in 1995.

Zasak Jigme Taring, architect of the 14th Dalai Lama, fled to India after 1959 and soon set about drawing maps of Lhasa and its surroundings from memory. He also drew a detailed plan of the Jokhang. In 1984 Taring completed his 'Map of Lhasa', and though physical relationships are rather distorted, the map gives a fine account of the town's religious, cultural and physical components, information that conventional geometrical maps sadly cannot include.

Many photographs, mostly from the 1920s and 30s, offer a valuable and accurate record of what Lhasa was, and a number of them are quite beautiful as well. These are supplemented by satellite imagery and contemporary colour photographs that add up-to-date views and information.

The Lhasa Atlas is a book about the topography, environment, historical development, buildings and townscape of old Lhasa, and it also discusses future plans and issues concerning the protection of Lhasa's historical townscape in the face of urban development.

Despite the ravages of time and the folly of human destruction, there is still some hope for Lhasa old town. If *The Lhasa Atlas* can make a contribution to its conservation, and if readers and travellers come to understand the evolution of this unrivalled place, then this book will have fulfilled its purpose.

Few maps or sketches of Lhasa exist before the 20th century. Tibetan culture certainly produced maps, but not necessarily in the factual tradition of the West. Old Tibetan maps tend to be more 'ideogramatic' and illustrative of important features, and often depict spiritual and cultural relationships more clearly than topographical ones, bringing in themes of religion and geomancy.

A number of known historical maps of Lhasa – and some not so well known – are presented in the book. The early 20th century saw a major turning-point, with several conventional surveys made of Lhasa. Other maps are interesting in the way creative imagination combined with the skill of observation and a steady hand. The first Western-style map dates back to 1884, though it was not until 1904 that two British officers, as

Topography of Lhasa within the Lingkor. Scale 1 : 20 000. The interval between contours represents 1 m for the plain and 5 m for the hills. The numbers indicate altitudes starting at 3,600 meters. The plain slopes almost unnoticeably (1 : 500) from east to west following the flow of the river, and the central area of the old town is slightly elevated. This elevation has probably resulted from original topography and the build-up of cultural layers from centuries of town building. The flat plain experienced frequent flooding; numerous faulty dykes were attempted before Peter Aufschnaiter built the first successful ones in the late 1940s.

'Panorama of Lhasa'. J. Claude White, 3 August 1904. This is one of several panorama photographs from this point on Chakpori from the early 20th century. The Barkhang Chenmo in Shöl and the stairs down Marpori from the Potala's Namgyal monastery have not yet been built. The old town is almost hidden by a 'forest' of trees, but Yuthok Bridge is visible. Sera monastery can be seen at the foot of the mountains to the left of the Potala. John Claude White, long-time Political Officer in Sikkim, was appointed second in command to the British mission led by Colonel Francis Younghusband that invaded Tibet in 1903-04 to force open relations with the country. He was chosen for his years of experience in the Tibetan border areas and his knowledge of regional politics. His many fine photos of southern Tibet and Lhasa, as well as of Bhutan and Sikkim, exist in rare albums; this image was taken the day after the British forces entered Lhasa.

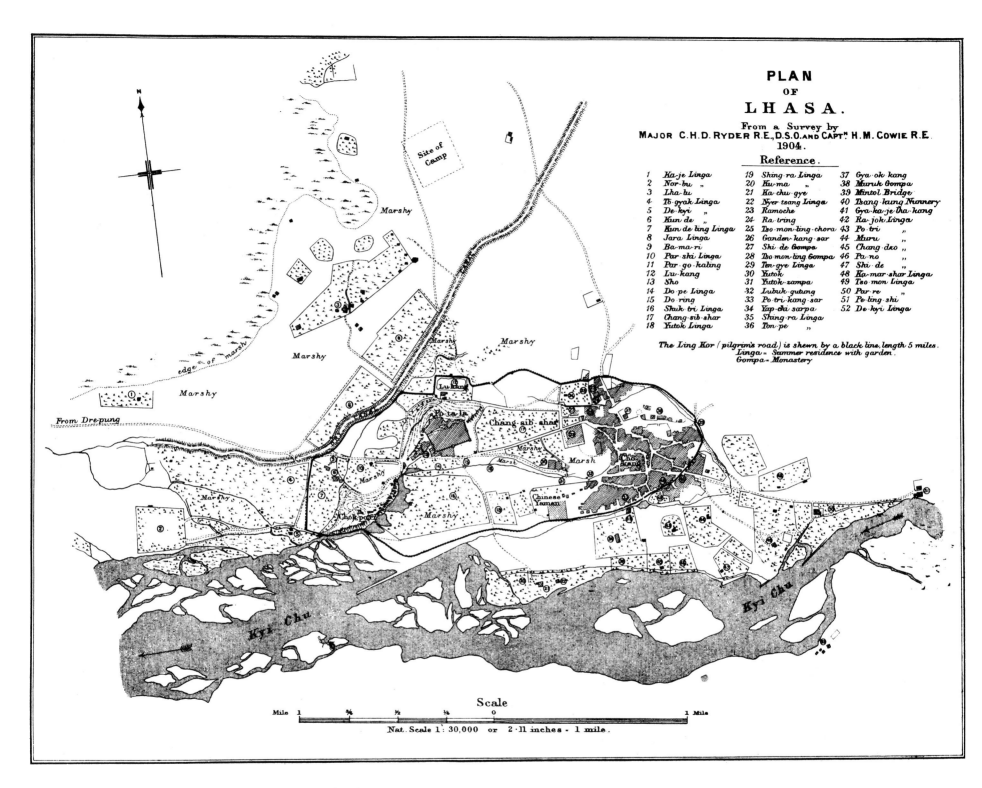

PLAN
OF
LHASA.

From a Survey by
MAJOR C.H.D. RYDER R.E., D.S.O. AND CAPTᴺ H.M. COWIE R.E.
1904.

Reference.

1	Ka-je Linga	19	Shing-ra Linga	37	Gya-ok-kang
2	Nor-bu „	20	Ku-ma „	38	Muruk Gompa
3	Lha-bu	21	Ka-chu-gye	39	Mintol Bridge
4	Tö-gyak Linga	22	Nyer-tsang Linga	40	Tsang-lang Nunnery
5	De-kyi „	23	Ramoche	41	Gya-ka-je tha-kang
6	Kun-de „	24	Ra-tring	42	Ra-jok Linga
7	Kun-de-ling Linga	25	Tso-mon-ling-chora	43	Po-tri „
8	Jara Linga	26	Ganden-kang-sar	44	Muru „
9	Ba-ma-ri	27	Shi-de Gompa	45	Chang-dzo „
10	Par-shi Linga	28	Tso-mon-ling Gompa	46	Pa-no „
11	Par-go-kaling	29	Ten-gye Linga	47	Shi-de „
12	Lu-kang	30	Yutok	48	Ka-mar-shar Linga
13	Sho	31	Yutok-zampa	49	Tso-mon Linga
14	Do-pe Linga	32	Lubuk-gutang	50	Par-re „
15	Do-ring	33	Po-tri-kang-sar	51	Pe-ling-shi „
16	Shuk-tri Linga	34	Yap-chi-sarpa	52	De-kyi Linga
17	Chang-sib-shar	35	Shing-ra Linga		
18	Yutok Linga	36	Ton-pe „		

The Ling Kor (pilgrim's road) is shewn by a black line, length 5 miles.
Linga = Summer residence with garden.
Gompa = Monastery

Scale

Nat. Scale 1: 30,000 or 2·11 inches = 1 mile.

'Plan of Lhasa'. Ryder and Cowie, 1904. Scale 1 : 30 000. This survey made by Major C.H.D. Ryder and Captain H.M. Cowie, published by the Royal Geographical Society in 1904, is almost certainly the first true survey of Lhasa. The authors, both members of the British expedition that invaded Tibet, have evidently observed on the spot and used the best available survey methods of the period. The map and town plan, naming and placing 52 locations, remained unrivalled for almost 50 years. Minor shortcomings indicate that the authors may never have been inside Norbulingka, the Summer Palace.

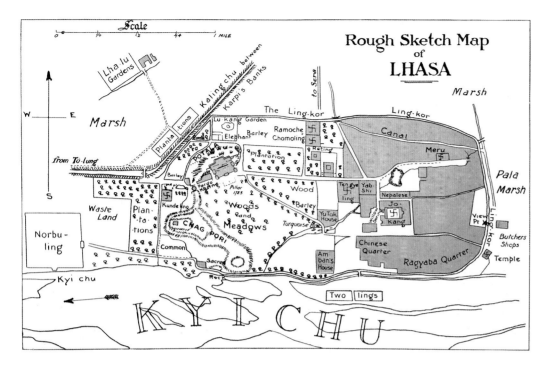

'Rough Sketch Map of Lhasa'. P. Landon, 1905. Not to scale. Perceval Landon and L. Austine Waddell, in addition to Ryder and Cowie, also published surveys of Lhasa in their accounts of the Tibet mission. Landon, special correspondent for The Times, was an eyewitness to all major battles and events that led ultimately to the entering of Lhasa. The outside world was intrigued by news about Tibet; Landon felt he could not wait for the official survey of Lhasa (presumably the Ryder and Cowie map) to reach London before publishing his book, so he included a preliminary rough sketch, clearly the result of direct observation and with a value of its own.

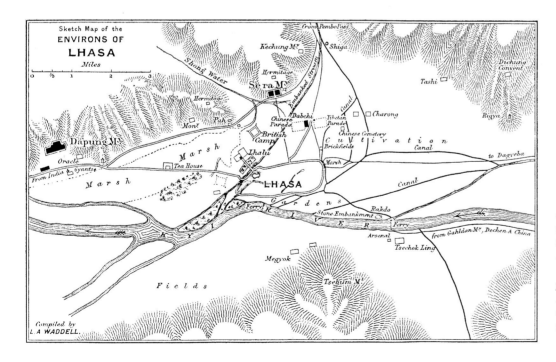

'Sketch Map of the Environs of Lhasa'. L. Austine Waddell, 1905. Not to scale. This map shows the Lhasa valley with its main built structures along the river and below the mountains. As a sketch it is surprisingly accurate. The road west towards Gyantse passes closely under the foothills of Drepung monastery, unlike today where it follows the Kyichu river. The road east towards Ganden and Sichuan crosses the river and follows the Kyichu's south bank, as it does today. Waddell wrote several books on Tibet, and in Lhasa and its Mysteries he published two interesting maps, both reproduced here. His long career with the Indian Army, especially at Darjeeling, allowed him to pursue numerous interests: natural history, archaeology, languages, medicine and especially Tibetan civilization. He accompanied the Younghusband mission to Lhasa as an officer and 'cultural expert'.

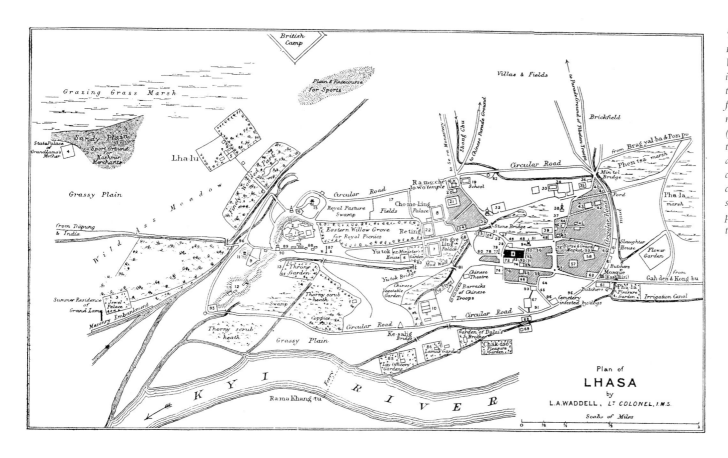

British Camp

Grazing Grass Marsh

Plain & Racecourse for Sports

Villas & Fields

Brickfield

Sandy Plain

State Palace Grandlama's Mother

Sport Ground for Kashmir Merchants

Lha-lu

Circular Road

Circular Road

Min tol Bridge

Phen tsa marsh

Ford

Pha la marsh

Grassy Plain

Royal Pasture Swamp

Ramo-che Jo-wo temple

School

Wild Ass Meadow

from Dapung & India

Eastern Willow Grove for Royal Picnics

Cho-mo-Ling Fields

Re-ting

Stone Bridge

Slaughter House

Flower Garden

Yu-tok ex-Minister's House

Ten-Gye Palace

Horse & Grass Market

from Gah den & Kong bu

Summer Residence of Grand Lama

Jewel Palace

Thorne's Garden

Mud Wall

Chinese Theatre

Chinese Vegetable Garden

Butchers Mosque (Kashmiri)

Barracks of Chinese Troops

Butchers Camels infected by dogs

Pha La Pleasure Garden

Irrigation Canal

Masonry Embankment

Swamp

Thorny scrub heath

Coppice

Yutok Bridge

Circular Road

Ke-saling Bridge

Garden of Dalai's Brother

Lamas Garden

Chak-dsot Pleasure Garden

Grassy Plain

Thorny scrub heath

Lay Officers' Gardens

Ramu Khang-tu

Ferry

K Y I   R I V E R

Plan of
LHASA
by
L.A. WADDELL, Lᵗ COLONEL, I.M.S.

Scale of Miles

'Plan of Lhasa'. L. Austine Waddell, 1905. Not to scale. This town plan by Waddell is clearly not surveyed with instruments, but is the result of observation and investigation. It contains much factual information though of a different nature than the Ryder and Cowie map (p. 23). In addition to text on the map, the author includes a list of 96 names and explanations. Waddell was a medical officer and may have been more concerned with culture and society than strict topography. The map key, which provides a glimpse of social life at the time, is presented without changes.

1. THE GREAT CATHEDRAL, THE TRUE "LHASA" OR "PLACE OF THE GODS"
2. GRAND LAMA'S PALACE ON POTALA HILL
3. GRAND LAMA'S SUMMER PALACE (NORBU LING)
4. GRAND LAMA'S MOTHER'S PALACE FOR RECEPTIONS
5. GRAND LAMA'S PARENTS' PALACE, OR PARADISE (LHA-LU)
6. EX-PRIME MINISTER YUTOK'S HOUSE
7. RESIDENCE OF THE DEPOSED KING-REGENT (GYAL-PO)
8. RESIDENCE OF THE EX-REGENT OF TSO MO LING
9. RESIDENCE OF THE OF KUN-DE-LING
10. CHINESE RESIDENCY OF THE AMBANS
11. BA-MO (BONG-BA) HILL, SURMOUNTED BY CHINESE TEMPLE TO KESAR
12. CHAG-GA OR CHAG-PA HILL, SURMOUNTED BY TEMPLE OF MEDICINE
13. THRONE GARDEN, WITH A STONE OR BRICK SEAT FOR GRAND LAMA
14. A HEATH, CALLED THE "CENTRE SNAKE-WAITING," ALLEGED TO HAVE BEEN VISITED BY BUDDHA SAKYA MUNI
15. A SNAKE-DRAGON TEMPLE, SURROUNDED BY A MOAT, AND CONNECTED BY A LOCK WITH MARSH TO THE EAST
16. ELEPHANT STABLE OF DALAI LAMA
17. CAMPING GROUND FOR TROOPS GOING TO THE RACECOURSE AND SPORTS IN FIRST MONTH OF YEAR
18. RA-MO-CHE TEMPLE, ALLEDGED TO BE ERECTED BY THE CHINESE PRINCESS KONJO OR TARA (DOL-TANG) IN SEVENTH CENTURY A.D.
19. UPPER SCHOOL OF MYSTICISM
20. TEMPLE OF THE BUDDHA OF BOUNDLESS LIFE
21. KANG-DA KHANG SAR, PALACE OF FORMER LAY "KINGS"
22. RESIDENCE OF THE LATE DEPOSED REGENT RE-TING, A LAMA OF SE-RA, WHO DIED IN BANISHMENT TO CHINA, ABOUT 1860. NOW USED AS AN ACADEMY
23. ASSEMBLY HALL OF TURKI MERCHANTS
24. "NAM-DE-LE" CROSS-ROADS
25. RESIDENCE OF DOWAGER MOTHER OF (PREVIOUS) GRAND LAMA
26. CHANG LO-CHEN
27. CHINESE RESTAURANT

28. TIBETAN RESTAURANT
29. JAIL
30. CHINESE TORTURE-CHAMBER
31. POTTERY MARKET
32. CHINESE GYA-BUM-KANG CHORTEN, AND BY ITS SIDE A TEMPLE ERECTED 1891
33. LOWER SCHOOL OF MYSTICISM AND PRINTING-HOUSE
34. MURU MONASTERY
35. RESIDENCE OF THE GENERAL (DAH-PON) WHO VISITED DARJEELING IN 1892 (NGA-PÒ-SA)
36. GUARD-HOUSE
37. TANNERY
38. PHUN-KANG CHORTEN
39. ORACLE OF DARBOLING
40. SADDLERY AND HARNESS BAZAAR FROM EASTERN TIBET
41. SALUTATION POINT (AS HERE THE PILGRIMS BY THE CIRCULAR ROAD CATCH A GLIMPSE OF THE GRAND LAMA'S PALACE OF POTA-LA, WHICH THEY SALUTE)
42. CHINESE "VALLEY" (GYA-MO-RONG)
43. GRASS MARKET
44. NUNS' RESTAURANT
45. CHINESE DRUG SHOP
46. EATING HOUSE
47. INNER CHINESE MEAT MARKET WITH DOUBLE ROW OF STALLS ENTERED THROUGH CHINESE ARCH
48. SHOPS OF NEWARS FROM NEPAL
49. RICE MARKET AND LARGE PRAYER FLAG
50. MOHAMEDAN CHINESE EATING HOUSE
51. BHOTANESE AND CHUMBI SHOPS
52. SUMMARY MAGISTRATES' COURT FOR DISPUTES
53. SU-KHANG
54. SUR-GYAR-KHANG
55. LARGE PRAYER FLAG, "THE EASTERN MOUNTAIN"
56. CHINESE EATING HOUSE
57. BANKYE-SHAG (PHALA) PALACE
58. KARMASHAR ORACLE
59. HORSE MARKET
60. CHINESE MILITARY PAYMASTER

61. SLAUGHTER HOUSE
62. GYE-TON JONG-PÒN
63. HOUSE OF KASHMIRI MAGISTRATE FOR MOHAMEDAN DISPUTES
64. RAB-SAL
65. KUN-SANG-TSE
66. SHATA PALACE
67. THE LAMA-DEFENDER OF RELIGION
68. SHATA-LING
69. NEPALESE CONSUL'S SUMMER HOUSE
70. SAM-DUB PALACE
71. OLD PALACE
72. KAH- SHAG
73. GAH-RU SHAR.
74. SQUARE OF SONG-CHO RA WHERE THANKSGIVING IS HELD IN FIRST MONTH AND WHERE WHIPPING IS INFLICTED FOR THIEVING, ETC.
75. MEAT AND LEATHER MARKET
76. RAG-GA-SHAG.
77. EDICT PILLAR.
78. WHITE TARA'S SHRINE
79. DANCING HALL
80. LODGING HOUSE FOR TASHILHUMPO PEOPLE
81. MI-SAD BRIDGE AND CHINESE ARCH
82. FAIRY SPRING OF CHINESE PRINCESS
83. TRIAD CHAITYA, CHORTEN
84. TURQUOISE-TILED BRIDGE (YUTOK SAMPA)
85. SUMMER GARDEN FOR MINISTERS AND CIVIL OFFICERS
86. SUMMER GARDEN FOR LAMAS
87. EDICT PILLAR
88. BAZAAR AND FOUNDRY
89. GRAND LAMA'S STABLE
90. GATEWAY OF PARGO-KALING
91. TEMPLE OF THE THREE LORDS
92. COUNCIL CHAMBER
93. NEPALESE CONSULATE
94. FOUR-DOORED CHORTEN
95. GALLERY OF ROCK PAINTINGS ON MEDICAL COLLEGE HILL
96. BEGGAR'S HORN HUTS

'View from Potola showing the Medical College on the hill'. J. Claude White, 1904. The photographer, looking south-west from the roof of the Potala, is standing on the site now occupied by the funerary chapel of the 13th Dalai Lama. The Gesar Lhakang is seen on top of Bhamari hill and right behind it sits Kundeling monastery. The Kyichu river with its many meanders runs westward and the Lhasa valley extends to the distant mountain, where the river turns south towards the Tsangpo valley. Most of today's industrial development is located in this western part of the valley.

'View across Kyi Chu valley from Potala Sho'. Charles Bell, 1921 (?). This photograph, taken from Marpori hill above Shöl, shows the open landscape of green meadows and trees in front of the Potala. Charles Bell, a political officer in the Indian civil service and probably the greatest authority on Tibet for a generation, wrote extensively about the country. He was sympathetic towards Tibetans and counted many of them as his friends, particularly the 13th Dalai Lama, who invited him to stay in Tibet. Bell remained in Lhasa from the end of 1920 through most of 1921, during which time he put forward recommendations for reform of the Tibetan government and army.

Potala from the Banak Shöl area. Hugh Richardson, 1936 (?). Here is the same general view as Kanwal Krishna's watercolour (p. 19). The two-storey southern wing of Meru monastery stands to the right and the lane going towards the Potala is today's Beijing Shar Lam. To the right, the square structure of Jebumgang chapel rises above the townhouses. Hugh Richardson's remarkable collection of photographs is but one small part of his huge contribution to Tibet studies and understanding. Between 1936 and 1950, he spent a total of eight years in Tibet, most of them as head of the British Mission. He travelled widely in the countryside, always alert to monasteries, shrines, local histories and early inscriptions. After leaving Tibet, Hugh Richardson's career as an independent scholar won him great respect among Tibetans and all others interested in the Land of Snows.

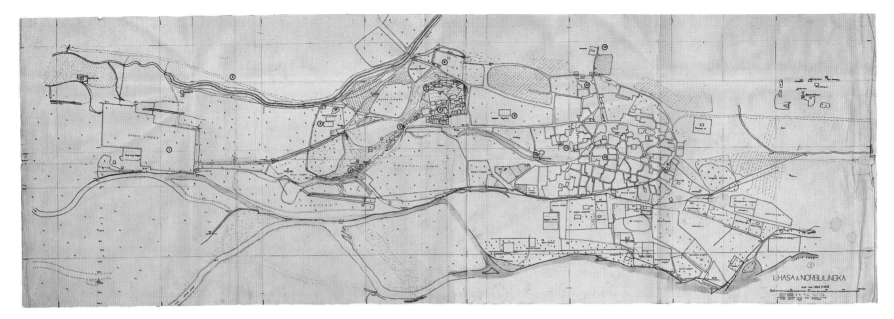

Above: 'Plan of Lhasa and Norbulingka'. *Peter Aufschnaiter,* *1948. Folded colour facsimile. Not to scale. (see Bibliography, Martin Brauen). Important features of this map are the Lingkor surrounding old Lhasa and the Potala; Norbulingka perimeter walls with the (then unsurveyed) Summer Palaces of the Dalai Lamas to the west; the water channel from the Sera area in the north to the Kyichu river; and new houses along the Kyichu river.*

Below: Lhasa Old Town, c.1955. Scale 1 : 10 000. This map fragment was given to the authors by a Lhasa resident and initially filed with other maps of minor interest. A second look, however, showed it to be the only map in the 17-year period (1948–65) between Aufschnaiter's map and the first satellite photo, and therefore of considerable interest. It reveals little physical development in the first five years (1950–55) of the Chinese presence. Clear elements are the new road between the Yuthok bridge's north end and the Jokhang, the extent of marshland in the eastern part of Lhasa, the Lingkor track to the north-east and Yabshi Taktster (residence of the Dalai Lama's family) close to the map's western border. The map is redrawn and coloured by the authors.

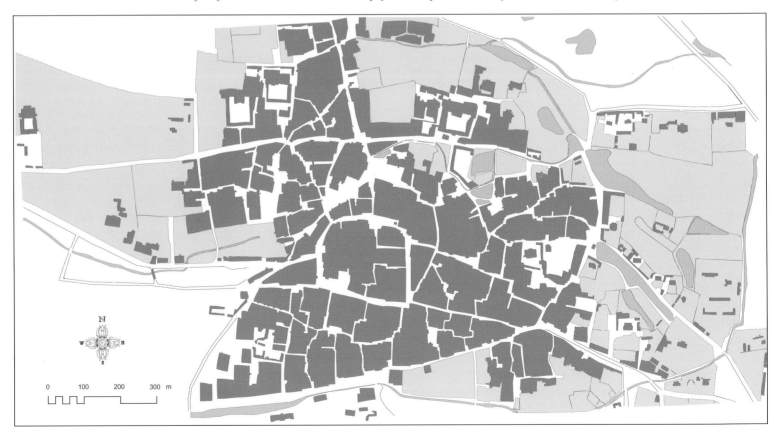

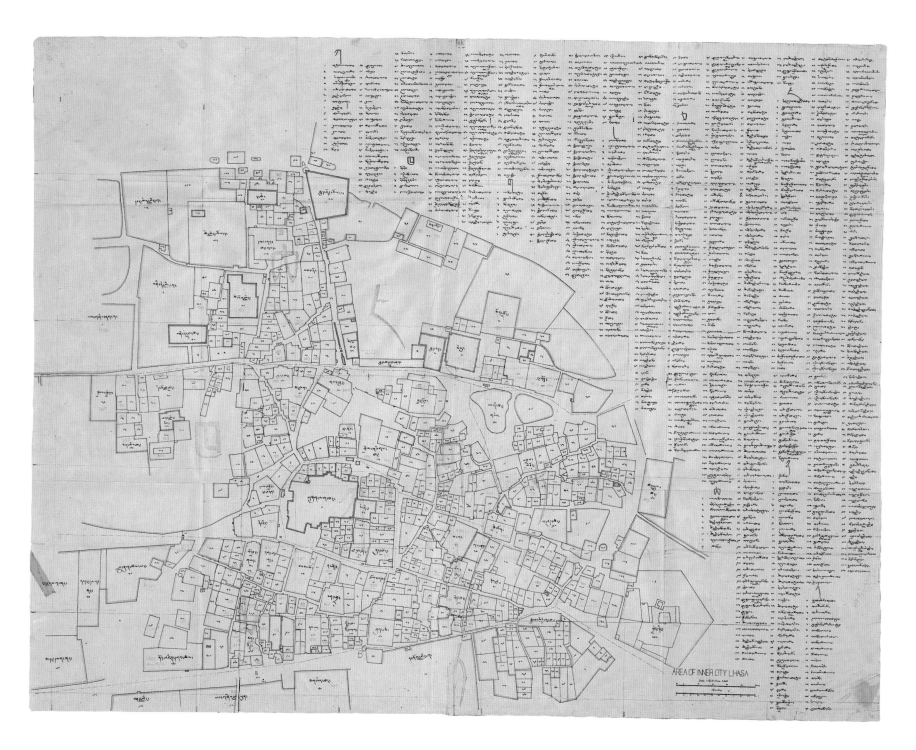

AREA OF INNER CITY LHASA

'Area of Inner City of Lhasa'. Peter Aufschnaiter, 1948. Not to scale. This beautiful map shows Lhasa town with its eight districts marked in large Tibetan letters, and approximately one thousand identified and numbered properties, with the property names in Tibetan listed adjacent. The LHCA registration work was based on this map, being the only detailed map available to the authors in 1995. Aufschnaiter's numbering system proved invaluable for identifying the old buildings and was used in the LHCA survey.

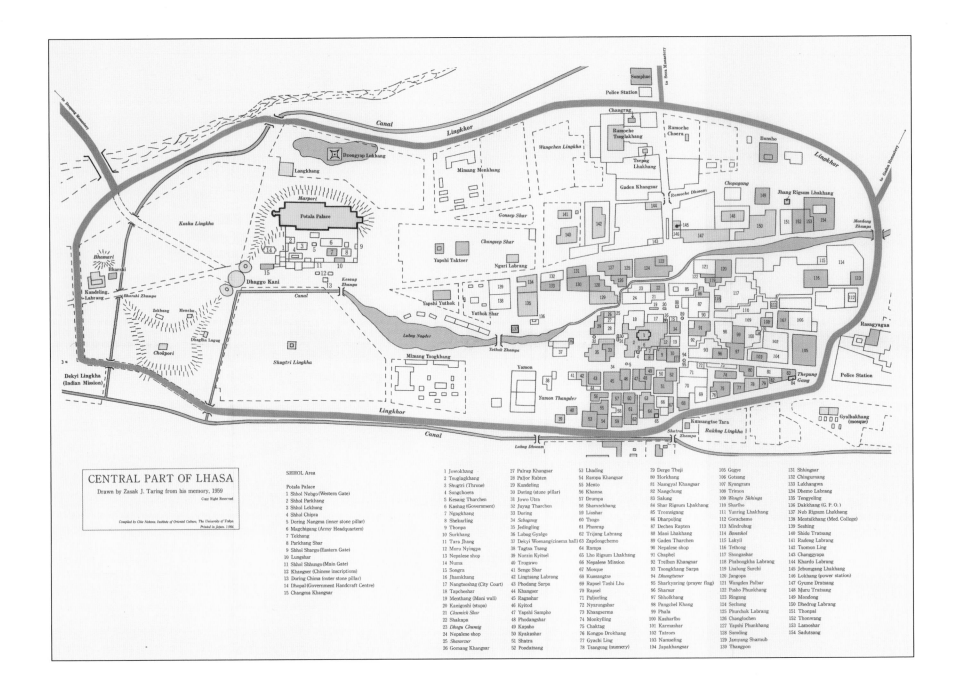

'Central part of Lhasa'. Zasak J. Taring, 1959. Not to scale (compiled by Chie Nakane, Institute of Oriental Culture, University of Tokyo, 1984). This map, drawn from memory, emphasizes the Lingkor and has an index that identifies 169 buildings. Ramoche Temple is shown to be the same size as the Jokhang, but in fact is much smaller. This 'exaggeration' must derive from the fact that Taring's is a 'cognitive map', sometimes unreliable. A riddle is the location of the North (Jhang) Rigsum Lhakang, one of four ancient protector chapels. It stands on Ramoche Lam, just north of Jebumgang, but Taring locates it much farther to the east. Fernand Meyer, in Demeures des Hommes, Sanctuaires des Dieux (p. 389), locates the Jhang Rigsum Lhakang at the same place as Taring.

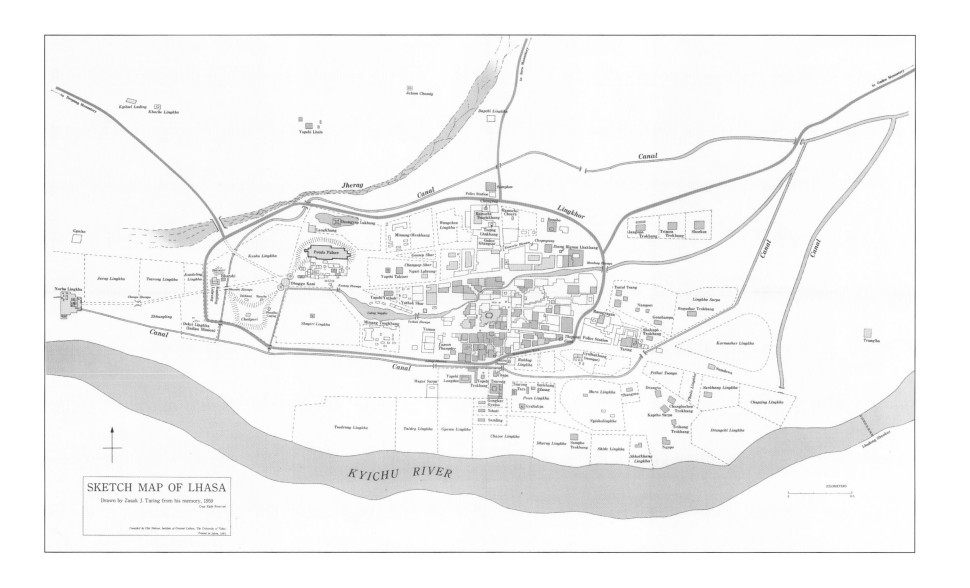

'Sketch Map of Lhasa'. Zasak J. Taring, 1959. Not to scale (compiled by Chie Nakane, Institute of Oriental Culture, University of Tokyo, 1984). This map of Lhasa focuses on the Lingkor and main roads leading towards external destinations. The road to Ganden is here indicated as following the Kyichu's northern shore, but maps from the turn of the century show the road crossing the river – by ferry – and then following the southern shore as today. Other main features are the large water channel from Ser, here called 'Jherag', other 'canals', new residences for the nobility outside the old town and the (compressed) Norbulingka.

Above: 'The Potala Palace seen from the west across the plain'. F. Spencer Chapman, 1936. The stark, open landscape west of Lhasa contrasts with the charming, park-like landscape east of Chakpori and Marpori hills. The West Gate is almost hidden by the high dykes, resembling sand dunes, that border the large diversion channel.

Below: Potala with West Gate and lake, from the south-west. C. S. Cutting, 1935. This remarkable photograph gives a fine impression of the entranceway to Lhasa from the west. The West Gate, consisting of three huge stupas, stands between Marpori and Chakpori hills. The entire city is hidden behind the hills, and only the Potala Palace is visible. One can imagine the dramatic entrance into Lhasa through the central stupa's small gate. To the right are doctors' dwellings on the lower ridge of Chakpori. The enclosure at front is possibly the special well that supplied water for the Dalai Lama alone. C. Suydam Cutting, a wealthy traveller and adventurer from the United States, visited Tibet three times, in 1928, 1935 and 1937.

Inside right: Historical Lhasa. General map of the LHCA project, 1999. Scale 1 : 7 500. This new map, here published for the first time, is a result of repeated missions by the authors.[1] Official maps that provided the basis and outlines for this map were obtained only with difficulty, and rapid construction of buildings and roads over the last decade made these 13- and 15-year-old maps obsolete, demanding significant amendments and supplements. The new map's main focus has been on traditional buildings and townscape features. All such old buildings (red) in the map are drawn from new surveys by the project; most new buildings (grey) are drawn from the official Chinese base maps and therefore have not been brought up to date. The urban structure of Lhasa is today considerably denser than indicated in this map, and the authors have incorporated a few new roads, squares and parks to approximate the present situation. These include the large square in front of the Potala and the new diagonal main road with roundabout just west of the Potala. The map is prepared for GIS (Geographical Information Systems), enabling easy production of the other theme maps in this book. Map contours (1 m on the plain, 5 m for the hills) are generated by the authors from point information in the official base maps. Coordinates establish a grid of squares, each 200 by 200 m, for easy reference. The map reveals features hidden from normal observation, such as the former alignment of the Lingkor north of the old town and the former near-diagonal track between Shöl and Yuthok bridge, which before 1950 ran more or less across open fields west of the old town. Today this connection is entirely gone. Obvious features of change are the new straight streets rather than old crooked lanes. Lhasa's main street, Beijing Shar Lam, cuts the old town in two and looks like a modern street, though in fact it runs along an old lane. The old town is crisscrossed by a dense web of narrow lanes. The grain of the new urban areas is entirely different, however, characterized by very large residential quarters, defined as closed compounds that vehicular and pedestrian traffic cannot cross. The entire inner city consists of only eight or ten of these forbidding blocks, the largest being about 350 by 600 m – this is considered unusually large for any city.

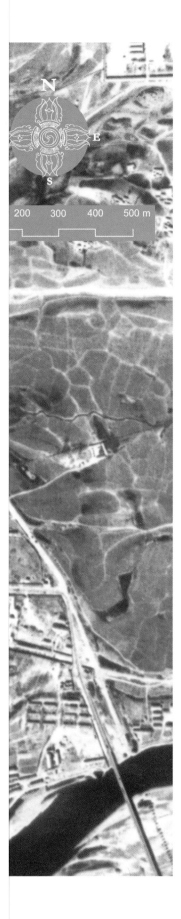

200   300   400   500 m

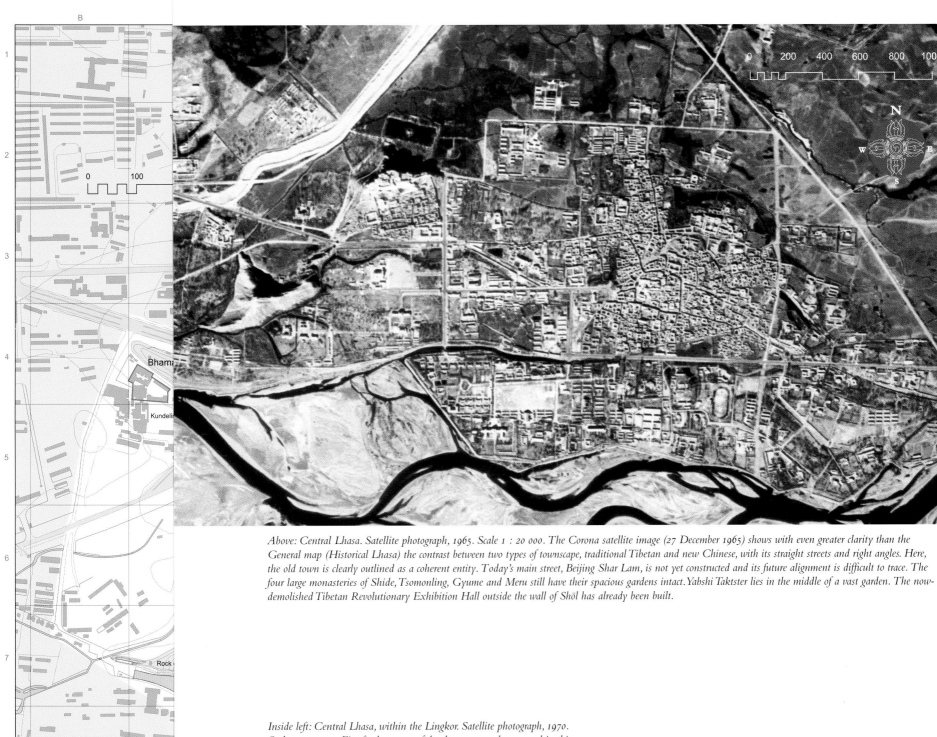

Above: Central Lhasa. Satellite photograph, 1965. Scale 1 : 20 000. The Corona satellite image (27 December 1965) shows with even greater clarity than the General map (Historical Lhasa) the contrast between two types of townscape, traditional Tibetan and new Chinese, with its straight streets and right angles. Here, the old town is clearly outlined as a coherent entity. Today's main street, Beijing Shar Lam, is not yet constructed and its future alignment is difficult to trace. The four large monasteries of Shide, Tsomonling, Gyume and Meru still have their spacious gardens intact. Yabshi Taktster lies in the middle of a vast garden. The now-demolished Tibetan Revolutionary Exhibition Hall outside the wall of Shöl has already been built.

Inside left: Central Lhasa, within the Lingkor. Satellite photograph, 1970. Scale 1 : 10 000. Five further years of development are documented in this digitally manipulated Corona satellite view (21 November 1970). Little has happened compared to the development between 1960 and 1965, years of major Chinese presence in Lhasa. Events of the Cultural Revolution (1966–76), when politics, not construction, dominated, are a probable explanation. Some road building has taken place north of the Potala, the channel across the road from Shöl has been filled in, Mentsikhang Lam has been built in a formerly marshy area and construction of Beijing Shar Lam has started east of the old town. Kundeling monastery, totally destroyed during the Cultural Revolution, seems still intact.

Lhasa from mountain south of the town. F. Spencer Chapman, 1936. This is among the earliest known photos of Lhasa seen from this mountain. The main features of the town are exposed with near-perfect clarity. Both Drepung and Sera monasteries are outside the frame but would have been visible in a panorama.

Lhasa from mountain south of the town, 1999. This modern view from the same position as F. Spencer Chapman's photograph shows the explosive development of Lhasa. The old town is just discernible around the Jokhang Temple, but no longer as a clear structure. The river is being tamed and its shallows filled in for housing and institutions. The city seems to spread to all part of the valley, stopping only at the mountains.

Architecture

CHARACTER AND SOURCES

Tibet is a country of vast arid spaces enclosed by mountain ranges. From the air the land looks deserted. Before the age of paved roads and airstrips, very little indicated human presence from a distance – a few cultivated fields along river valleys and isolated villages dotting the landscape. The traditional Tibetan building is modest and blends into this huge landscape. Even buildings as monumental as the Potala Palace result from a humble, low-key architectural tradition, which pays little attention to symmetry, axes and other conventional tools of architectural style.

This chapter describes Tibetan architecture with a focus on Lhasa, its townscape, architectural monuments and so-called vernacular architecture – buildings and structures that are simple, which meet normal habitat needs, and are native to the place. In physical form and content they reflect the material and immaterial components of cultural traditions, building traditions and the natural environment. A specific vernacular architecture may be found across a broad geographical region of diverse cultures with similar material conditions. Such a tradition contrasts with formal, learned architecture – buildings for the elite – where achievement of aesthetic effects, often according to principles of style specific to a certain period or cultural area, are deemed most important.

Tibetan architecture is clearly founded on principles seen across the Himalayan region, but with individual characteristics that make it unique as a cultural expression. There may be few apparent 'academic' or theoretical elements, because its character and content are generated from practical needs, the constraints of building materials and the harsh physical environment. Strong formal models and rules have come from the Buddhist architecture of India and China, so Tibetan architecture as a whole belongs to both vernacular and formal categories. Without oversimplifying, we have chosen to use the term 'traditional architecture' throughout.

The architectural style that characterizes old Lhasa largely developed in the 17th century, when the 'classical order' reached its peak in expression and refinement.[1] This style, characteristic of the buildings and artistic activity of the Gelukpa school of Tibetan Buddhism, differs somewhat from the other schools.

In Tibetan architecture it is sometimes difficult and artificial to distinguish sharply between 'architecture' and 'decoration' – the two are aspects of an architectural assembly often of rare integration and quality. Individuals with different training and background perform the work, and still the result appears strong, handsome and integrated. Art historians, conservators and architects clearly have different opinions on Tibetan architecture, as evident in many publications. Our approach is concerned with what can be observed and reflected upon, with a focus on architectural character, rules, construction and building types rather than the origins and nature of Tibetan architecture.

In uniting Central Tibet in the 7th century, Songtsen Gampo initiated a process of nation building. Successive powerful secular and religious rulers contributed to this process, each adding his own stamp of authority to society and its spiritual-physical environment. Urban culture only developed in Lhasa during and after the 5th Dalai Lama (d. 1682), a period assumed also instrumental for the growth of the main monastic centres.

To appreciate the symbolism, aesthetics and meaning of Tibetan architecture it is necessary to understand the broader approach to the world and the cosmos.[2] From earliest times, the role of religion, including its rituals, goals, habits and wonderful unseen world of gods, demons and deities, has formed the basis for an entire approach to life. In Tibet, this approach binds together the environment, the people, their arts and activities and, by extension, even their homes and buildings. Tibetan architecture is considered by some to be of minor artistic importance if compared to other aspects of the country's rich material, intellectual and religious culture. Yet a closer study reveals that such a comparison fails when appreciating the architecture's unique qualities and full heritage.

In India and China, architecture had little place in the traditional hierarchy of artistic and aesthetic activity or cultural thought. Indian religious architecture may nevertheless be said to reflect Indian culture as much as any other means of artistic expression. In China, architecture became a valued aspect of artistic activity only during the last two hundred years, even though the creation of such carefully thought-out complexes as the Forbidden City and Temple of Heaven in Beijing (both 15th century) display many aspects that today are considered artistically outstanding. Architectural style, despite a low status through much of history, clearly existed and was consciously used to promote worship and to enhance the importance of rituals. In time it also reflected the power of the rulers and their institutions.

In most societies it would be absurd to detach architectural work from a concept of durability. From the standpoint of

Opposite: Potala and Shöl, 1994. The village of Shöl, claimed to be much older than the Potala Palace, still has one-storey 'farmhouses' that could be part of any village in Central Tibet today and resemble those from a millennium ago. This view can be seen to illustrate the 'start' and culmination of Tibetan architecture.

Tibetan farmhouse, village and land-scape, 1987. This timeless, typically understated architecture is the basis for all Tibetan buildings. The lower part of the farmhouse walls is built in stone, the upper part in sun-dried clay bricks. On top of the walls are stored firewood (background) and dried yak-dung 'cakes' for fuel.

Potala Palace, 1995. A long distance separates the farmhouse from the awe-inspiring monumentality of the Potala, masterpiece of Tibetan architecture. Yet the basic materials and principles of construction have changed little.

Buddhism, the considerable religious merit acquired by building – often a main purpose for both initiator and builder – would be unaffected even if the building was never completed, or collapsed: the overall activity would be seen as a votive offering.[3] As a result, construction work in India could sometimes be carried out hastily with little concern for durability. This seems not to have been the case in Tibet, where severe climate and scarce resources demanded solid and lasting work.

The oldest structures in Lhasa known today are considered to have originated in the 7th–8th centuries during the height of the Tibetan empire. After internal struggle and confusion, there followed some 200 years of social and cultural unrest. Only in the 11th century did relative stability return, and with it a revival of Buddhism. It seems unlikely that many structures existing today would pre-date the 11th century.

Buddhism and with it Indian architectural knowledge is considered initially to have reached Tibet from China, and perhaps Central Asia. Tibetan contacts with India and China were probably quite extensive already during or even before the 7th–9th centuries, and with them came inevitable architectural influences, from east and west; they must have contributed fundamentally to the character of built form, as seen in parts of the Jokhang and Ramoche temples and Samye monastery.

Classical Indian texts came with the new religion and set clear rules for the design of buildings. Tibetan religious architecture was modelled on that of India, especially at the symbolic level, when architecture transforms into sacred art. In the words of the great Italian Tibetologist Giuseppe Tucci: 'to construct means to remake the world by following the pattern of the mandala'.[4]

The square, with a focus on its centre, the *axis mundi*, was in India and China the symbol of the ordered world. This feature is present in all religious structures; the sacred centre marks the point where celestial, terrestrial and nether worlds meet. The circular or round plan concept may have come from outside the region – at a very early time from as far away as Egypt and the Mediterranean.

In a 'combined' Indian-Chinese tradition, the very act of building establishes by magical rites a necessary rapport between the universe and a chosen site. Geomantic appraisals were used to cleanse and prepare the site and its surroundings for the sacred purpose of construction. The relationship between architecture and nature was based on invisible and empowering forces rather than as part of a quest for aesthetics and harmony. Nevertheless, in Tibet the patrons, designers and builders never lost touch with the practical aspects of life and construction.

Alongside Indian influence, China probably contributed significantly to Tibetan architecture and culture, especially in eastern Tibet, from the Tang dynasty (618–907) onwards. Complicated constructions in wood emerged – an extraordinary craftsmanship, with multiple layers of structural and decorative members filled with complex spatial concepts. At this time contacts between Tibet and the Newars of Nepal were also strong, as seen in the involvement by Newari builders and artists in Central Tibet from the 7th century onwards.

Tibetan architecture, emphasizes an overall simplicity of form and calmness that has come from native genius melded with foreign forms. At one level it can be understood as a manifestation of Buddhism's quest for peace, truth and serenity, particularly if compared to the dynamic nature of its close cultural relative, Hindu architecture.[5] Above all, Tibetan architecture seeks to link the cosmos and man through a symbolism closely related to human needs and experience.

Ruin, Shide monastery, 1995. Shide monastery, even in its dilapidated state, stands as one of the finest examples of the 'classical' building tradition. A wealth of information comes from its proportions, materials and details, such as the fine benma *frieze with a rare triangular 'window', the characteristic masonry and the black frames around the windows, here seen to be a thin layer of plaster.*

UNIQUE TIBETAN ARCHITECTURE

Unlike the stone buildings of India, which are often totally covered in carved decorations, or the glazed tile architecture of Islam, with its carpet-like decorations of geometrical patterns, exterior decorations of Tibetan buildings are confined to wood and metal. The stonework is normally decorated very little if at all; this perhaps reflects architectural style, or tradition, or simply the fact that local stone, due to size or hardness, is difficult to decorate. Tibetan architects and master builders seem to convert this potential limitation into a creative advantage. An important characteristic of Tibetan architecture is its refined, rhythmic play of large, 'empty' surfaces contrasting with small surfaces where a maximum of form and colour is concentrated with astonishing impact and richness.

The combination of crystal-clear air, distant vistas and architectural character makes it possible to discern building details and nuances at considerable distances. This visual quality is another important feature of expression. Blazing sunshine produces from afar pitch-black shadows that up close reveal forms and colours of unusual intensity.

In Tibetan religious buildings the contrast between exterior and interior spaces might raise speculation that the 'architect', constrained by the limitations of building materials and methods, only reveals his true intentions inside, in spaces that can seem over-articulated and over-decorated. Here every surface is covered with wall paintings, metalwork, woodcarvings, thangkas and decorative textiles. The overwhelming result may indeed accentuate the experience of worship, for a temple interior represents the heavenly abode of deities, a world naturally rich in every aspect, and shows the limitless affluence bestowed on them.

Alternatively, contrasting exterior and interior forms may result from the architect shaping and decorating the interiors according to another set of specific traditions, those of the monastic community and priesthood. Tibetan Buddhist buildings – as opposed to those of Japanese Zen Buddhism – have little place for minimalism as a spiritual quality or necessity.

A typical Tibetan building, although formed in unity with the landscape, often appears larger than life in this realm of few features and ungraspable scale. The building volumes are rough, as if hewn out of the rock or merged together with the landscape itself. The result is nearly always one of grandness, be the building large or small; the monumentality emerges from the interplay of the man-made and the natural. Its severe exterior character takes form from the nature of building materials, the harsh climate and the need of inhabitants for protection. After crossing the entrance threshold, though, warm and friendly spaces reveal themselves, often of small scale but always well formed and decorated in ranges of rich colours – deep red, brilliant yellow, intense blues and greens. In Tibetan interiors, little seems to limit the extent of decoration.

Tibetan architecture can be seen as obsessively symbolic in its overall architectural character: orientation, planning and design, decoration and artistic detailing. Classical Buddhist texts set rules for exterior and interior layouts, defined proportions and even dictated the number of columns to be used in various types of interior spaces. The mandala, a mystic circle of great symbolic power, forms the base of all architectural concerns. Despite such strong guiding rules, Tibetan architecture is firmly based on common sense and practical needs.

Tibetan buildings may appear rather uniform. A single building is normally square, rectangular or trapezoidal in form, with a massive stone base and battered walls built in fine masonry or with simpler mud bricks for the upper floors, topped

Yumbu Lagang, 1997. Yumbu Lagang in the Yarlung valley, 120 km south-east of Lhasa and south of the Tsangpo river, is believed to resemble Central Tibet's first buildings. Songtsen Gampo is said to have lived here before moving his capital to Lhasa. The small fort, integrated with the natural rock formations it stands on, overlooks the valley from a steep hill. It was most likely destroyed and rebuilt many times through history, and although a few parts of the building might date to the first millennium, Yumbu Lagang as it stands today – mixing traditional and popular Tibetan and Chinese architectural features – probably shares little with this early period. During much of Tibet's history, warfare required important buildings, whether on hills or in the plains, to be built for defence.

Courtyard in Lhasa, 1997. This courtyard of a small two-storey mansion typifies most secular buildings in Lhasa. The original building is nearly hidden by additions in the courtyard, at the wings and on the roof, but the main structure is intact and basically sound. Many families now share what was before the home of a single noble family and its servants. In such modest buildings one can find most elements used in Tibetan architecture.

with a flat roof. The strong, sloping verticality of external walls is cut in long horizontal lines towards the top; the walls of monastic and other religious buildings are bordered in a dark band known as the *benma* frieze. In a number of monastic buildings, the flat roofs contrast with the violently curved, Chinese-style golden roofs of their most sacred structures.

Windows are usually grouped and become larger towards the top floors respecting sound principles for distribution of static loads and the need for more light in the upper domestic rooms. The positioning of windows may also let the wall grow lighter towards the top where the building requires less girth for defence. External building components in wood are painted in strong colours.

Tibetan forts (*dzongs*) are austere and clearly 'military' in format, fortified and unapproachable with tall bastions and heavy, easily defendable confined points of access.

The rural residential building consists of a main house of one or two storeys with an enclosed courtyard to the south, inside of which are smaller structures and sheds. An 'isolated' residential building sits within a strong enclosure; clustered houses are more open in character, as if relying on the strength of their neighbours. In rocky landscapes, the village clusters often form naturally fortified structures.

TOWNSCAPE

Tibetan cultural history pays scant attention to the differences between a rural or nomadic way of life and life in the towns. The rural character of the Tibetan habitat made such concerns largely irrelevant until recent, rapid urbanization. Even towns such as Gyantse and Shigatse existed largely as agricultural villages up to the 20th century. Development of an urban culture, with the growth and interdependence of commerce, art and science, is in most societies regarded as a cultural high point. One wonders whether this has ever been the case in Tibet, or whether this 'cultural climax' might have evolved in other directions within a theocratic society.

Little is known about urban form in Tibet before the 5th Dalai Lama made Lhasa his capital in the mid-17th century. Earlier towns are assumed to have been dense village communities of farmers and servants, located near the monasteries and estates of feudal lords. Lhasa, too, was probably just a very small town before the 5th Dalai Lama reconstructed and expanded the Jokhang Temple and encouraged rural noble families to move from the countryside to settle in the town to be part of the new government and bureaucracy. These strategic moves contributed significantly to central control and to the expansion of Lhasa.

Tibetan towns have an organic character – Lhasa of the pre-1960s had no straight streets. According to legend, Lhasa was founded around the Jokhang, a temple built over the heart of a demoness whose ferocious size and power needed to be controlled for Buddhism to flourish. It seems Lhasa may have developed as a concentric structure around the Jokhang, though its exact development remains unknown. In contrast, Gyantse grew along a long, naturally curved street connecting the monastic and secular power points, monastery and fort. Gyantse and Lhasa illustrate two archetypal patterns of townscape and urban development that are found in many cultures. Reasons for their differences may be equally found in the constraints of topography and environment as in the purposes for why each community developed.

The rural character of early Lhasa stands out in clear contrast to the dense urban qualities of, for instance, Bhaktapur, the historical town in Nepal's Kathmandu valley. In Lhasa the generous spaces between large residences and estates only filled very slowly. Strong enclosing walls protected a number of important monastic communities. Samye monastery, on the north bank of the Tsangpo, was built with a near-circular wall enclosing it. The monasteries at Sakya, Shigatse and Gyantse were well protected, with access through only a few gates. Written sources indicate that Lhasa may also have had protective walls during some periods.

ARCHITECTURAL 'RULES'

Location

Important for all Tibetan architecture are the qualities of protection, merging into the landscape and commanding a view. Forts, monasteries and ordinary houses chose easily defensible locations with good views to warn of visitors. Most farms and village clusters are located away from scarce arable land, often built into the landscape with materials from near the site itself.

Height and high points are auspicious. In Tibet's hierarchical society, the symbols and functions of authority occupied the 'higher' places. The first fortified palaces on Marpori were located there for protection and for power. The Potala of today remains a fortified hilltop construction.

It is hard to imagine the practical reasons for locating the Jokhang Temple and thereby the town of Lhasa in the middle of an open plain, had it not been for the special circumstances around the vision of a geomantic demoness whose body lay across Tibet. Once built, the Jokhang became auspicious, a site considered desirable to live near. In Buddhism it is important to perform clockwise circumambulations of sacred sites, buildings and other constructions. Such routes are called *koras*, and all major sacred places and objects have at least one kora. In Lhasa one can imagine that the koras – a series of concentric walking paths – were established when the Bhrikuti temple (later named Jokhang) and its mandala-like structure of supporting temples and shrines were completed. Maybe the koras even pre-date the installation of the Buddha image in the temple. A kora is not a planned structure but a physical result of religious practice.[6]

Orientation

Orienting buildings towards the south is a general rule in Tibet;[7] orientation towards the east is common in neighbouring Bhutan, Sikkim and Ladakh.[8] In Tibet the custom might come from the need to catch as much sunlight as possible, or perhaps the practice reflects early contact with China, where a north–south orientation for buildings and towns has always been the predominant custom.

Lhasa's two most important temples, the Jokhang and Ramoche, are rare exceptions to the rule. Ramoche faces east and the Jokhang faces west. A hypothetical explanation is that the orientation of each building reflects the place of origin of Songtsen Gampo's two queens. Bhrikuti came from Nepal (west) and Wen Cheng from China (east).

Another exception to the rule, which could indicate the preference for an eastern orientation for religious structures, is Jebumgang temple in Lhasa, north of the Barkor. Jebumgang is a square building with double symmetry and identical entrances to all four outer walls, but with the entrance to the inner sanctum facing east. Where exposure towards the sun is unimportant, facing east might be preferred.

Axial quality

Tibetan architecture contrasts sharply with Chinese and Western concepts of axial symmetry. In China and the West, an axis may be described as functional and directional in guiding linear movement towards a point – an important urban feature, an altar or the emperor's throne. The axis may also underline a material or spiritual wish to control the landscape, superimposing the building complex, the townscape or the intention of the ruler on the environment in an act of strong will. In contrast, movement connected with Tibetan ritual buildings is circular. In Buddhism, worshippers and ritual processions move around a centre, manifested or not, in a clockwise direction. The axis exists in focusing attention on the centre, or *axis mundi*, of the sacred space. And though of central importance, this concentration of focus is done in a seemingly passive way.

In contrast to Tibetan townscape, a building in Tibet seeks frontal or façade symmetry if possible. Also, in highly irregular and complex building assemblies, such as the Potala, different components are often individually symmetrical on the exterior. Residential mansions may have a similar single-axis layout and massing, with interior spaces of the main building organized according to domestic functions in clear hierarchical order. In monastic building complexes, exterior and interior spaces are often organized with apparent symmetry around the direction of access, even if the movement is asymmetrical.

Concept of space

Monasteries are ideally located at the foot of a south-facing mountain slope towards a valley with a perennial river, to

Kelsang Dekyi Palace, Norbulingka, 1997. This small, elegant building was built in 1922 for the 13th Dalai Lama, who is said to have used it as his bedroom. The corner windows and details around the edges of the roof – conceived as a thin slab – are in line with similar expressions in the West at the same time, under the name Modernism.

Temple hall, Drepung, 1987. This temple hall at Drepung monastery, like other sizeable interior spaces, is filled with pillars. Tibetan architecture could be called an 'architecture of pillars', with such 'forests' of columns subdividing the main area into many small uniform spaces, which makes it difficult to grasp the overall space. Like Gothic form, Tibetan architecture is preoccupied with construction and form in the spatial design.

catch the low winter sun, to preserve scarce arable land and to find protection under a hilltop-castle, as seen in Shigatse, Gyantse and Lhasa.

In principle, Tibetan monasteries and large domestic buildings come from the same generic plan: the courtyard layout. A courtyard contains one- or two-storey outbuildings, which enclose a three-storey main building on the north side, facing south. The monastery court serves as the social space, with major events often taking place under tent canvas to protect from a hot summer sun. In Western terms, this could be called a 'Renaissance space' with the emphasis on the spatial qualities. The courtyard serves to unify; its continuous walls, controlling, comforting and relatively distant, hold within them the space for ceremonies, lectures, music and dance performances and gatherings.

Approaching an urban monastery or temple from narrow, shadowy alleyways, one enters through a small porch into the clear sunlight of the spacious courtyard. From there another small porch leads into the dark, mystical interior of the temple's main area. A total change in the character of space has occurred during this small transition. Inside the temple, darkness takes over and it becomes difficult to grasp the overall dimensions because dominating pillars subdivide the hall into many smaller spaces. To emphasize its symbolic purpose, the central space in the main temple is often of considerable height, stretching up two or three storeys, with the focus on centrally placed votive sculptures. Natural light enters from skylights only; searching shafts of sun illuminate colourful wooden construction, textiles and golden images in an embracing space of varied depths, contrasts and hues. Internal circulation always follows the massive dark walls that compress the space; the overall spatial experience becomes one of contrasting opposites, as part of a conscious and highly developed architectural and ritual approach to space, which creates an intimate and proper atmosphere for devotion.

The formal space of the courtyard is private, whether sacral or secular. It is closed off from the public urban space by heavy doors. Formal public space does not exist. The few public squares in Lhasa are self-grown extensions of streets, either functioning as markets or as 'outdoor' extensions of the temple hall. This may indicate that Lhasa had a primary network of monastic institutions and communities, with secondary residential areas, and that public secular life did not develop a need for formalized space.

Houses for the rural aristocracy were built in the courtyard layout. A large, rectangular main house on two or three floors faced south, with a courtyard in front and quite narrow buildings on one or two floors providing space for servants, animals and storage. All activities connected with the daily running of an extensive estate centred on the courtyard. With sunlight essential, the main building had several small courtyards, useful and charming, screened from wind and an outside world.

In Lhasa, the building type most used remained a rural fortified dwelling. In a few of the more recent traditional buildings one notices certain international architectural influences. Here, particularly with windows set into the masonry, architectural elements are connected by breaking them down into their constituent elements, as slabs and lines and points, as if in the Modernist tradition of Western architecture of the 1920s and 30s. Examples are pavilions in Norbulingka and Shöl Lekung. Especially in Norbulingka an intention to architecturally connect interior and exterior spaces seems evident in the more recent buildings. Large windows are set on the corner of heavy masonry walls and a thin slab of flat roof protrudes; the look clearly resembles ideas of Modernism. Could there have been some form of cross-fertilization? It is well known that the great American architect Frank Lloyd Wright was a serious student of Tibetan architecture. Whether this Lhasa 'sub-style' was imported or indigenous is not altogether clear, but it was most likely connected to the introduction of steel beams at the start of the 20th century.

STARTING CONSTRUCTION

The master builder (*wuchen*) is responsible for the layout and main geometry of the building. He determines the overall height, and from this he calculates the width of the walls at their bases, and also the foundations. Artists sometimes draw plans and elevations for important buildings; this was the case in the 17th century when the artist Choying Gyamtso did so for the regent, Desi Sanggye Gyatso, at commencement of the Potala Red Palace on Marpori.

The 'masonry wuchen' is in charge of the overall building work and supervises activities without taking direct part in the actual construction. The master mason and master plasterer (*shalbon*) together are responsible for laying the *arga*, a fine clay used to make roofs and floors. Most plasterers were – and are – female, but they could never achieve the wuchen or mastercraftsman level due to the low status of women.

Tibetan building work is carried out according to firm rules and unique measurements. The smallest measurement is *karma* (9.5 millimetres). Four karmas make one *tsun,* a Tibetan standard equal to the length of the thumb's middle joint. Seven tsuns minus one karma make one *jongdo* (256 millimetres). It is believed the jongdo standard was defined by the measure used to build Samye, Tibet's first monastery, towards the end of the 8th century. It was revived in the 1940s during repairs to Samye, and the jongdo is used to this day as a unit of measurement.

Construction activity in most cultures still involves the performance of certain ceremonies, though in the West such things are almost forgotten. In Tibet, religious rituals take place throughout the building process, the most important ones at the start and finish. Offerings of butter, tea, beer and rice are made to the earth deities at the very beginning. *Khatas*, long white ceremonial scarves, are presented to the head craftsmen, and during the completion of each stage to thank the construction team for their skill and hard work. At the conclusion, the 'releasing celebration' inaugurates the building and honours the master builder. In Lhasa, these traditional rituals which punctuate the building process seem to be disappearing, though in West Tibet, Ladakh and other remote areas the ceremonies carry on.[9]

Nunnery, Chakpori, 1994. Here is a typical 'three-pillar room' in a religious setting. The dimensions and proportions of the space are pleasant but the pillars dominate.

SPACE AND CONSTRUCTION

Interior Tibetan space is dominated by a layout of pillars placed in a remarkably uniform grid, regardless of building type. Tibetan architecture can therefore adequately be called an 'architecture of pillars', in which the grid is a consequence of the length of timber beams – between 2.0 and 2.2 metres – that could be transported on animals across high mountain passes to Lhasa.

A square room has 1, 4, 9 or 16 pillars, or more, depending on its size; a rectangular rooms has 2, 3, 4, 6 or 8 pillars, or more. The basic domestic unit of space is a one-pillar room with an area of about 4 by 4.4 metres. A poorer urban family may have two such rooms, one with a window facing the street, the other a kitchen with a skylight or window towards a courtyard. Each room has two kangs (heated platforms) for sitting and sleeping, a few cabinets and a few small tables. Larger tables and chairs were never part of the traditional Tibetan interior. This standard space module, the basic geometric unit of practically all traditional buildings in Tibet, was seen as a limitation only when it became possible to replace the construction of short beams and pillars with long steel beams. High costs of transport prevented the new fashion of steel from becoming widespread.

Stone foundations of even large buildings are quite shallow, normally not deeper than 300–400 millimetres below ground level, being as wide as to 1.5 times the width of the wall at its base. The most important foundations were those for the columns, receiving a concentrated heavy load. With changes in ground conditions (changes in groundwater level etc) and erosion from below and above ground, many buildings

are affected by differential settlement and partial fallout of the wall construction. Increasing water content in the ground and high water absorption in the stonework is seen to lead to frost damage.

Construction of the main loadbearing walls starts with the master craftsman controlling the main geometry and setting out of all main walls. In the loadbearing walls, often 1 to 1.5 metres thick at the base, an inner and outer layer of stone are separated with a wide gap filled with crushed stones and clay. The clay acts as a strengthening agent that cements together the two stone 'skins'. The walls are built layer by layer; traditionally, workers would build only three layers of stone per day, allowing the construction to settle and dry before continuing. The interior skin of stone stands vertically and the outside face of the wall slopes inwards (battered wall). This construction is a natural way to give the structure sufficient rigidity and flexibility while still limiting its overall weight.

Every course of stone is turned up towards the corners, giving the stones near each corner an increased capacity to accommodate lateral disturbances, such as earthquakes. A course consists of a row of aligned large stones, each separated from the next by a layer of small stones or chips surrounding it. Most stonework is set in a mortar of specially selected clay. The construction with alternating layers of small and large stones gives the walls added strength to limit any

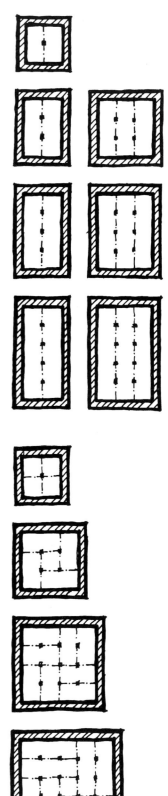

Multi-pillar rooms. Scale approximately 1 : 400. The basic 'one-pillar room' developed by the addition of pillars into larger rooms. The main beam normally follows the direction of the room, but in wider rooms, here shown as a square, the direction sometimes shifts for reasons of stability.

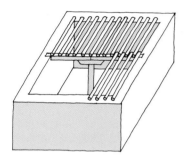

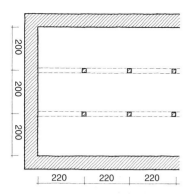

Four-pillar room. Plan of a room's four-pillar section, with dimensions. The main beams often span about 10 per cent more than the secondary beams.

One-pillar room. A one-pillar room with main beams and secondary beams.

Above right: Building. The construction system of a typical Tibetan building with a depth of one-pillar and a gallery for access. This could be the wing of a large monastery, with monks' quarters. The main beams follow the direction of the building and the secondary beams span between the walls and main beams.

Right: Karmashar temple, Lhasa, 1994. Though Karmashar is said to date back to the 8th century, this wall is probably not that old. The quality of the masonry is very high and the colour indicates that the building is more than two hundred years old.

lateral damage. Such building methods require considerable skill from the masons, resulting in beautiful and well-built traditional stone walls. Despite the high skills of masons, traditional Tibetan and Himalayan architecture never developed the stone arch. In Lhasa, the buildings' main walls have relatively little internal cross-bracing or reinforcing in timber and stonework, a sign that earthquakes are fewer and less punishing here than in many other parts of the Himalayan region.

The loadbearing elements of a Tibetan building, those elements that bring the loads down to the foundations, are the thick external walls, thinner internal walls, which divide rooms and serve as horizontal bracing, and columns. The walls are made in stone or clay blocks and columns and secondary construction elements are made in wood. Columns or pillars were commonly made of the hardwood juniper, usually about 200 by 200 millimetres in size. Before transport to the construction site for assembly, the pillar, brackets and main beam assembly would be mounted (upside down) and adjusted, the final construction erected as parts of a prefabricated system. In large constructions the pillars were made from several lengths of wood, sometimes expressed in a cross section in the form of a mandala. Similar to columns in for instance Gothic architecture, the structural aspect is enhanced by forming a larger column from a bundle of smaller ones. This also adds an impression of relative lightness to the construction, as seen in the outer entrance of the Jokhang and Ramoche.

Pillars are the most important elements of interior construction, and when possible they were traditionally made of monolithic tree trunks; the oldest part of the Jokhang retains such examples. There is a story of a Mongol ruler who visited Sakya monastery, south-west of Shigatse, and brought as his gift an enormous tree trunk to be a pillar of the new temple hall. That a piece of untreated timber would be an appropriate gift between heads of nations tells a lot about its value, its rarity and the problems of transport in those days.

The top part of a Tibetan column, the capital, has three components. The top is formed as a small square block cut out of the column itself. On top of this sits squarely the 'short bow', a horizontal bracket with a length about twice the column width. The 'short bow' can be plain but in finer buildings is usually carved. On top of the 'short bow' sits the 'long bow,' often as long as the column itself and tapered towards both ends in more or less elaborate ways. The main beam, normally in pine and around 150 by 210 millimetres in section, is supported on the 'long bow'.

The picture emerges of a squat construction with short columns regularly spaced, all dictated by short lengths of available timber.

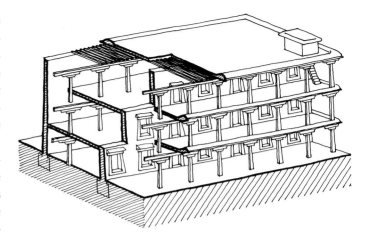

In cases where the ceiling height needed to be higher than was possible with the standard pillar and beam system, a composite framework was introduced. Tie-beams, brackets and corbels – long and short and stacked and cantilevered in layers widening towards the top – would sit on top of the main beams. Such composite beams could add significantly to the room

height, and would mainly be used in spectacular central spaces of important, usually monastic, buildings.

The beams in one room are often laid perpendicular to the beams in adjoining rooms in order to strengthen the rigidity of the overall construction. For the floor or flat roof construction, the secondary layer of beams - traditionally of round timbers – is supported by the main beam and the structural wall. Secondary beams of 70–100 millimetres in diameter are laid at a distance of 200–250 millimetres from each other. In a larger, high quality building, such as a monastery or mansion, builders use secondary beams of 100–120 millimetres. In between the beams, smaller timbers are placed to support the heavy construction fill on top. These in-fill timbers or slats are in section up to 25 by 45 millimetres, often shaped and decorated and sometimes even cut and planed as small planks. In simpler buildings more irregular round branches are used.

On the layer of beams and small timbers is placed first a layer of cobblestones, often as large as 100–150 millimetres across; on top of this comes a layer of yellow mud, about 100 millimetres thick. The stones serve to separate the wood from the clay in order to prevent the wood from rotting with the clay's humidity. On top of the yellow mud come layers of clay of different granular quality, known as the arga.

Openings for doors and windows are formed as part of the main loadbearing construction, with secondary door and window frames put in only after the main structure is completed and allowed to dry.

In high quality buildings, all horizontal surfaces, mainly roofs and floors, are always made with arga clay. On top of the yellow mud or clay, the first of three layers of arga clay has granules of 15–30 millimetres in size. The clay is watered while being continuously tamped and rammed with traditional tools for compaction and smoothing by the arga team. Through at least one day – always accompanied by singing and dancing – the clay is worked into a quite moist and pliable mass to an overall thickness of some 20–30 millimetres. For ramming, the tool used is called *babdo* (*bok-do*), a wooden stick with a flat, rounded stone fixed to the bottom. The top two layers of arga clay are much finer than the first, with the top layer of clay granules being very fine, like rough silt. After days of compacting, smoothing and watering, the arga surfaces become remarkably smooth. They are laid to be continuous, and all flat areas, parapets and other exposed surfaces are covered in arga with rounded, smoothed edges. As a final activity, and to provide water resistance, the top layer is first impregnated several times with extracts of a tree-bark (*yon bok*) and then several times with a resin (*pokar*) that has been boiled in rapeseed oil. This method is very similar to that used for building flat

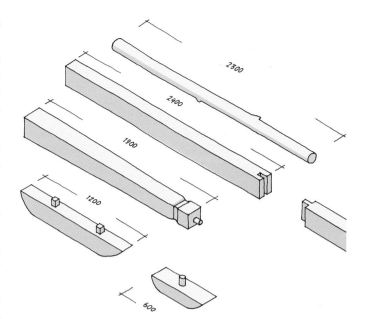

Wood elements. Major parts of a Tibetan timber construction, to distribute the interior loads of a building, are the tapering pillar with its capital, the 'short bow' and the 'long bow', the main beam slotted together over the pillars to form one long member and the round secondary beams.

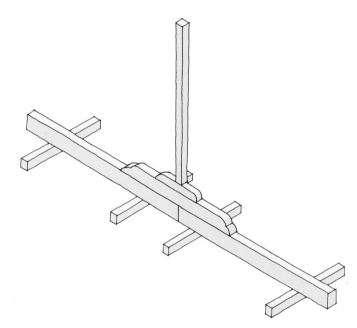

Workshop assembly. Fitting the wooden elements together upside down in the workshop before final mounting on site.

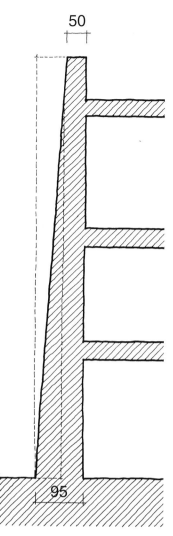

Wall section. General section showing the sloping outside and vertical inside of a wall.

Ruin, Shide monastery, Lhasa, 1994. This section of wall shows the outer and inner 'skin' of masonry and the rubble filling the cavity.

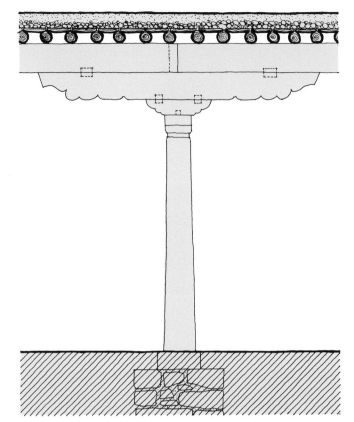

Clockwise from top middle:

Main entrance porch, Jokhang, 1995. The heavy pillars are assembled from several pieces of timber to create a mandala-like cross section held together by metal straps. Comparison with a Gothic approach to decoration is tempting.

Pillar and beam. This schematic section presents the principles of timber construction.

Arga teams, Potala, 1995. Arga roof being laid by two teams singing and dancing in competition. They tamp and pound the wet arga clay with bok-dos.

Arga edge, Shöl Dekyiling, 1995. The cornice of an arga roof being impregnated with oil and resin to become waterproof.

Laying arga. On a roof, workers lay the first coarse layer of arga clay on top of the stone layer. They level the arga with bok-dos, tamping tools made of a round piece of slate fixed to a long stick.

Interior roof. Typical interior roof. The main beam, decorated with lotus and chötseg (carved or painted pattern of tiny cubes), carries the blue secondary beams, which support the small yellow infill timbers. The floor/roof construction rests on top of them.

Capital and bow. A pillar, bow and main beam construction of extraordinary quality. The beam is built up with several expanding layers of smaller members.

waterproof surfaces in Yemen, another arid mountainous region. In contrast to Buddhist Tibet, in Yemen animal fats are used to waterproof the top layers of finely crushed and compacted clay. In both cases, the finished surface needs to be maintained regularly with plant or animal oil, preferably each year.

ARCHITECTURAL DETAILS

The benma frieze

The purple benma frieze, a unique feature of Tibetan architecture, is a structural decoration that tops façades. It appears as a long horizontal band terminating the white, red or ochre battered stone walls of monastic and religious buildings. The frieze is made of thin branches of the tamarisk bush (benma) that are cut in short lengths, about 40 centimetres, bundled together with leather string, reinforced with clay and wooden pegs, cut evenly and stacked with the end showing. Painted purple, benma looks like velvet from a distance.

In contrast to the sloping or battered masonry wall of the building, the benma frieze is a horizontal element that in section is vertical, both a decorative and a practical element. It is the lightweight part of the parapet and begins where the main wall has reached the uppermost point determined by its minimal thickness; sometimes it is found between two floors as well. In some cases the normal double-skin wall, with sloping external skin, may terminate lower than calculated. In this case the benma frieze, with its lighter construction and vertical section, can assist to 'complete' the wall by achieving the required room height. This is one reason for the frieze being built in many differing heights, to suit specific circumstances.

Windows

A room needs fresh air, daylight and warm sunshine. In Tibet there is plenty of each. Tibetan buildings are not artificially heated; most warmth enters the building as natural solar heating through window openings, so the orientation of buildings and living rooms towards the sun becomes critical. Before window glass became available in Tibet, the windows were closed with wooden shutters that permitted some air and light to enter but kept the worst cold out. As soon as the sun was up in wintertime, the shutters would be opened to let the sunshine in. In summer they would remain closed to keep the comfortable temperature inside.

External windows range from narrow slots, as seen in the lower parts of the Potala and Jokhang walls, to the large win-

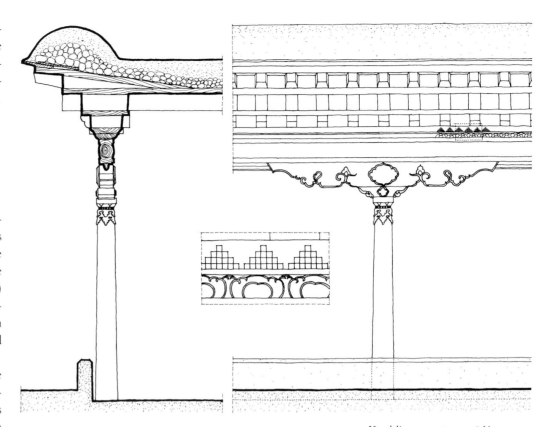

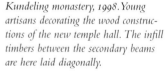

dows of mansion living rooms and the Potala's main upper façade. The Potala main façade, from bottom to top, displays the entire 'catalogue' of window shapes and sizes – in a way that beautifully expresses the tectonic character of the construction.

Windows always have loadbearing wooden elements with secondary frames and shutters. Because the masonry arch is an unknown feature in Tibetan architecture, the openings are limited to relatively modest sizes depending on the amount of timber available for supporting the opening in a masonry

Kundeling monastery, 1998. Young artisans decorating the wood constructions of the new temple hall. The infill timbers between the secondary beams are here laid diagonally.

Pillar and beam, Potala. Section and front view of an open gallery towards a courtyard. The multi-layered expanding build-up of the main beam carries a cornice of arga-paved roof. Only the middle layer of secondary beam ends are the 'real' beams; the others are only short decorative pieces of wood. Detailed are the common lotus and chötseg frieze.

Benma, Potala, 1987. Enormous double benma panels separate the White Palace and Red Palace. The 'start' of the benma panel has no relation to the floors of the building. The white, round beam-ends are only for decoration.

The benma frieze. The cornice of a major religious building shows the construction of the benma frieze, which is vertical in contrast to the sloping masonry wall. This is a visual refinement as well as a practical advantage.

construction. This also explains why large windows are 'stacked' on top of each other to constitute one large wooden construction, often over several floors. The most spectacular example of this is the enormous 'window' at the Potala that spans over seven floors in height. The norm in large mansions is a two-storey sun-window.

Broad, black frames, both decorative and symbolic, border the standard Tibetan window. The border is traditionally made of special clay, 20–30 millimetres thick, and is applied to the stone wall as a final finish after the window is put in place. Many people believe the border has a practical function by

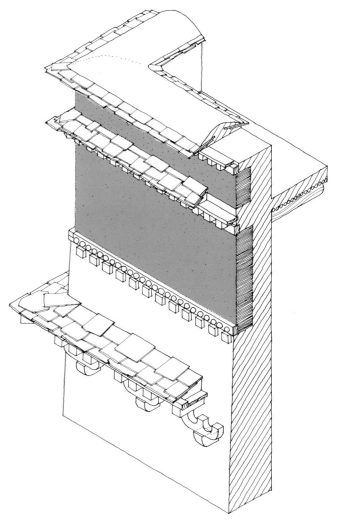

somehow reinforcing the wall, which is weakened by the opening. In structural terms this sounds quite doubtful. Another more likely opinion is that the black pigment applied to the plaster, or integral with it, collects heat from the sun and then, by natural ventilation, 'wafts' heated air into the building.

Doors

Doors and windows pose different problems of construction. A door opening may be large while at the same time being located at the bottom of a tall, heavy stone wall – a definite structural disadvantage. The heavy dimensions and elaborate constructions of door lintels are therefore often necessary and not just for decoration. If a door opening is very wide, it is divided into several doors separated by loadbearing pillars. The result looks like a large unifying framework, often with very high thresholds.

USE OF MAIN COLOURS

Tibetan architecture is colourful to an extent almost over-whelming to the first time visitor. Traditional symbolism of colour in Tibetan art and architecture relates each of the five colours – properly ordered blue, white, red, green and yellow – to one of the five main elements. Blue symbolizes air or space, white symbolizes the Buddha-condition or absolute emptiness, red symbolizes fire, green symbolizes water and yellow symbolizes the earth.[10]

The symbolic meaning of the Potala's two colours – red and white – is considered to pre-date Buddhism, to a time when the culture was nomadic. The two staple foods, red meat (*mahr*) and white dairy products (*gahr*), permeated life. Meat-ceremonies (*mahr-dun*) were common when nomads fought and leaders met. Dairy-ceremonies (*gahr-dun*) were usually linked to religion; the Yoghurt Festival is still celebrated each July in Lhasa.

White by this interpretation symbolizes luck, gentleness, good fortune, and good deeds for the benefit of others. White makes people feel peaceful, clean and beautiful. The colour red symbolizes power, strength, dignity and honour in memory of religious leaders and heroes and consequently is more re-stricted.[11] The external use of colour at the Potala may support

Window, Shatra mansion, 1995. A typical window on the first floor of the wing, towards the lane, has fine proportions although it is neglected like the rest of Shatra. When new, the border would be painted black, the woodwork would have bright colours and a red and white curtain would hang from the awning. Finally, a perforated and decorated piece of cloth would cover the window shutters.

Awnings

Windows and doors exposed to the heavy rain showers of a limited but intense rainy season can be given elaborate awnings that cantilever up to one metre out from the wall. The awnings are intricate constructions, much as are the larger constructions of tie-beams, brackets and consoles of the interior ceilings. The awnings, covered in slate tiles, are an absolute necessity and their prominent position, intricate design and colouring make them a major architectural element in shaping a façade.

Textiles

A feature that gives Tibetan buildings a distinct, friendly appearance is the use of textiles as permanent elements of the exterior. The most common expression, found in every house no matter how simple, is outdoor curtains topping the windows and door hangers in the warm seasons. Tent canvas covering a courtyard is also common with all building types, from farmhouses to monasteries. The Jokhang reveals a range of vertical outdoor textile sunshades, with fine perforations that create delightful sun spots in a room.

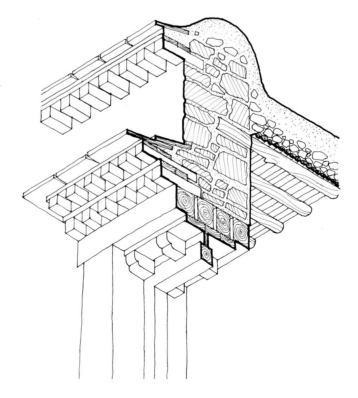

Above left: Sun-window, Shatra mansion, 2000. Large south-facing 'sun-windows' give heat and light to the main living rooms on the first and second floors of the main building.

Window section. The cornice above a window shows the supporting construction, the arga roof and the slate covering of the awnings.

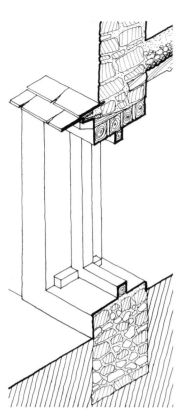

Door section. Door section with modest awning; heavy timber beams carry the wall above the door. The door frame is mounted at a later stage of construction.

these interpretations. The primary use of red and white is such that the White Palace, built by the 5th Dalai Lama, accommodates the domestic and administrative quarters, and the Red Palace, built after his death by a regent, contains the funerary chapels of past and future reincarnations.

External walls of secular and religious buildings are usually whitewashed or left untreated. Monastic buildings may also be painted in yellow-ochre or, more commonly, in various shades of red and orange. This tradition of colouring has not been used on new buildings for the last two hundred years, except for the funerary chapel of the 13th Dalai Lama, erected in the mid-1930s on the west side of the Potala.

Monastic and secular interiors frequently use a blue of brilliant intensity on the secondary ceiling beams, and green only much more rarely. Pillars and main beams are often painted red. Yellow can substitute for gold on metal roofs and other metal fixtures on religious buildings, as seen at the Potala and the Jokhang.

When inaugurating a new building, it is still a living tradition to apply tsampa (barley flour), yoghurt and milk to the walls. In the same way, pilgrims apply butter to temple doors and offer butter on the knees and aprons of Buddha images.

The importance of colours, in particular red and white, was once apparent in all aspects of life. In clothing, white was the colour of common woollen dress and of the winter sheepskin coat. The wedding dress was a white *chuba* (long dress tied at the waist with a sash) and white khatas were and are still given at all appropriate occasions. The colour of the Tibetan king and his court was an all-embracing red – red palace, red clothes, red flags, even red face paint. Ceremonies with food offerings require *tormas*, ritual cakes of varied shapes in red and white. White tormas are offered to Buddha, and red tormas, shaped as pyramids, are offered to protector deities. Before Buddhism, funerary tombs are believed to have been common in Tibet; the tombs of laymen were painted white and the tombs of kings and aristocracy painted red. With Buddhism the tomb took the shape of a stupa. The Potala Red Palace is in fact a huge stupa-temple that continues to respect the tradition of symbolic colouring.

The Potala, if painted entirely red, could be seen as a structure expressing supreme power. One practical explanation why it is not all red concerns the enormous amount of paint and render needed, the difficulty of producing such materials and the great costs involved to cover such huge surfaces. The method of application, throwing bucketfuls from windows and rooftops to produce rough layers centimetres deep, is wasteful. Whitewash, on the other hand, is easily available and relatively cheap.

Doorway, Shöl house (291), 1995. This fine nobleman's house from the 18th century has especially fine proportions and details. The awning above the door is among the most elaborate preserved in a secular building.

DECORATION

Looking at a Tibetan building, decorations are normally limited to thresholds and borders, edges between solids and void, and between inside and outside. It is this juxtaposition of the relatively small but heavily decorated areas and the large 'clean' wall surfaces that gives Tibetan architecture its aesthetically pleasing and harmonious expression. In the interior, structural decoration is concentrated around the main constructive wooden elements; tops of pillars, brackets and main beams.

The horizontal band of the benma frieze, with its golden shields and decorative beam-ends, articulates the border between wall and sky. The transition between inner and outer spaces may be emphasized in railings, thresholds, doors and windows. In the structural components, decoration focuses on the zone of actual transition, that of the supporting and supported members, as with column and bracket, suggesting a tectonic aspect of this seemingly purely visual style.

Left: Awnings, Shatra mansion, 1995. These awnings are 'miniature roof constructions' made by a multitude of small pieces of wood, normally painted in bright colours.

Textiles, Jokhang, 1999. Special gold brocade textiles hang from the cornice and the entire main courtyard is covered with a decorated tent canvas to celebrate a three-day prayer session by monks from Ramoche.

Architectural decoration is carried out by sculpting structural members or by applying decoration to their surfaces. Both have long traditions and play equally important roles in Tibetan architecture. Main decorative elements in the exterior of a Tibetan building are the windows and doors and – where they exist – the benma frieze and golden roofs.

The 'clean' wall mentioned above has its decoration, too, either from the way the masonry wall is built or by patterns in the plaster of mud brick walls. The masonry wall can have different forms of expression depending on the degree of dressing of the single stone, and the quality of the actual wall construction. In high quality buildings, external walls may be adorned with a few specially sculpted stones that tell a religious or secular story. The quality of workmanship is clearly shown in the careful fitting of small stone flakes in between the layers of construction stones, and at corners in the way the

Ceremonial tents below a mountain, Charles Bell (or Rabden), 1921. The tent has always been very important in traditional Tibetan culture, where much of the population still lives semi-nomadically. Also, picnics in the countryside, in tents and under sunshades, are universally popular.

layers are curved up and around the corner. In plasterwork, patterns are made by applying the plaster differently. A pattern resembling 'topped waves' is common.

The parapet that terminates the battered wall of an ordinary building is made in a row of slate to protect against rain; in large buildings of monastic origin or ownership, the parapet is built as a benma frieze that can be several meters high. The dark, purple band of the benma is often accentuated by rows of decorative white beam-ends, no longer elements of construction, and circular shields with symbolic motifs that are hammered out in copperplate and gilded or fire-gilded.

One interpretation of traditional use of colour claims that the white walls of a monastic building represent the common people and the purple benma border on top represents the ruling power; here visual symbolism connects and holds the society in place. The benma might also represent the night sky, its round golden shields symbolizing stars and other celestial bodies – only celestial power can be above the ruling power.

In Tibet as elsewhere, the window is associated with legends, folklore and magic. The façade of the Tibetan building symbolizes the human face; the word for façade, *dong*, means face. This might help explain the Tibetan preference for symmetrical façades. In East Tibet windows are called *karmik*, or bright eyes, and the small protective and decorative awnings above windows are *mikched*, or eyebrows. Thus windows are conceived as the eyes of a house, though this does not explain the broad, black surround to the window. One popular belief, perhaps from nomadic Tibet, states that the complete window symbolizes the face of a yak, with horns, eyes and other features. In West Tibet, traditional houses can still be seen where black window frames are made with 'horns' extending beyond the trapezoidal surround.

In Tibet as in many rural cultures it remains common to hang the head or horns of a strong animal – a yak, for instance – outside the house, inside a gate, under a bridge etc. This is done to protect the structure and its residents or users and to scare away evil spirits. Protecting a house from evil spirits by giving all openings a black surround, which is a difficult barrier to cross, offers a plausible explanation for its use.

Traditional wooden doors are often framed with colourful painted borders. Common motifs are the lotus flower and an intricate pattern of tiny cubes called *chötseg*, 'the stacking of religious law'. The 'lintel' is often built as a composite timber framework with tie-beams and brackets in layers of increasing

Entrance porch to a temple hall, Drepung, 1987. The glowing red pillars in dim half-light make the forms stand out with great intensity. Blue beams and yellow ceiling add to the shock of colour. In Western culture, such pure colours are found only in powder form.

Red wash, Meru Nyingba, 1999. Red wash for outer walls is here being cooked in a huge cauldron. The mixture consist of 1 kg tsag, powder from a red stone, with 0.6 kg glue to each 5 litres of water.

Potala, 1997. The Potala is divided into a White Palace and a Red Palace. The two colours, highly symbolic with meanings, are said to date back to the pre-Buddhist period of Tibetan culture (pre-7th century).

width, all allowing ample opportunity for colourful decoration. In a few high quality examples the lintel construction is seen topped by a row of carved lions which symbolically carry the heavy wall.

Doors in most ordinary buildings use wooden pivots. The doors in richer buildings have long handmade iron hinges and a central handle in the form of a large ring attached to a circular bowl-shaped disc. Such metal elements can show craftsmanship of the highest quality in detail and refinement. The long hinges may be furnished with plant ornaments or reproductions of humans and animals inlaid as gold and silver in the iron.

Awnings above windows and doors provide protection against rain and sun and constitute a vital part of the architectural expression of the building by adding horizontality, colour and rhythmic shadows to the white walls. The awnings act to introduce the decorative and built character of the building, as 'miniatures' of the type of construction found inside the building (with a multitude of small wooden members carrying slate roofs). The outside white window curtains attached to the awnings add a rare element of liveliness to the austere

façades. When walking down a lane it touches one to observe curtains moving in the breeze, as if to ease the severity of the black window frames.

In the interior, decoration of main construction elements is restricted to the wooden pillars, brackets and main beams. These are usually carved and painted, often with an elaboration that

Lubu Gowa Khangsar, Lhasa, 1997. This residential house is one of very few yellow secular buildings in Lhasa; coloured walls were almost always reserved for religious buildings. Lubu Gowa Khangsar is said to have been painted in memory of a visit by the 6th Dalai Lama (1683–1706).

Masonry wall, Yabshi Phünkhang, 1994. Example of a good quality old wall with quality craftsmanship.

Jokhang roof, 1994. The decorative, colourful elements of Tibetan architecture are here brought together in a small corner of harmony and peace.

Farmhouse outside Lhasa, 1997. Firewood is stacked on top of the walls. The benma frieze is said to originate from this motif.

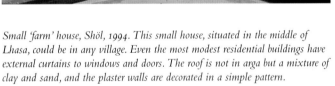

Small 'farm' house, Shöl, 1994. This small house, situated in the middle of Lhasa, could be in any village. Even the most modest residential buildings have external curtains to windows and doors. The roof is not in arga but a mixture of clay and sand, and the plaster walls are decorated in a simple pattern.

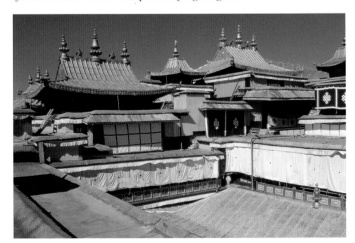

Jokhang roof, 1997. Many important details of Tibetan architectural design appear here in a compact area. From top down: arga cornice with protective slate slabs; curtain with symbolic colours; benma frieze with a golden shield; and awning with 'fake' beam ends covered with slate slabs.

Potala roof, 1995. Golden roofs, used normally only to cover the most important parts of monastic buildings, are built in a composite framework of tie-beams, consoles and brackets – typical of Chinese architecture – whereby the weight is brought down onto a few points of support. The structural needs and behaviour of the construction create a composition of high elegance.

Left: Windows and wall. Typical windows with black frames. Are the frames' stylized yak heads intended to scare away intruders or evil forces, or are they simply for heating incoming air? Perhaps both. The increased width towards the upper floors is characteristic for Tibetan windows.

Jokhang Nangkor, 1987. A corner of the Jokhang's inner gallery shows delicate decoration of timber construction at its best. The 'long' bow has been shaped in accordance with the common 'cloud motif' to project an impression of effortlessness. The lotus and chötseg friezes are clear and the curtains protect the colours from the sun.

Horns, Delin Khangsar, Lhasa, 1997. An example of the custom to exhibit horns or skulls above windows or doors. They are supposed to be a threat to unwanted visitors, but also to show the power and strength of the house owner. In West Tibet, this custom developed in such a way that the window itself, symbolizing a head, is painted with 'horns' extending from the black frame.

would surpass most known Western traditions. The most aesthetically pleasing decorations, however, are often those of a simpler form where the hand of the artist can be imagined.

The lower part of a pillar is most often smooth due to direct contact with people; only the upper part supporting the small square 'capital' is decorated and carved with floral motifs. The two horizontal brackets, the 'short' and the 'long' bow, on top of the pillar are more elaborately carved and generally taper towards the ends. The forms are often stylized clouds to give the impression of weightlessness, combined with the floral motifs. Carvings can in the most elaborate cases become entire scenes of three-dimensional animals, plants and humans, sometimes carved separately and attached to the structural elements. The decoration is usually restricted to the brackets but can also engage the main beam in its full length, often in the form of a narrow frieze with the much used lotus and chötseg carvings.

All the woodwork is painted in bright colours with highly symbolic meanings, as any use of colour is based on a system of symbolism. In a typical entrance to a temple the pillars, brackets, main beam and walls might be painted red, the secondary beams blue and the ceiling itself yellow, all three colours with an almost fluorescent quality. In some cases the pillars are clad in red velvet, reinforcing the intensity of the colour.

Central Tibet displays different types of timber construction. One type is the system of interior load-bearing short-span construction of pillars and beams that developed within the restrictions of limited building materials. Details of jointing and decoration are believed to have come to Tibet from India. Another type is the so-called free standing Chinese pavilion, often located atop monastic buildings and temples. A third type is the Chinese roof construction, with its composite framework of tie-beams, brackets and consoles, in Tibet used in buildings of traditional masonry construction. The two latter types

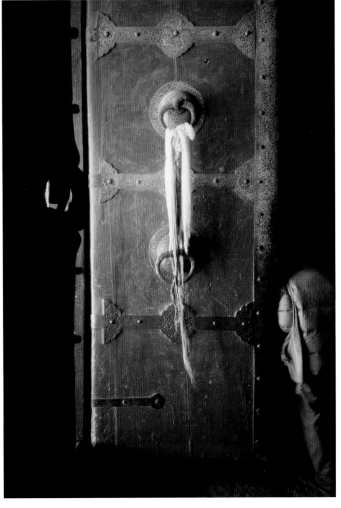

Door handle, Gyume monastery, 1994. An example of the superb craftsmanship found especially in metalwork on doors. The decoration culminates where the hand touches the building in the handle, which allows transit from the sunlit courtyard to the mysterious interior of the temple hall.

Norbulingka, 1987. Heavily decorated entrance, between the park and inner areas. The chötseg frieze is recognizable.

Temple door, Ganden monastery, 1994. Large temple door with fine metalwork. The door is hinged in the traditional way, fastened to a vertical piece of timber with extensions at both ends that fit into holes in the floor and lintel.

Awnings, Yabshi Phünkhang, 1994. This entrance from the courtyard to the main building displays different types of awnings, curtains and sunshades.

Bracket, Jokhang roof, 1998. One half of a 'long bow' shows a very clear example of the cloud motif. The relatively simple execution, the faded colours and the hand of a fine artist make this outstanding.

Jokhang roof, 1997. Chinese-style construction of free-standing pavilions.

Gallery towards interior courtyard, Potala, 1987. In summer, sun-screens afford protection and give pleasant light to the space.

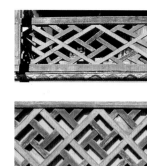

Railings, Sera monastery, 1994. Four railings with diagonal patterns.

probably had their origins in the architecture of China's Tang Dynasty, and as architectural concepts they may have come with Buddhism to China from India.

In the oldest parts of the Jokhang there is evidence of Indian influence in the detailing, sculpting and assembly method used in the column-beam construction. The wooden pillar components seem to be 'stacked' on top of each other as if made in stone; parallels can be seen in real Indian stone architecture.

Wooden railings are pained in bright colours, often creating cheerful, richly coloured surprises in courtyards and building interiors. Railings are often physically detached from other architectural elements and can be seen in various designs. Maybe the craftsman-designer eagerly grabbed this opportunity to create individually crafted elements in intricate patterns,

but always as a derivative of classical geometrical patterns and incorporating the structural diagonal. Used externally, well crafted and colourful railings add liveliness and individuality to an otherwise severe façade.

The external use of textiles on buildings is a feature that most likely combined the influences of nomad and religious culture. Use of awnings and conventional tent structures for religious and secular functions is well known, but textiles used as a permanent architectural element in combination with stone, clay and wood seems unique to the area of Tibetan cultural influence. Perhaps their use is linked to the concept of the 'wind horse' (*lungta*) prayer flags, which, printed with mantras and activated by the wind, endlessly spread prayers and good will into the universe. Where else can one find curtains

Left: Decorated pillar and beam assembly, Norbulingka, 1987. Typical elaborate decoration with attached woodcarvings.

Right: Main entrance, Jokhang, 1987. Different types of textiles used for different purposes. The brown curtains are wool; the upper left gallery is in front of the Dalai Lama's quarters, and the sun-screens have small 'windows'.

A

B

C

D

E

F

on the outside of every window? The textiles are normally of white cotton fabric adorned with sacred symbols and geometrical or floral patterns. Only in rare cases are they made of wool, such as the huge 'curtains' or sunshades hung from central balconies of the Potala Red Palace or the heavy fabrics hanging above the entrance porch in front of the Jokhang.

Until Lhasa developed a dense townscape, areas quite near the Barkor were at festival times each year turned into tent-towns, which would grow up to accommodate tens of thousands of pilgrims and visitors, including Mongol black tents in the area of Banak Shöl. Such scenes are illustrated in wall paintings. As late as in the mid-1980s, tent-camps were common in the fields north of the Potala, areas now taken over by the growing city. In Tibet, picnics are still an important social-cultural institution, and a true Lhasa picnic naturally involves a tent. At festival times entire tent-towns emerge in Norbulingka.

Smaller residences owned by ordinary townspeople were noticeably less decorated than the opulent houses of nobles or merchants, and often built in mud brick on a stone foundation. Almost all of these buildings in the old town have today disappeared. In Shöl, a few such houses still stand (293, 294, 303).

BUILDING TYPES

Tibetan religious structures constitute an essential part of the architectural environment. They include stupas (*chorten*), koras (circumambulation routes), mani walls (walls made of stones inscribed with mantras), rock art, steles (*doring*), flagpoles or prayer masts (darchen) and incense burners. A rich literature exists on these spiritually and culturally important structures, but in this book, devoted to townscape and buildings, they are considered of secondary importance within the sacred and profane public landscape.

Most buildings are built on the concept of an 'architecture of pillars,' in which materials and practical loadbearing limitations define the dimensions of structures and interior spaces. The buildings may appear to be quite similar, yet this very similarity of form and architectural expression often conceals the fact that they are adapted for widely different uses and could therefore be described as representing different building types.

A full typology of Tibetan architecture still awaits its researcher. It is nevertheless useful to categorize the buildings in Lhasa into groups, mainly according to their function, in order to present a complete list of historical buildings. With these categories or 'types', it is possible with a few key letters to indicate whether, for example, a house along a street has shops or whether a large house is a mansion or a residential yard. A building can of course represent several categories of functions at the same time.

At the overall level, two categories of building types exist: religious and secular. Here are the main types.

Religious buildings

A. Temple complex or compound. Example: Jokhang (313).

The Tibetan temple is often a square hall with a flat roof and skylight carried by a 'forest' of columns. The entrance is from the south. Facing the entrance along the northern wall is a long altar with Buddha images and saints. In the centre of the assembly hall, long rows of maroon mattresses between the columns indicate the area where monks sit during daily chanting sessions. Wall paintings cover the walls and thangkas hang from the beams. Major temples have over long periods of time developed into large building complexes with several courtyards and a multitude of functions.

B. Temple or chapel. Example: Lukhang chapel (317).

Smaller temples are often built in special places for special purposes. A small number of resident caretaker monks or nuns from the overseeing monastery take turns being responsible for the temple's upkeep.

C. Monastery. Example: Tsomonling (308).

A Lhasa monastery consists typically of four wings around a rather large courtyard. The northern wing functions as the main building with three to four floors and with one or two separate temples. The main building is attached at both ends to the side wings over two floors, with monks' cells reached from a gallery. The layout is symmetrical, with the entrance normally through a gate in the centre of the south wing. A monastery can also be integrated into a temple complex, in which case it is adapted to the overall layout of the temple.

Secular buildings

D. Monumental official building (palace, fort, military building, governmental production building). Examples: Magshikhang (army headquarters) (296) and Barkhang Chenmo (Gangjan Pende Terdzökhang, printing house) (288).

Inside Lingkor, the only buildings of this category are the Potala and some in Shöl on the slopes of Marpori.

E. Other official buildings

These are mostly found in Shöl: Shöl Barkhang (printing house) (305), Ngü Barkhang (money printing house) (298), Shöl

Lekung (administrative building) (289) and Shöl Dekyiling (prison) (290). The only building of this type in the old town is Nangtseshar (prison) (8).

F. Mansion. Example: Shatra (143).

A mansion is the residence of an extended aristocratic or wealthy family. The typical configuration consists of a main building with up to three storeys on the north side of a courtyard. To the east, south and west stand secondary buildings or outbuildings. The main building is usually symmetrical and always socially and functionally hierarchical. Its layout resembles a monastery, except that the main building of the mansion occupies the entire northern part of the site with the secondary buildings attached to it (the main hall of a monastery is enclosed on both sides by its secondary buildings). The urban mansion is adapted from the traditional rural family compound, a large walled-off yard in mud brick or stone construction with a main house oriented east-west to expose its long side to the sun at the back of the yard. The entrance to the mansion compound is normally from the south and, if possible, should lie in the north-south axis that runs through the building complex. The main building is normally built in stone, with the outbuildings often a combination of stonework (lower level) and mud brick construction. Large ornate windows and balconies make the main building's top floor appear rich and monumental. These large sun-windows and balconies probably derived from 19th-century influences. Courtyard buildings, usually one storey lower than the main building, have rooms and spaces on the upper floor that are reached from a gallery. The ground floor of each building provides space for stables and storage rooms.

A generally high level of workmanship and decoration, with finest materials available for construction, characterized these mansions. Noble families in Lhasa were the first to import materials such as glass and steel beams for their houses.

G. Townhouse. Example: Trapchishar (1).

The townhouse is a further example of the most common traditional residential building type, adapted to suit often quite confined urban sites. Each townhouse has a courtyard, often small but essential for light and ventilation, which acts as an arena for outdoor domestic activities. On the Barkor and many other market lanes, the ground floor shops connect to dwelling areas above by means of steep ladders and trap doors.

H. Streethouse. Example: Shamo Karpo (7).

This term describes a hybrid of the townhouse when the site is too restricted to allow for a courtyard. The streethouse is lit only from the street, and is often located on corners to

increase the number of windows. Adjoining buildings behind it allow little space for the normal facilities of an independent building, and therefore the streethouse normally lacks its own latrine-tower. The streethouse type most likely developed as the town grew denser and as more marginal sites were used for commercial and residential construction. The streethouse always has shops on the ground floor.

I. Residential yard (or building). Example: Delin Khangsar (106).

The residential or tenement yard in old Lhasa is clearly an urban creation. Originally, it was privately owned by rich monasteries or the government, and built to generate rental income as well as to provide much needed housing. Unlike most other buildings, the residential yard is normally asymmetrical, built to fit the given site configuration. It is often an assembly of small, terraced and uniform two- or three-storey townhouses. A common courtyard provides access to a well and latrines.

J. Clustered housing. Example: Shöl East cluster (301–303).

Lower social strata in Lhasa lived in simpler single-storey, mud brick buildings, often clustered with animal pens and outbuildings. Very few of this building type remain, with some examples in Shöl. They are in many respects similar to the traditional rural housing cluster.

K. Summerhouse. Example: Tsomonling Drokhang (252).

The summerhouse emerged as an urban phenomenon towards the end of the 19th century, when noble families built summer houses in the open landscape, away from their main residence in the increasingly dense, warm and smelly old town. Gradually, many well-established families sold or rented out their residence in town and moved permanently to the new 'suburbs'. Located in a large garden, the original summerhouse has a generous south-facing window front, a separate kitchen and servant buildings. A monastery often has a summerhouse for the abbot in an adjacent garden.

L. Outbuilding. Example: Chibra (169).

All major compounds or estates have outbuildings located both inside and outside the main enclosed courtyard. As Lhasa grew denser, outbuildings were gradually upgraded or replaced by buildings of a higher category. Today, stables and other secondary structures are nearly entirely gone.

G

H

I

J

K

L

Townscape

INTRODUCTION

The Potala rises high above the plain of Lhasa as a welcoming and unmistakable beacon for any approaching visitor. It appears long before any other sign of the town, whether arriving from east or west. In olden times it must have been with special excitement that travellers came upon this spectacular, relatively large town. The distinct form of early 20th-century Lhasa contrasted sharply with the surrounding open landscape, but already in the late 1950s the borders of the town were becoming 'blurred' with many new buildings on the outskirts. Today the city fills almost all available space in the valley.

'Townscape' often refers to the activity of planning and building structures with a particular concern for pleasing and aesthetic results. In this book, townscape means the combined fabric or grain of buildings and open spaces that physically make up the environment of the town. For townscape a single building is less important than the coherence and integrity of the public space. In the dense, traditional townscape of Lhasa it is sometimes hard to distinguish one building from another. Earlier this was not the case; buildings spread out with gardens and open space between them, the battered walls of the buildings reinforcing a life quite independent of others. Simply put, townscape features were less prominent.

Lhasa as an architectural composition is, like most other towns, a result of the ordinary life of generations of residents, the interventions of its leaders and the accumulation of all historical events that the town has experienced. Neolithic finds might indicate that the Lhasa valley supported village structures already in the 7th century. The traditions of building and architecture that have formed Lhasa were strongly rooted in rural culture, perhaps developed partly in the Lhasa valley itself. In trying to understand the complex, multi-layered nature of a townscape, it is rewarding to try to build imaginary bridges to these events and personalities of long ago.

The urban environment in Lhasa consists of the urban structure or grain combined with its urban life. It is composed of the following:[1]

– a physical dimension that describes buildings, building patterns, densities, architectural and aesthetic values and concerns;

– a functional dimension that describes land use, localization of functions, infrastructure etc;

– socio-economic dimensions concerned with demographics, living conditions etc;

– network dimensions of traffic and communications, energy, resources and environmental relationships.

As a pre-industrial Buddhist town, Lhasa was confronted with the force of modern life only a few decades ago. New social and physical models introduced to the old structure produced tremendous changes to traditional architecture and townscape. Traditional townscape during the past 20–40 years has disappeared fast in Lhasa; this is typical for most historical towns worldwide.

Contrary to modern urban landscape, traditional townscape is considered to be sustainable and in need of relatively small investments to maintain itself. In a traditional townscape respect for the environment and the balance between requirements and resources somehow manages to prevail. This is not the case with modern, ever-expanding cities.

Contemporary society acts as if the myths of progress and development will go on forever. Such a view easily overlooks the formidable cultural resources that exist in the traditional townscape, resources that could help renew and regenerate the very same urban environment. In Lhasa, historical townscape and the lessons of living, accumulated through a thousand years, could be immensely valuable as a 'seed-bag' for future cultural transformation.

A town is a composition of elements, patterns of buildings and structural features with 'veins' – streets, alleys, lanes, public spaces – that make each townscape different from every other. A town may be described as young, mature or old. A mature town is coherent, having reached a form in harmony with needs and use. After dramatic shifts in values and circumstances, an urban community may split into a 'new town' and an 'old town' – often leading to the deterioration of the old town as it becomes culturally and economically marginalized.

The question of what constitutes the qualities of an old town can be answered in different ways. Some emphasize the presence of important and representative old buildings, others the entire environment of anonymous or vernacular buildings. Others again claim public space to represent the most important quality. Whether to protect and maintain a traditional town after its original functions no longer exist presents a dilemma. Should it be turned into a giant museum, or should it be reinterpreted or allowed to disappear as a historical environment? Parts of old Lhasa are already turning into museums – the

Potala is a prime case – and others are now under protection – the Jokhang, the Barkor area and a number of individual buildings. Serious international efforts now revolve around how to protect the values of traditional cultural heritage in urban settings.

RECORDING TOWNSCAPE QUALITIES

Lhasa's new townscape, introduced with modern town planning in the 1960s, is not discussed here although it has of course strongly affected the character of the old townscape.

Architecture can be defined as the aesthetic, physical organization of human activities. With this definition in mind, we concentrate on formal and informal structures in the townscape, in order to provide descriptions and commentaries on its most important aspects. Our work involved the investigation of topography, history and architecture, and required the definition of two main components, 'developed structures' and 'individual buildings'. We then recorded, described and analysed aspects and dimensions of townscape in text and maps; all this was done with a focus on selected, appropriate themes. The objective was not to devise a strict methodology that could be seen as rigid in approach, but to encourage a considerate and creative planning process with the goal of protection for old buildings and traditional townscape. We identified about 60 townscape features but in the end, for reasons of space and priority, have here presented only 20.

'Developed structures' may be described as coherent entities or independent sections of townscape, comprising anything from just a few buildings to entire streets and urban districts.[2]

There are three categories of 'developed structures':
- Townscape features;
- Townscape patterns;
- Townscape elements.

Townscape features describe the overall physical grain of the townscape, the spatial compositions, sequences and objects that affect the town and give it character. Examples are silhouettes, main streets, large squares and dominant individual buildings. In Lhasa, the Potala Palace and the Jokhang Temple, the relationship of Lhasa to the surrounding mountains and the relationship between the local hills and the old town are good illustrations of townscape features.

Townscape patterns include the diversity of building patterns that exist in a townscape to give it a special quality and the way buildings relate to each other as groups in the physical environment. Examples are a characteristic grouping of buildings or an urban block whose physical form came from

original property lines, new planning policy, old street patterns or topography.

Townscape elements reflect traditional use in town life and provide direct visual links to the history and events that shaped the town. They are individual spatial elements or details of special interest that provide identity. Examples are an urban space, a park, a section of a street and a façade.

LHASA TOWNSCAPE

The pattern of human settlement in the Lhasa valley probably did not develop as increasingly wide circles of habitat spreading around and out from the Jokhang and the Barkor, but rather as a scattering of widely spaced but historically linked structures in the town area, throughout the valley and beyond. Intermediary spaces in the old town only filled in gradually. This accords with a general pattern of habitat in Tibet and the Himalayan region, where each building is a small fortress in itself, surrounded by a walled enclosure and open land. Neighbours reside at a respectable distance. Such is the general rule of life also in nomad encampments. Ancient stacked cave dwellings and villages of clustered, labyrinthine houses, with access to all buildings across terraced rooftops, are further examples of habitat. Lhasa old town before the mid-1950s may represent yet one more type, with a dense urban area linked through a maze of narrow dirt alleyways to markets, holy places and the other parts of the city. Growth was organic, with new individual structures being added as and where needed.

The survey component of the LHCA project focused on the fine traditional townscape and historical buildings of Lhasa. This study proceeded because little documentation existed on the architecture and townscape, and rapid changes in the creation of a modern city were overwhelming and obliterating the assets of cultural heritage.

In Tibetan Buddhist society rituals embrace many aspects of life and remind everyone of the ever-present importance of religious activity. Sacred hierarchies in the natural and cultural landscape are 'present' and vital for pilgrims and residents alike. Lhasa's urban environment over time became filled with sacred places and elements and developed into a potent destination of pilgrimage. Townscape became a physical manifestation of human beliefs in the dimensions of space and time; old Lhasa illustrates how prototypical patterns of behaviour contribute to create specific architectural form.

The growth pattern described here appears to be the case in larger towns and villages, and in the monastic universities that came to form small towns in themselves. An overall, defining conception for constructed space seems only to have arisen in a few cases, such as Samye and Drathang monasteries, built from the start according to concepts of classical Buddhist cosmogony and given an idealized physical layout, in the form of a mandala or a universe.

Lhasa at first had the appearance of loose clusters of individual buildings forming the nucleus of a townscape with structures located quite freely in a larger landscape, each building or estate competing for the most desirable site. An early village community may have existed at the foot of Marpori, protected by fortified buildings on Chakpori and Marpori. Pilgrims and traders must have provided useful additions to the Lhasa community up through the centuries, adding fresh blood and new energies. With varying fortunes in power, prominence and riches, Lhasa may not have experienced a permanent urban community, with established social standards and a controlling elite, until the reign of the 5th Dalai Lama in the 17th century.

For the non-monastic community it was auspicious and often necessary to live near sacred structures. A house located near the Barkor became a high priority for many families. The resulting fight for space and position seems nevertheless to have affected Lhasa townscape less than in many other famous historical towns.

The Jokhang's sacred role at the centre of the town acted to generate the Nangkor, Barkor and Lingkor circumambulation routes, all of which changed their courses over the centuries. The activity of circumambulation has clearly affected the layout of the town greatly, but not exclusively. During the Barkor circuit, the flow of pilgrims turns around prayer masts (darchen). These may appear at first glance to form part of Lhasa's sacred cosmography, but history shows them to vary widely in date and purpose. In total, seven have been erected – two of these at Ramoche. The earliest prayer mast went up at the Barkor's south-east corner in 1409. Another from 1720 stands south of the Jokhang, and the most recent was set up in front of the Jokhang in 1986.[3]

This remarkable human behavior of circumambulation adapted the paths to follow the evolution of the holy place and the changing townscape. The interior Nangkor and exterior Barkor form the core circuits, and the 7.5-km-long Lingkor traces the outer kora. This outer limit encloses a sort of 'island', which includes the Jokhang and the old town, Ramoche, the Potala, Chakpori and Bhamari. Its exclusion of Norbulingka suggests that the present circuit dates to the time of the 5th Dalai Lama. Earlier lingkors were probably smaller, although Ramoche would surely have been one of the earliest points of delimitation. Some weak traces in street patterns in the old town do suggest the formation of other circuits.

Other sites in Lhasa perhaps add to a sacred pattern, although a chronological analysis may not support the concept of a conscious layout of holy places. In the early 15th century a disciple of Tsongkhapa, the great religious teacher and reformer, described this region on the Kyichu river as the 'Mandala of Lhasa'. This seems to hold true only in the case of the four Rigsum chapels, dedicated to Tibet's holiest protectors, which stood at the four cardinal points surrounding the Jokhang.

Another sacred 'group of four' in the cosmography of Lhasa is the four 'Lings', residences of the regents of Tibet. These four 17th-century Gelukpa institutions are Tengyeling, Tsomonling, Kundeling and Tsechokling.

Lhasa town had a number of residences known as labrangs, built specially for incarnate lamas. The earliest is Labrang Nyingba, where Tsongkhapa stayed during the first Great Prayer Festival (Monlam Chenmo) in 1409. This fine structure on the inner Barkor is also known as Thonpa and may be the oldest noble residence remaining in Lhasa. From 1757 onwards, other important regent-lamas were allowed to build new residences in the central town, but private labrangs were forbidden. Examples are Takdrak Labrang and Radreng Labrang.

Although religion and politics have always been intimately linked in Lhasa, many residences or mansions belonged specifically to the secular world. These were the homes of nobles and government officials, merchants and foreigners, princes and diplomats, such as Nepalese ambassadors and the Manchu Ambans, China's representatives in Tibet.

Special laws developed to govern construction in the inner town. No building could be as high as the Jokhang, nobles could build to three storeys in height, but buildings for ordinary people could be only two stories. With the exception of two or three specially privileged residences, no lay houses, noble or otherwise, could have the benma frieze at the top parapet – this was reserved for religious structures.

TOWNSCAPE FEATURES

High mountains bordering the Lhasa valley visually dominate the town, which sits on the flat valley floor just north of the Kyichu river. In the middle of the valley rise two steep hills, Marpori (98 metres) and Chakpori (100 metres), and near them a much smaller one, Bhamari (17 metres). The top of each hill held an institution; the Potala on Marpori, the Medical College (Mentsikhang) on Chakpori and Gesar Lhakhang on Bhamari. These hills function as landmarks and project an extraordinary power across the wide plain.

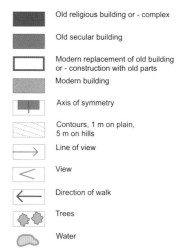

Key to Townscape maps

Old religious building or - complex

Old secular building

Modern replacement of old building or - construction with old parts

Modern building

Axis of symmetry

Contours, 1 m on plain, 5 m on hills

Line of view

View

Direction of walk

Trees

Water

Townscape features. Scale 1 : 20 000. Townscape features here mean spatial compositions, sequences or objects that affect the town and give it character, as for instance silhouettes, main streets, large squares or dominant individual buildings. In Lhasa the Potala and the Jokhang, the relationship of Lhasa to the surrounding mountains, and the relationship between the local hills and the old town may be used as illustrations of townscape features.

The four main features:
1. *The hills, especially Marpori with the Potala and Chakpori with the (former) Medical College.*
2. *The old town, the flat, dense building mass which once stood out as a distinct form but now has diffused into the general fabric of Lhasa.*
3. *The Jokhang Temple, at the centre of the old town, formerly dominant for its size, height, golden roofs and historic importance.*
4. *Beijing Shar Lam, the main street that earlier connected the Potala and the Jokhang. Today it divides the old town in two.*

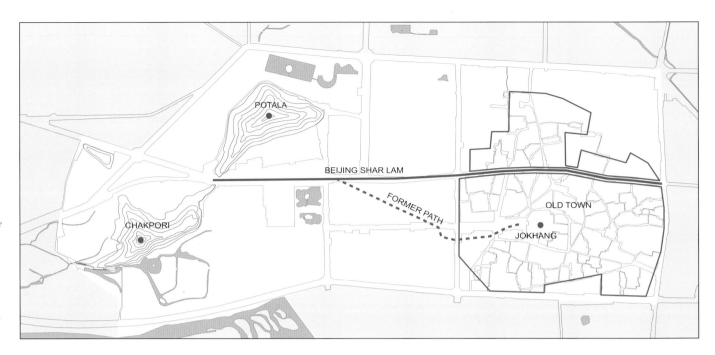

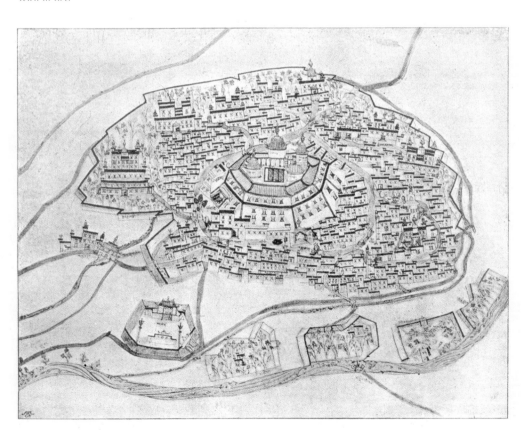

Marpori

The curved hill of Marpori stands one km north of the river and the slope facing south seems somehow protected from the winds that sweep through the valley. A very early habitat was probably established here and today's Shöl, the administrative village below the Potala, is quite likely a descendant of this first community.[4] Marpori was a natural location for a fort. Massive defensive structures built into the rocky formation transformed the hill itself into a stronger, more dominating presence that radiated power and control over the surroundings.

Chakpori

Chakpori, slightly taller than Marpori, must have appeared impressive with the small, concise structures of the Medical College at its summit. Much of the drama of Lhasa's silhouette is due to the Marpori-Chakpori formations, seen in contrast to the restrained shape of the historical town.

Bhamari

The low hill is hardly more than a mound. Before modern buildings surrounded it, Bhamari was a pleasant hillock on the valley plain that stood out in counterpoint to the hard, rocky character of the two larger hills.

Old Lhasa

In a nondescript flat and exposed area of marshy scrubland, almost two km east of the hills, the old town of Lhasa took form as it grew up around the Jokhang Temple. In time it would come to stand out distinctly as large flat clusters of grey stone buildings, flat roofs with colourful prayer flags, coloured walls and a few curved and pointed golden roofs, all interspersed with open spaces, wooded areas and agricultural gardens. During some periods, a protective town wall may have underlined its shape. The Lhasa of yesteryear – a defined form on the flat plain at a distance from the river – can be called in the vocabulary of townscape 'a major developed structure'.

Centuries before the towering Potala Palace was built on Marpori, the Jokhang Temple, with modest height but considerable mass, lay almost by itself in a marshy spot, first as a symbol of kingly power, then as a major magnet for religious and secular activity. The Jokhang experienced many ups and downs through history, but always retained its central role as a destination for pilgrimage and worship, thanks largely to the sacred Jowo Buddha image within. The temple was a natural nucleus for a town that expanded in the 17th century and culminated in the early part of the 20th century.

In the greater valley landscape, the hills of Marpori and Chakpori constituted one power point and the Jokhang another. In some respects they can be seen as vertical and horizontal emanations; their roles as centres of power, at least in legend, affected the growth and form of the communities surrounding them.

Lhasa Old Town. This 'pilgrim's map' comes from a photograph of a painting, first published in 1894 in L. Austine Waddell's The Buddhism of Tibet or Lamaism. *It describes in an unusually clear way the circular, distinct form of the old town centred around the Jokhang. Apparently a perimeter wall encloses the town on all sides except towards the river. The Lingkor is outside the wall and follows it for long stretches. Remarkable are the mansions in their large, walled gardens by the river. The Yuthok bridge is also a focus.*[5]

View from the Potala roof, 1995. Looking towards the centre of the old town, one first sees in the foreground the Shöl perimeter wall with its towers. The large Taktster mansion (at centre, one-fourth in from the left margin) was once the only building in the expanse between Shöl and the old town. Today (2000), several semi-high-rise buildings disturb the skyline.

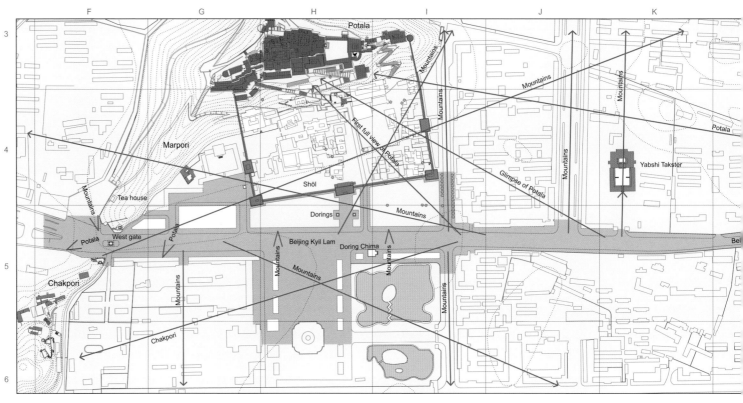

Beijing Shar Lam. Scale 1 : 6500. Beijing Shar Lam's streetscape maintains close visual contact with the mountains, seen to the north and south, a quality that is very important for the entire old town. This is indicated on the thematic map, which also identifies the four monasteries located along the street as well as Jebumgang, the unusual temple dedicated to Tsongkhapa, with 100,000 images (now destroyed) of the Gelukpa founder. The splendid view of the Potala rising above the townscape, especially from Beijing Shar Lam near Meru monastery, must be preserved. The two Yabshis, family residences of the Dalai Lamas, lie along this street. Yabshi Phünkhang is today the only remaining old building located directly on Beijing Shar Lam (severely exposed to traffic). Two other old structures shown on the map were recently demolished. Meru monastery earlier had direct access to Beijing Shar Lam, as recorded in satellite photos and old maps, but is now largely obscured behind modern buildings.

Beijing Shar Lam

A track or lane that approached Lhasa from the west connected the hills and the Jokhang. It passed the West Gate (Bargo Kani), the foot of Marpori outside Shöl and continued on a rough diagonal towards the Jokhang, on its way crossing a small stream by means of a covered stone bridge (Yuthok Zampa). This lane has been identified as Beijing Shar Lam. Most of the track has disappeared, but some sections connect to the present Beijing Shar Lam and one part survives as the largely reconstructed stone bridge in the midst of modern commercial buildings. The lane in its modern form continues to be an important link between major townscape features.

The east part of Beijing Shar Lam follows the route of a narrower, earlier lane that served the four large monasteries of old Lhasa which were located along it, and connects with sites east of town. The manner in which Beijing Shar Lam cuts the old townscape in two is of considerable consequence – mostly

West Gate, main street and remodelled outer Shöl, 1997. This view from the southern stupa of the West Gate shows the main street, here called Beijing Kyil Lam, paved with granite, almost 50 m wide and 600 m long. This is a far cry from the dirt tracks of 50 years ago. If the monumentality of the Potala is not in danger of being dwarfed by this gigantic linear exposure, the original charm of approaching the town has definitely been lost.

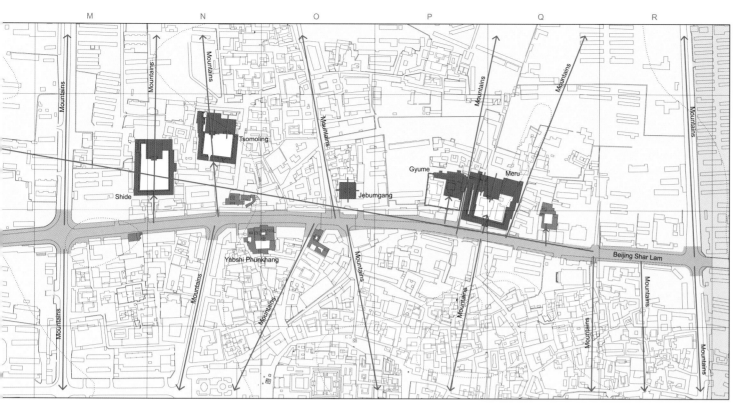

negative. Despite its present appearance as a modern and hap-hazard urban collage, the streetscape of Beijing Shar Lam still contains so many historical elements that it seems justified to describe it as a major developed structure – a dominant and ordering element in the townscape.

Points of Reference

The Potala on Marpori and the Medical College on Chakpori were the two obvious visual points of reference; they acted as magnets to attract all visual attention in the central parts of the Lhasa valley. They also functioned as navigational points, making it easy to identify a location almost anywhere in the townscape.

Other traditional reference points in Lhasa, man-made or religious in nature, are smaller and generally more difficult to detect. But a number of them are so important on the basis of age, size, appearance or cultural significance that we have here named whole areas of townscape after them: the Jokhang area, the Ramoche area, the Mosque area.

Beijing Shar Lam, eastern end, 1994. The street here follows the line of the original lane. The Potala, 2 km away, stands exactly at the end of the view.

Points of reference. Scale 1 : 20 000. Points of reference are based on visual features and other qualities that identify important points in a rough mental map of a town. In Lhasa, the Potala is by far the most important reference point, a visual anchor for the entire valley. The Jokhang is equally important as the spiritual focus for the old town.

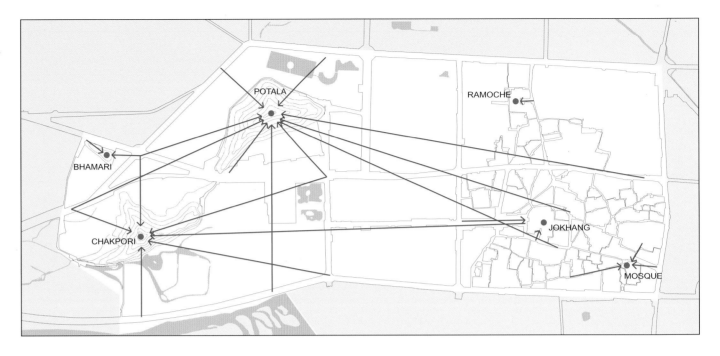

View north from old Lhasa, 1997. Ramoche Temple is a major point of reference but hardly noticed when walking the streets. Its golden roof and spires stand out against the surroundings only when seen over the rooftops.

TOWNSCAPE PATTERNS

Harmony, scale, variety of composition and use of materials distinguish the four townscape patterns discussed here:

 - Lhasa old town in a flat river landscape;
 - Potala Palace and fort on Marpori with the fortified village of Shöl below;
 - Chakpori village cluster;
 - Yabshi Taktster, an individual building in a natural landscape.

Lhasa old town

The central focus of old Lhasa is the Jokhang Temple and the buildings that gradually developed around it. Townscape growth and change over many centuries resulted from numerous layers of historical and physical 'events', including topography and the evolution of age-old paths or lanes. Sacred circuit routes (koras) and radiating tracks encircled and connected the Jokhang with all important places: the Barkor and Lingkor, Marpori and Chakpori, Sera and Drepung monasteries, and

Potala from the Jokhang roof, 2000. From one important reference point to the other; this photographic view is luckily able to avoid modern constructions. The city's rooftops, far from staying level, are continuing to grow higher as new, larger buildings replace traditional structures in the old town.

Townscape patterns. Scale 1 :20 000.
Townscape patterns identify different ways that buildings relate to each other as groups in the physical environment. The pattern may be identified in the form of a characteristic group of buildings or an urban block that is given its physical form as a consequence of original property divisions, new planning policy, old street patterns, topography or other factors.

The four areas indicated have distinctly different patterns:
1. Centralized town on the flat plain.
2. Palace/fortress on top of the hill with fortified village below.
3. Caves and minor buildings in a miniature mountain setting.
4. Detached mansion.
    Each of the four patterns is shown in the following four detailed theme maps.

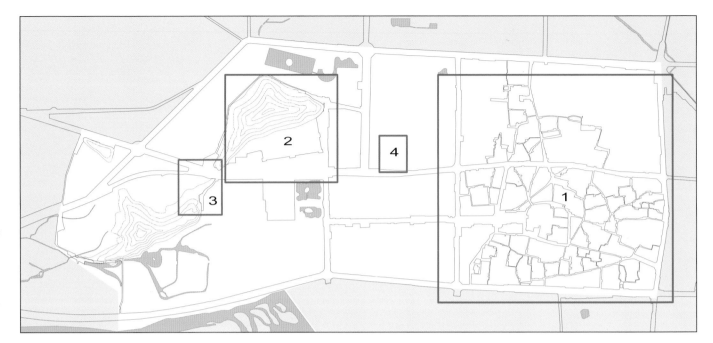

Lane in the old town, Tsonak Lam, 1997. The lanes are often so narrow and crooked that vehicular traffic is impossible. It is lanes such as this that make the old town special and vital.

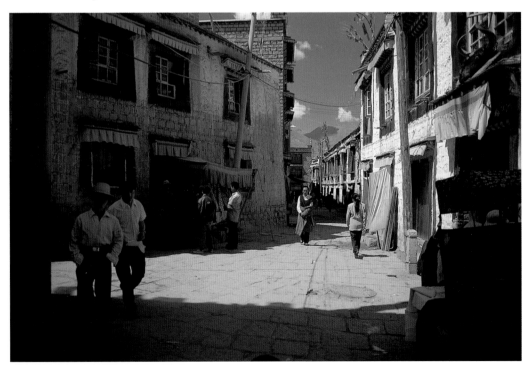

outlying religious and secular centres beyond the borders of Lhasa.

The map of the old town (p. 73) shows all old buildings still standing in 1994, with existing lanes and alleyways. The Barkor (intermediate kora) remains intact, but the original Lingkor (outer kora enclosing old Lhasa) now only exists as fragments.

It is not yet known how and when Lhasa developed into a complex, mature townscape from the original, solitary Jokhang structure. Geomancy almost certainly played a part. One notices that the two oldest, most important temples, the Jokhang and Ramoche – and also Jebumgang from the 17th century – are oriented almost exactly on the cardinal axes. It is assumed that this orientation was of central importance, and that the buildings were constructed in an open landscape. Almost no other buildings in Lhasa, perhaps with the exception of Shide monastery, adhere to this strict orientation. Rather, buildings grew up in relation to the direction of koras and the radial routes connected to these koras. It is natural to assume, therefore, that this layout of paths formed the oldest pattern in historic Lhasa.

As seen in the map, the large monasteries and mansions always follow the same layout: a main building to the north faces a courtyard to the south. An interesting exception to this is the Gorkha Nyingba mansion (former Nepalese embassy), where the main building sits freely inside a surrounding courtyard and is oriented almost exactly north–south and east–west.

The people of Lhasa have always felt it important to locate their buildings inside the Lingkor and as close to the Jokhang

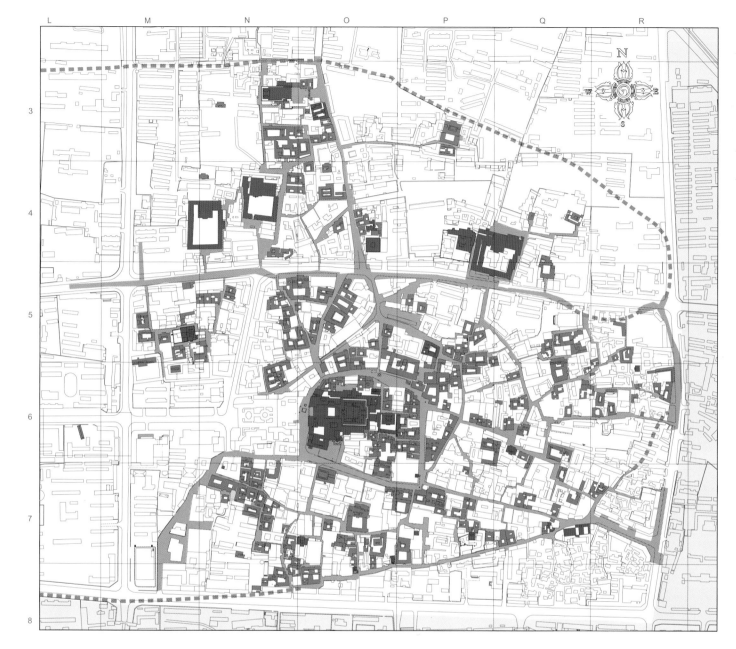

3

4

5

6

7

8

Pattern 1. Centralized town on the flat plain. Scale 1 : 7500. Here presented are buildings, old lanes and alleyways that still existed in 1994. Parts of the Lingkor and streets that have gone are shown with a dotted line. Koras around the central Jokhang Temple have generated the street pattern, and fragments of probably 'dissolved' koras are visible. Radiating streets connect centre and periphery. The important Ramoche Lam links the Jokhang with Sera monastery. Main buildings generally face south, taking their orientation from already existing lanes. It was desirable to locate buildings inside the Lingkor and near the Jokhang, but it seems there were never rules to dictate where the buildings were to be placed.

as possible. Lhasa's first Muslim mosque stood outside the Lingkor, but otherwise temples, monasteries, mansions and smaller buildings seem to be distributed inside at random, though paying attention to topography. Exceptions are the four monasteries that lie almost on a line perpendicular to the Jokhang-Ramoche axis. These institutions – Meru, Gyurme, Shide, Tsomonling – were established at very different times; the oldest, Meru, in the 9th century and the youngest, Tsomonling, in the 18th century. During this long period large parcels of land between the Jokhang and Ramoche probably existed as natural landscape and cultivated land. Otherwise these religious institutions would not have been able to create their extensive gardens. This belt of wealthy, important monasteries may have defined the northern edge of the built up townscape, with Ramoche in fields behind them to the north. Reminders of the character of the area are the two small summerhouses that are today entirely enclosed by modern buildings.

Potala and Shöl

The pattern of built form found on Marpori, a fortified palace protecting a village at the foot of the hill, is well known

Pattern 2. Palace/fortress on top of the hill with fortified village below. Scale 1 : 3 000. The entire top of Marpori hill has been transformed into a series of terraces, partly hollow, as bases for a great number of complex buildings woven together to form one of the world's most impressive architectural compositions. Major elements in the architecture are the enormous sloping supporting walls that recapture the natural form of the hill and the fragile cloud-like golden roofs that crown the Potala. The village of Shöl is possibly the oldest inhabited area in Lhasa. Shöl's organization follows a largely rectangular pattern with many variations. Here, as in the old town, the delineation of routes and tracks seems to have directed the location and form of the buildings. Most evident is the track from the main Shöl gate to the foot of the great stairway; this testifies to the lack of architectural axes in Tibetan townscape.

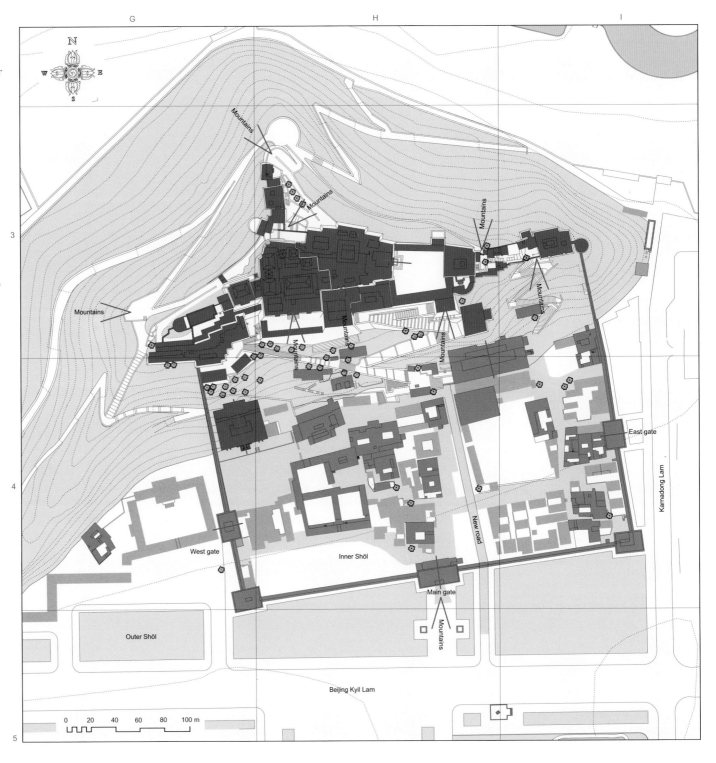

Opposite left: Shöl, 1994. A small part of central Shöl still has a rural, idyllic character, until recently even with cows and sheep. Less central parts of the old town had areas with similar buildings.

*Right: Shöl and Potala, from the roof of Shöl's main gate, 1994.
The irregular track from the gate zigzags up to the foot of the Potala's giant
stairs. The row of old houses to the left form the original front facing the track;
similar houses on the other side have disappeared to make way for the new
entrance road east of the main gate.*

from other Tibetan towns – Shigatse and Gyantse, for instance
– and elsewhere in the Himalayan region. The Potala, however, stands alone for its clarity of architectural composition
and richness of architectural and artistic execution. It seems to
form a crystallized extension of the Marpori rock; the main
walls reinforce the irregular slopes to create an awesome, highly
unusual barrier between the Potala's spiritual and physical im-
mensity and the surrounding world.

Shöl has a village character with traditional buildings protected inside a high enclosing wall with watchtowers and heavy
guarded gates. The layout of buildings follows an almost rectangular pattern, most unlike that of the old town but familiar
in freer townscape not affected by internal ritual routes.
Whether Shöl could be described as being 'more planned' than
the old town remains uncertain. Regardless of its semi-
orthogonal geometry, no rules may be detected regarding location of functions or spatial hierarchies. The largest open space,
used for religious festivals, was the area in front of the large
printing house, Barkhang Chenmo, by the western perimeter
wall. This area is now partly filled with new housing.[6] Outside the fortified walls, Outer Shöl was a village of its own;
today only one building remains. The pattern of townscape as
well as building types in Outer Shöl seems to have more re-
sembled Lhasa old town than Shöl.

Clockwise:
Pattern 3. Caves and minor buildings in a miniature mountain setting. Scale 1 : 3 000. The topography here on the north of Chakpori totally dominates the arrangement of buildings and architecture. Access to the ridge is only by very narrow footpaths.

Pattern 4. Yabshi Taktster, detached mansion. Scale 1 : 3 000. This large mansion, built for the family of the 14th Dalai Lama in the 1940s, was situated by itself in a large garden like countless other mansions all over Tibet, then as the only detached mansion inside the Lingkor.

Yabshi Taktster, 1997. There is still space around the mansion but it has more the character of a backyard with the garden gone. The building that once dominated the space between the Potala and the old town is now hard to find.

Chakpori houses from above, 1996. The small Chakpori housing group clings to the ridge. Today they are in ruins, but this unique type of buildings should be preserved.

Caves at Chakpori North, 1994. Modern buildings hide the entrance to the meditation caves assigned to King Songtsen Gampo and his Nepalese queen. Together with the small housing group and a nunnery, they constitute the pattern of minor detached structures in a mountain setting.

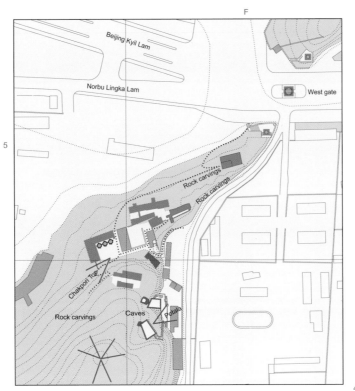

Chakpori village cluster

At the northern end of Chakpori, close to the West Gate, a small group of clustered houses clings to the narrow ridge. Shaped as a small village cluster in a rocky terrain, they are unique in Lhasa. Together with the nearby Tangtong Gyelpo temple, they may have formed a small community of their own, housing mainly medical monks and lamas from Mentsikhang, the Chakpori Medical College. Almost all the buildings are today dilapidated or ruined.

Yabshi Taktster: individual building in a landscape

This large mansion, built for the family of the 14th Dalai Lama, is a recent traditional construction and today the only building in old Lhasa situated in an open landscape unattached to other structures. Yabshi Taktster represents a distinct building type: the free-standing larger residence in extensive gardens, found all over Central Tibet. It is assumed to have developed from a more or less fortified or protected farmstead, imported into a semi-urban setting as here in Lhasa. Gradually it turned into a townhouse. Yabshi Taktster is difficult to find because the modern townscape surrounds it on all sides.

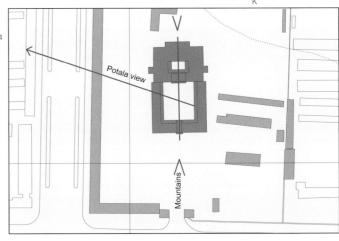

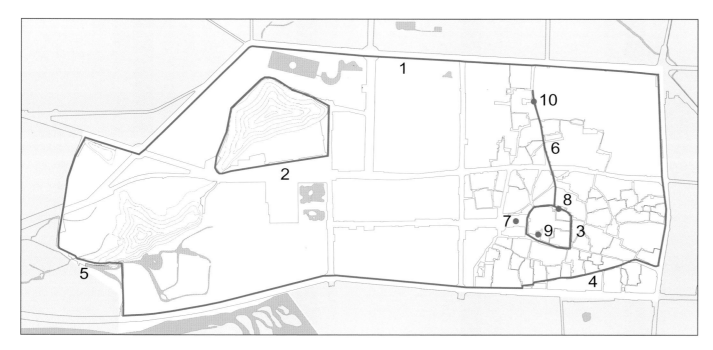

Townscape elements. Scale 1 : 20 000. Townscape elements are individual spatial elements or details of special interest that provide identity, often playing important roles as backdrop to traditional public life. Such elements might be an urban space, a park, a section of a street, a façade or a smaller component.

The ten most important townscape elements of old Lhasa:
1. *Lingkor: outer kora.*
2. *Tsekor: Marpori kora.*
3. *Barkor: intermediate kora.*
4. *Lingkor South-east.*
5. *Lingkor South-west.*
6. *Ramoche Lam.*
7. *Jokhang square.*
8. *Barkor Tromshung Jang: Barkor North square.*
9. *Sungchöra: Barkor South square.*
10. *Ramoche square.*

TOWNSCAPE ELEMENTS

Ten townscape elements are included here from a total of about 50 investigated, based on observations of daily life and familiarity with the overall functional-ritual townscape of Lhasa.

1. Lingkor: outer kora

The Lingkor today varies considerably from the traditional Lingkor. In fact, only two sections exist in more or less authentic shape, described below as separate elements. The map (p. 78) shows the old and new Lingkor. With the construction of large modern residential compounds north-north-east of the old town, the Lingkor today runs along a new major street, Lingkor Chang Lam. To the south it also follows a new street, Jingdrol Shar Lam, the longest and widest straight street in Lhasa. Only to the south-east and south-west does the original Lingkor remain nearly intact.

Citizens and pilgrims walk the Lingkor in their hundreds as part of daily worship, to accrue personal merit and to honour the religious institutions located inside its perimeter. On the map each dot represents one such major religious institution. Numerous older Lhasa citizens walk the Lingkor each morning – alone, with grandchildren and neighbours or with a pet animal. Along the way they might pause at a traditional teahouse. There are also several 'stations' along the route where small offerings are made, especially along the western section.

These stations are marked with prayer flags or incense burners. Also, large mounds of hand-sized stones, some inscribed with a sacred mantra, have accumulated at strategic points where the route may change direction, for example where it turns sharply right upon leaving the riverbank or where it meets the rock face of Chakpori and turns left. An old stone mound by the river can be seen on Aufschnaiter's 1948 map (see p. 28). It disappeared in 1998. A circuit of the Lingkor is said to refresh both body and spirit.

2. Tsekor: Marpori kora

The kora around Marpori and the Potala is in character, form and function changing fast. Until a few years ago, the Tsekor was a simple gravel footpath around the base of Marpori with open views across the landscape. Today it is a broad paved pedestrian road enclosed by high walls on both sides, with the Potala visible over the inner wall and a modern cityscape closing in from the other directions. Market stalls have moved in, first with items for the pilgrims and recently with food and consumer goods. In 1999, for the first time, meat was sold here. The Tsekor is becoming a market street, but koras have always more or less been religious and secular entities.

To the east, Karnga Dong Lam, with its long established market activity, extends up to Nyangdren Lho Lam. To the south the kora runs along the pavement of Beijing Kyil Lam and the huge new Potala square; most pilgrims use a newly evolved footpath directly under the perimeter wall of Shöl.

Townscape element. Lingkor: outer kora. Scale 1 : 20 000. The Lingkor is a long, 7.5-km kora that entirely encircles old Lhasa. It was for centuries an important outer boundary of the spatial-religious landscape of the town, to which the 'memory map' made by Zasak Jigme Taring bears witness (see p. 30).

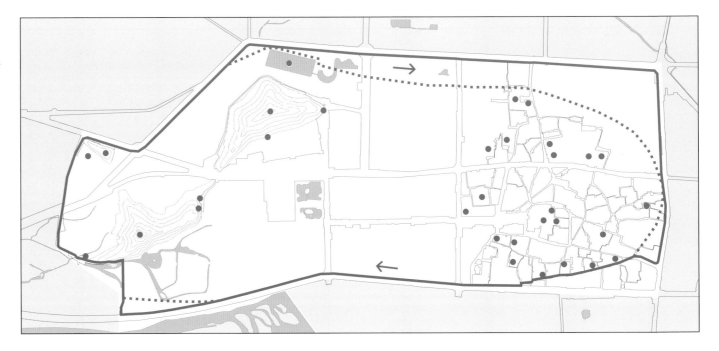

Lingkor passing along Kyichu river, 1987. This scenery may have changed somewhat during the previous 30 years, but that is nothing compared to the changes between 1995–2000. The island has been enlarged and a huge housing scheme with hundreds of dwellings and shops has turned it into an entirely new city district. The Lingkor remains.

Outer Shöl, with buildings several hundred years old, faced demolition in 1995 when the area between the West Gate and Karnga Dong Lam became upgraded. Only one small building survived. Until 1995, the outer face of the wall enclosing Shöl revealed its rammed earth construction. Now exposed in its entire length, the wall has been faced with granite blocks.

With a length of 1900 metres, the Tsekor is twice as long as the Barkor and significantly less crowded. The invasion of market stalls is gradually changing this and the Tsekor is becoming increasingly popular for both pilgrims and ordinary pedestrian traffic. During the main summer pilgrimage season several thousand people circle the Tsekor each day, many for the first and only time in their lives. It is a varied and visually stimulating walk, with the Potala and distant mountains as foci. Long stretches of the Tsekor are lined with prayer wheels. Incense burners set into the wall face Marpori, as do numerous charming stone images of gods and auspicious signs.

Outside the main gate of Shöl two small pavilions each house a historical stele. In 1995 they were restored and returned from Lukhang park to a site near their original location.[7] The yellow pavilions are constructed in granite blocks, each topped by an elaborate Chinese-style roof with green glazed tiles. The 18th-century steles have beautifully carved capitals, and one of them rests on the back of a tortoise. They give accounts of different successful battles against the Gorkhas. Across Beijing Kyil Lam stands an 8-metre-tall stele on a small mound inside an enclosure of recent construction. Known as Doring Chima, it was erected during the reign of Trisong Detsen in the 8th century and commemorates the general whose Tibetan troops conquered Chinese territories and occupied Changan, the Tang-dynasty capital.

The stupas of the West Gate, demolished decades ago when modern vehicular traffic started to affect Lhasa, were rebuilt in 1995. In former times the only access from the west was

Clockwise from top left:

Lingkor, stone pile. 1997. The Lingkor, turning from the river towards Chakpori, passes a huge pile of stones put there by pilgrims and local devotees. This pile disappeared during construction work on the new island in 1998.

Tsekor, 2000. Devotees along the Tsekor in front of the Potala prostrate on the sidewalk.

Potala square, 1998. This area, formerly an open meadow, has never been built upon. The huge square is used for festivals and Sunday markets. The Tsekor passes between the square and the walls of Shöl.

Lingkor passing the Muslim market, 1997. The kora now passes along the market and past the old mosque.

Lingkor near its eastern extreme, 1997. View from the blind end of an inactive section of the old Lingkor; the minaret of the old mosque, just outside the kora, rises in the background.

through the largest central stupa; this entrance gate to a dramatic degree both linked and separated two huge landscapes. The entrance into old Lhasa would have been thrilling. In a single glimpse the traveller could take in the Potala towering to the left, the defence walls of Shöl below, meadows and fields and in the distance Lhasa's townscape surrounding the Jokhang's golden roofs – all dwarfed by majestic mountains.

Around Marpori are located a number of culturally and architecturally important structures. They were originally stations on the Tsekor, visited in conjunction with walking the kora. Some of these stations are included here and described briefly.

The Elephant House (Langkhang), situated on the Tsekor north-west of Marpori, was built to house four elephants

Outer Shöl, 1987. Outer Shöl, destroyed in 1995, once covered the area from the West Gate to Shöl's main gate and hid the Shöl wall, constructed of rammed clay. Only one house remains from the ancient village of Outer Shöl.

Tsekor West, 2000. The market developed explosively between 1998–2000, but in urban situations koras have always attracted commerce. The commercial 'outer' side and the religious 'inner' side of the kora are clearly separated.

received by the 13th Dalai Lama as an imperial gift from China. Skeletons of the elephants were found when the building was demolished in 1997. A restaurant, now closed, stands in its place.

Lukhang chapel, also known as the Naga pavilion, is located in the middle of the Lake of the Nagas (snake or dragon-like creatures) north of Marpori. The 6th Dalai Lama built the chapel on an artificial island in this large pond. The Lukhang chapel is closed off by a high perimeter wall around a park, guarded by ticket vendors.

Karnga Dong shrine on the Tsekor's north-east corner is taken care of by nuns from Michung Ri convent, located high on a mountainside east of Lhasa. The building containing the shrine is a recent construction. Large granite slabs carved with images of saints and gods perhaps originated from East Rigsum Temple, and are said to have been found after the Cultural Revolution in the foundations of a bridge. Some of the stones are believed to date back to the 7th-century founding of the Jokhang.[8]

On Chakpori south of the Tsekor proper is Palha Lupuk, an ancient cave with many Buddhist images cut into the rock face. Some say Songtsen Gampo used it as a retreat, others claim it to be the oldest known man-made cave in Tibet. Nearby sits a small convent-temple established by Tangtong Gyelpo, a multi-talented sage of the 15th century who founded Tibetan opera, practised medicine and built iron suspension bridges. The temple was originally located on the peak of Chakpori but in

Tsekor West, 1998. The Tsekor today is a wide, paved walkway enclosed by high walls. Prayer wheels line the wall towards Marpori. The market remains modest.

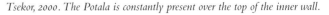

Opposite: Townscape element. Tsekor: Marpori kora. Scale 1 : 4 000. The Tsekor, nearly two km long, was originally a track in the open countryside. Today it is turning into a market except for the section in front of Shöl. Teahouses and stations along the kora make the circumambulation a varied and social experience.

Tsekor, 2000. The Potala is constantly present over the top of the inner wall.

Tsekor East, Karnga Dong shrine, 2000. This small modern shrine is a stations on the Tsekor. It holds some very old carved granite slabs with images of Buddha and deities.

Potala, viewed from the north, 1987. The entire public park north of the Potala, with Lukhang chapel and Naga lake, was formerly part of the Tsekor area. Now the Tsekor is confined to the walled-in path.

Tsekor, Doring Chima (stele), 1994. An 8th-century stele records the Tibetan victory over the Chinese. The text is still clearly readable on this beautiful monolith.

temple walls and gradually found its natural form; the kora today likely resulted from the boom in building during the time of the 5th Dalai Lama in the 17th century. With this expansion it became prestigious to live along the Barkor, which became the focus of Lhasa's religious and secular life. Here there were no formal squares, the largest public space being Sungchöra, the extension at the southern entrance to the Jokhang, where large gatherings and lectures for monks were staged. No square existed in front of the main entrance to the Jokhang — only steles and a sacred tree marked the site.

Chakpori caves, 1997. The caves and nunnery are among the stations within the Tsekor area. Cave entrances are more than 20 metres above the ground; the terrace of the upper chapel offers a superb view of the Potala.

Tsekor in front of Shöl, 1997. Two reconstructed pavilions house historical steles outside the Shöl main gate.

1695 moved to its present site to make way for the Medical College, which was demolished in 1959 by the Chinese.

3. Barkor: intermediate kora

The Barkor is the kora encircling the larger Jokhang complex (Tsuglhakhang). Meru Nyingba monastery and numerous residential buildings exist close to the Jokhang inside the Barkor. Meru Nyingba, built against the Jokhang's walls, perhaps dates from the 7th century. The Barkor's route has changed a great deal over the centuries, as seen in paintings and illustrations. During its first centuries the Jokhang may have stood alone on the marshy plain, surrounded only by simple buildings for the craftsmen who built it. A kora probably ran close to the

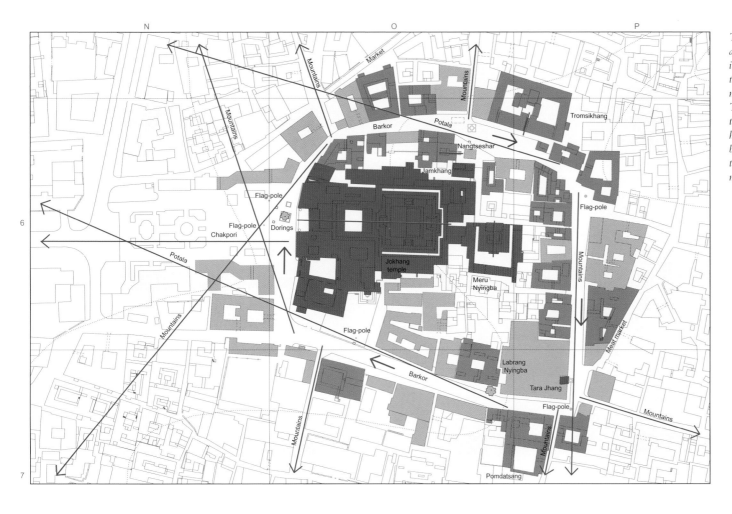

N   O   P

Market

Mountains

Mountains

Mountains

Barkor

Potala

Tromsikhang

Nangtseshar

Jamkhang

Flag-pole

Flag-pole
Chakpori

Flag-pole

Dorings

Mountains

Jokhang
temple

Meru
Nyingba

Flag-pole

6

Potala

Mountains

Barkor

Labrang
Nyingba

Tara Jhang

Flag-pole

Mountains

Mountains

7

Pomdatsang

Mountains

Meat market

Townscape element. Barkor: intermediate kora. Scale 1 : 3 000. This, the third in the series of koras revolving around the Jowo Buddha image, is both the most important devotional route in Tibet and the major market in the old town. Hundreds of new pilgrims throng here every day and at dusk the crowds become huge. Important views connect the kora with the Potala and the mountains.

Religious processions between the Potala, monasteries and the Jokhang are assumed to have been an important aspect of interlaced religious and secular life. These processions almost always included the Barkor, as recorded in murals and thangkas. The Jokhang, most sacred place in Tibet since the 7th–8th centuries, drew pilgrims to Lhasa in great numbers. They would stay for days or weeks, and their need for shelter and food contributed considerably to developing the town and its community.

From early days, the Barkor has been Lhasa's main market area. Even before a proper town grew up, market stalls and lodging tents may have lined the circumambulation route, and during religious festivals, complete tent towns mushroomed around the Barkor, adding to the bustling social, religious and commercial life.

The Barkor's physical form as we know it today probably took shape during the late 1800s and early 1900s. Newly added buildings lined the Barkor more regularly than before, some large and representative, others small and for residential purposes. Nearly all of them had shops facing the street. Today

the Barkor is almost 800 metres long, and 4–20 metres wide. Its walls are the linked façades of two- or three-storey buildings, the older ones with sloping walls that make the space between the buildings wider towards the top. This feature gives the traditional Tibetan streetscape a unique quality lost with the introduction of modern construction and uniform vertical walls. Along the Barkor as elsewhere in the traditional townscape, smaller elements, most with religious significance, dot the way: stupas, mani walls, giant prayer masts, incense burners, mani piles, steles, clusters of prayer flags and sacred trees. Each element is approached and venerated according to ritual forms – one walks to the left of a mani wall, stupa or prayer mast; one offers fragrant juniper to the burners.

It is religiously auspicious to walk around the Barkor, or any kora, and many of the local Tibetans take the stroll daily, to be alone with their prayer wheels or to socialize and chat. The Barkor, for all its sacred symbolism and religious import, also seems to be an ideal market street. It is not too long, yet long enough to maintain interest and variety with constantly changing internal and external views, and with a streetscape

Jokhang square, 1987. View towards the 'entrance' to the Barkor; the Jokhang is to the right.

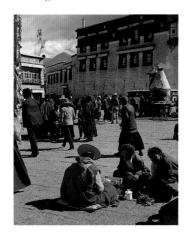

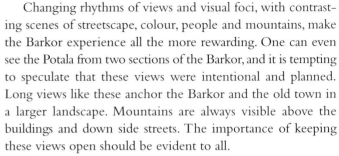

Barkor, 1987. The 'entrance' to the Barkor from the open square built in 1985. This view looks against the clockwise direction of walking. The Jokhang is to the left; a mountain view anchors the site into the larger landscape.

Changing rhythms of views and visual foci, with contrasting scenes of streetscape, colour, people and mountains, make the Barkor experience all the more rewarding. One can even see the Potala from two sections of the Barkor, and it is tempting to speculate that these views were intentional and planned. Long views like these anchor the Barkor and the old town in a larger landscape. Mountains are always visible above the buildings and down side streets. The importance of keeping these views open should be evident to all.

The Barkor contains some of Lhasa's most impressive secular buildings, yet a large number of these have been demolished since the LHCA survey and documentation work started in 1995. It is truly unfortunate that the finest and most important street of old Lhasa has changed to such a degree. A few new buildings are being successfully rebuilt in a near-traditional Tibetan style and some traditional buildings are now properly repaired and upgraded.

Still, all is not well on the Barkor. Towards the south-east corner one meets a modern shopping centre, built in the early 1990s to replace the large Surkhang family mansion. It is considerably larger than the old building, built in concrete with large steel windows and vertical, non-sloping walls. Inside one is introduced to a modern commercial world of glass, steel and marble. The new Surkhang severely breaks with the scale and harmony of built form on the Barkor. Attempts to add 'Tibetan style' details are crude pastiche. The Barkor deserves at least a competent reconstruction of the traditional buildings on this important corner.

Barkor North, 1987. The kora widens into an elongated square (element 8, see p. 93) with the main market activity on the Barkor. The three-storey building to the right is new but with traditional battered walls and materials and acceptable proportions. Across from this building stands Tromsikhang with the longest, finest and one of the oldest façades on the Barkor. A quiet architectural harmony reigns.

Barkor North, 1997. The same square as in the previous photograph. The three-storey building has been replaced by a new one about the same size but with different materials and detailing. This concrete construction with vertical walls, steel windows and quasi-Tibetan features destroys the former harmony. This type of 'renewal' is typical, though other cases are worse. Building turnover on the same plot is often amazingly fast. A five-year lifespan for a building is quite common in Lhasa.

of human proportions. Traditional Barkor buildings vary in size and expression within a common code. Architectural details, as well as artefacts for sale in shops and stalls, have a robust attractiveness characteristic for handmade objects.

Barkor East, looking south, 1987. The Barkor with traditional proportions and atmosphere.

Barkor East, 1987. Looking south. The Surkhang building, one of Lhasa's finest town mansions,[9] can be seen outlined at the end of the row of house fronts to the right. The streetscape has close contact with the mountains.

Barkor East, looking north, 1987. To the left is the north-east corner of the old Surkhang building.

Barkor East, 1994. The new Surkhang building on the Barkor's south-eastern corner. A modern shopping centre built in the early 1990s rises much higher than the original Surkhang building and totally crushes the scale and proportions of the area. Its huge overlit courtyard unconvincingly tries to disguise itself as a streethouse by means of quasi-traditional and fake detailing.

Barkor North, 1999. Barkor North and Barkor South have important 'view lines' that connect with the Potala.

Barkor South, with Potala. F. Spencer Chapman, 1936. Jokhang and part of the Sungchöra square to the right.

Right: Barkor South, 1997. Shortly after turning the south-eastern corner, the Potala appears over the roofs to connect the Barkor with the landscape and dominating point of reference.

Barkor North, street scene, 1997.

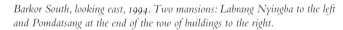

Barkor South, looking east, 1994. Two mansions: Labrang Nyingba to the left and Pomdatsang at the end of the row of buildings to the right.

Barkor South, looking east. F. Spencer Chapman, 1936. The mansion to the extreme left is Labrang Nyingba, the Barkor's oldest secular building. Next to it is the now-demolished Surkhang and across from it the three-storey Pomdatsang mansion. The Barkor was unpaved at that time.

Barkor West. Scale 1 : 200. Ancient stone steles (dorings) in their modern enclosures.

4. Lingkor South-east

This 700-metre-long section of the Lingkor is the only part of the circumambulation route that still touches the old town. From the narrow passage between Shar Rigsum Lakhang, the eastern protector chapel, and the Great Mosque, the Lingkor can be experienced to some degree as it once was. A few old buildings remain along the route, among them the Ani Tsangkung nunnery, with its temple built over a meditation cave of Songtsen Gampo. Further along is the charming Kunsangtse mansion and immediately after this the small mosque, recently demolished for a huge new replacement, completed in 2000. At the next crossing, Lho Rigsum Lakhang, the southern protector chapel, stands on the corner. Approaching the end of this section, where the Lingkor makes a sharp left turn to join the main street, the small manor house of Trijang Labrang – once owned by a tutor of the 14th Dalai Lamas – blocks the view.

Lingkor South-east, 1999. View towards the east. The ochre building is the Ani Tsangkung nunnery.

Townscape element: Lingkor South-east. Scale 1 : 3 000. The only remaining part of the historic Lingkor that touches the old town. A number of fine old buildings border the kora.

5. Lingkor South-west

At the western outcrop of Chakpori, the Lingkor enters a narrow 200-metre long section where it squeezes between the rock face and a marshy area. Steps are cut in the rock and the track rises 20 metres above the plain. Hundreds of rock carvings are scattered across the rock face, most of them painted in bright colours, some protected by tiny shelters. The rock carvings may be from only a few years to more than one thousand years old. From the top of the path the view over the river and mountains is impressive, in earlier times even more so.

Descending one enters a small open square at water level facing an enormous flat vertical rock face also covered with beautiful rock carvings. The rock, a natural oddity some 50 metres long and 5 metres thick, rises as a thin slab up to 20 metres above the ground. This perfect site for rock art, properly called Sanjia Gudong, has been a sacred place of worship perhaps for as long as humans have been in the area. Its dazzling array of art spans many centuries and styles, some dating back to the 7th century. Today the rock face is protected by an enclosing tall portico. Despite the beauty of this location, tourists rarely find their way here.

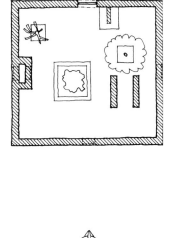

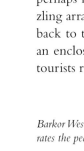

Barkor West. Scale 1 : 30. The 3.5-metre-tall stele, dating from 823, commemorates the peace treaty signed between Tibet and China.

Lingkor South-east, 1997. The old temple of Ani Tsangkung nunnery.

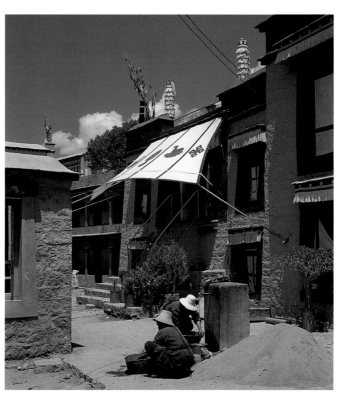

Lingkor South-east, 1999. South Rigsum Temple (Lho Rigsum Lakhang), one of the four old protector temples built as a mandala around the Jokhang.

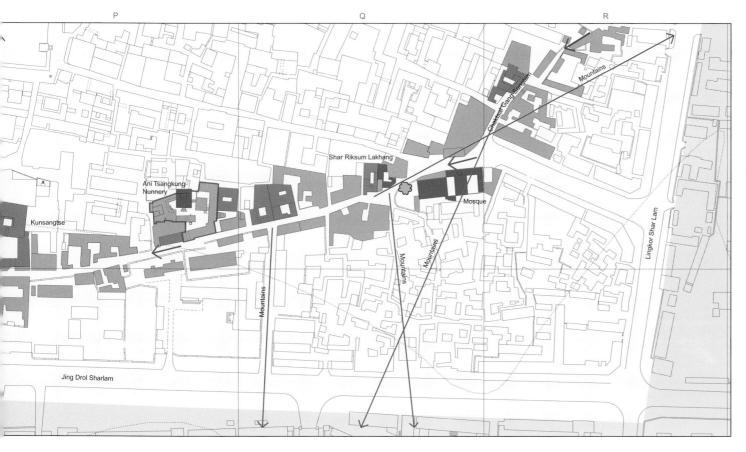

Lingkor South-east, 1997. The small mosque, demolished and replaced by a far larger mosque in 2000.

Lingkor West, 1997. Descending the stairs before reaching Sanjia Gudong 'picture rock'.

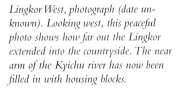

Lingkor West, photograph (date unknown). Looking west, this peaceful photo shows how far out the Lingkor extended into the countryside. The near arm of the Kyichu river has now been filled in with housing blocks.

Townscape element. Lingkor Southwest. Scale 1 : 3 000. One of only two remaining parts of the old Lingkor. Steps carved out of the rock face rise 20 meters, then descend to Sanjia Gudong, a magnificent 'picture rock' with hundreds of carved images of Buddhas, deities and spiritual masters. It stands at the extreme western outcrop of Chakpori hill and constitutes the Lingkor's westernmost point.

Townscape element. Ramoche Lam. Scale 1 : 3 000. Ramoche Lam is possibly the oldest street in Lhasa; it connects the Jokhang and Ramoche temples.

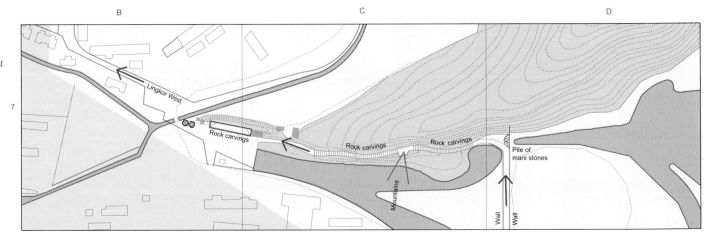

6. Ramoche Lam

Ramoche Lam connects the Jokhang and Ramoche temples. The two, built around the same time in the 7th century, probably had a connecting lane of at least of the same age; Ramoche Lam, a track that crosses the circular koras, may indeed predate them to be the oldest in the area, a link between early Neolithic settlements around Sera and the Kyichu river.

Today, Ramoche Lam seems to connect the front of Ramoche with the Jokhang's rear side. That both temples 'landed' on the same side of the track may be more coincidence than planning; the original connection between the temples might have followed Ramoche Lam on the upper part but then deviated to follow Shasar Zur Lam for its lower part through the waterlogged areas. Shasar Zur Lam appears to end very close to the assumed original Jokhang entrance, and is likely to be considerably older than Barkor Sang Trom Sanglam, which connects Ramoche with the Barkor today in an almost direct line. Only Shasar Zur Lam appears on the 1948 Aufschnaiter map; Barkor Sang Trom Sanglam apparently did not exist at that time. The undulating route of the connecting track would be explained by the marshy character of the land before these areas were developed. A former bridge on Ramoche Lam spanned the marsh (for its likely location, see map p. 28). Barkor Sang Trom Sanglam, the southern part of Ramoche Lam, is possibly an addition that became a lane or street with the last round of townscape infill in the early 1950s.

Ramoche Lam widens considerably upon entering present-day Beijing Shar Lam. As seen from the Aufschnaiter map, this was caused by a very long mani wall in this place. The mani wall, perhaps ancient, certainly pre-dated the surrounding buildings and confirms the importance of Ramoche Lam,

Ramoche Lam, looking south, 1997. The streethouses are lower and generally of a poorer standard than those on the Barkor.

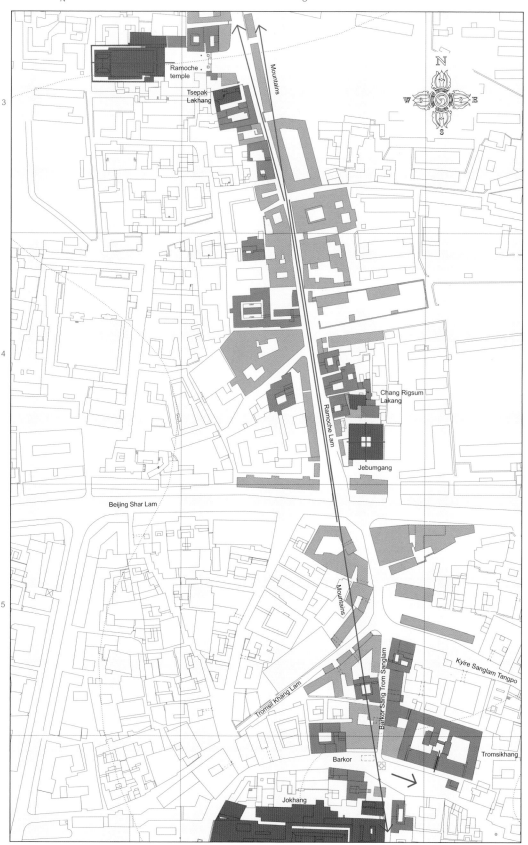

*Townscape element. Jokhang square.
Scale 1 : 1 000. The pre-1985 approach
to the Jokhang came from the west
through an area of natural landscape,
across a bridge, and up to buildings that
unevenly lined the narrow street leading
to the Jokhang's main entrance. At the
end of this short street one found oneself
already in the Barkor, with the main
entrance immediately to the right. The
great anticipation of arriving at the holy
Jokhang would keenly focus pilgrims and
visitors; they would certainly pay close
attention to all passing elements, including the sacred tree, steles, incense burners
and prayer masts. Originally, no square
lay in front of the Jokhang, as indeed
little evidence exists of planned exterior
spaces in traditional Tibetan townscape.
The monumental and sacred 'interior'
spaces of the huge courtyards in the
Potala, Jokhang and large monasteries do
not seem mirrored by any public or
external secular spatial compositions.*

*Integral to the Jokhang's main en-
trance are two giant prayer masts, two
large incense burners and two small
walled areas. The smaller enclosure –
four steps down from ground level –
houses a large stone turtle with a tall
stele supported on its back. The stele
carries a famous inscription in Tibetan
and Chinese of the agreement in 823
between Tibet's king and China's emperor; it affirms the peace treaty between
their countries. The other enclosure holds
two large steles, one with an inscription
on smallpox, its danger and its cure. This
dates from 1794 and is severely damaged
from scrapings and knife cuts, as if people
have tried to acquire pieces of the stone
itself for medicinal purposes. The other,
smaller stele, sunk into the ground, has
no inscription. Next to it a raised basin
holds the dead stump of a large willow
tree that legends say was planted by
Queen Wen Cheng in the 7th century.
In the summer of 2000, the Jokhang
square was redesigned and repaved with
new granite slabs.*

*Jokhang square, 1997. The Jokhang's
monumentality is clearly not built for the
long-distance view that the present
square offers. In fact, the exposed temple
looks rather small and insignificant.
Today, one can only imagine the earlier
experience of suddenly arriving and
seeing the monumental, imposing entrance portico from the dark, narrow
Barkor.*

which today is a busy market street. In Ramoche Lam shops
and workshops are mixed. The metal trade is prominent, particularly workshops for decorative copper and brass for religious buildings; noise and colourful activity spill out into the
street as well. The market activity is purely for locals and few
tourists ever find their way to Ramoche Lam.

About 600 metres long with a width varying from 5 to
25 metres, Ramoche Lam retains views of the mountains, which

are very important for a sense of place and belonging within
the greater townscape.

The buildings along Ramoche Lam are of the same architectural and functional character as in Barkor but generally smaller
and in some cases with only one floor. Today only four or five
old buildings remain on Ramoche Lam, but luckily the streetscape,
with its grain of lanes and alleyways, is close to the historical,

Barkor Tromshung Jang, 1987. Looking west from the middle of the square.

traditional one. A careful reconstruction could save special architectural qualities in this all-important street of old Lhasa.

7. Jokhang square

The popular square in front of the Jokhang does not belong to the category of traditional townscape elements because it was built in 1985. Its construction required the demolition of an entire quarter, originally created for the craftsmen who built and decorated the Jokhang. The map fragment from the mid-1950s (see p. 28) illustrates the grain of the earlier townscape of this area, an important part of the Barkor with interesting street elements. The square, a meeting point between the old and new town, has become the formal entrance to the Barkor where pilgrims and tourists encounter numerous market stalls. Many tourists only experience the old town by walking up this square from their bus and walking once around the Barkor.

8. Barkor Tromshung Jang (Barkor North square)

The urban space of Barkor Tromshung Jang is formed by a simple widening of the Barkor over a length of some 80 metres. Here Ramoche Lam (Barkor Changtrom Sanglam) enters the Barkor from the north, at a point previously marked by a stupa and mani wall. The stupa in this space must have been a magnificent discovery when making the first turn after passing the Jokhang's entrance portico. It is a great pity that the stupa has been demolished – one wishes it to be rebuilt. The stupa articulated the space of the square, 40 metres at its widest, 20 metres at its narrowest. On the sunny northern side the space is flanked along its entire length by a splendid building, Tromsikhang, with its outstanding symmetrical façade of three storeys. In the south-west corner is the former courthouse and prison, Nangtseshar, with its remarkable architectural integrity; the symmetrical front has two 'towers' that flank a high flight of steps. Next to Nangtseshar stands Jamkhang, a charming small temple. Between them there appears a glimpse of the Jokhang.

Barkor Tromshung Jang, 1987. The view of Nangtseshar, the old courthouse and prison, is today blocked by a new payer wheel building erected in the early 1990s. A corner of the Jamkhang temple appears to the left, and the Jokhang's wall is spotted in between. One of five large juniper (incense) burners on the Barkor stands here.

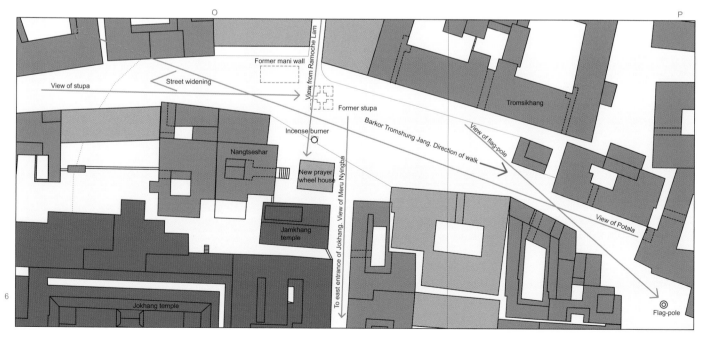

Townscape element. Barkor Tromshung Jang (Barkor North square).
Scale 1 : 1 000. A prayer wheel house (donkar) built in the early 1990s is perhaps a substitute for the demolished stupa. Unfortunately, its mass is so dominant that instead of merely being an object in the square it has become a new wall, reducing the size of the space and blocking the view of the old courthouse. This square is the liveliest part of the Barkor market; it branches off towards Ramoche Lam to the main old market, now an indoor market hall. Further along the Barkor, before walking around the prayer mast that marks the kora turn, one may on looking back catch a glimpse of a distant Potala above the roofs.

9. Sungchöra (Barkor South square)

Of the original two square-like widenings of the Barkor, the southern one (Sungchöra) was the largest public urban square in old Lhasa. It also merged with the Jokhang's southern entrance. A stepped podium built against the outer wall of the Jokhang indicates the place where religious functions were directed towards the public space. In former times, during the Great Prayer Festival, this space was used to address thousands of monks who gathered in Lhasa for the festival.[10] This square also saw the arrival and competition between huge decorative constructions (*chöpa*) made of coloured, sculpted butter. These offerings, elaborate pointed triangles as high as the houses, were exhibited for religious reasons and also to win prizes. Today's market activities are kept to the Barkor proper and leave the square a quiet place set apart from the daily hubbub.

10. Ramoche square

The square in front of Ramoche is the least architecturally defined of the spaces described in this book. It consists of an outer public section separated from an inner section by a large gate;

Sungchöra, 1997. The square seen from the roof of the Jokhang. Since the Great Prayer Festival celebrations were abolished, the square has become a quiet, closed off corner.

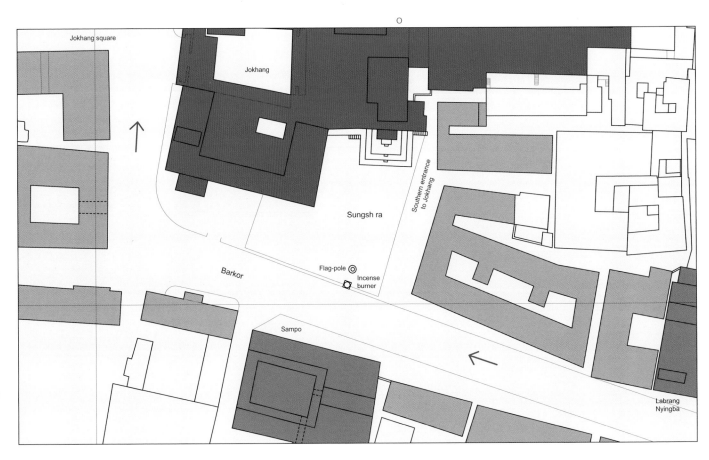

Townscape element. Sungchöra (Barkor South square). Scale 1 : 1 000. The square is merely a widening of the Barkor. Against the Jokhang's southern façade is a stepped podium for lama officials during major festivals. Up to twenty thousand monks would sit on the square and in the street for teachings and examinations. At such times the Barkor would be fenced off (see Potala wall painting, p. 62).

Sungchöra. Watercolour by Kanwal Krishna, 1940. On 24 February 1940, the day after the instalment ceremonies of the young 14th Dalai Lama in the Potala, huge triangular frames with butter sculptures were shown in the square; the best displays won prizes.

Townscape element. Ramoche square. Scale 1 : 1 000. Formerly, the square marked the end of Ramoche Lam where the Lingkor crossed immediately north of Ramoche. Here a town wall would have had a gate. Opposite Ramoche, on the other side of Ramoche Lam, was a garden belonging to the temple and used for philosophical debates, a practice still common in Tibetan monasteries. Today, residential buildings with shops border Ramoche Lam at this place. Old and new buildings in the area, lower than in the Barkor, give Ramoche square a more open appearance. The character of Ramoche Lam and its buildings is considerably more modest than along the Barkor, and perhaps embodies some of the Barkor atmosphere before the economic and social changes of the last 10 years. Here one also feels more in contact with the valley and the enclosing mountains, as if on the edge of town.

the inner space clearly belongs to the temple. This inner court-yard, open on one side, makes the approach to Ramoche quite different from the approach to the Jokhang.

Ramoche square, 1994. The gate to the temple forecourt is apparently a modern adaptation. Old photos indicate that there was originally only one large open space only, reaching from Ramoche Lam up to the entrance of the temple.

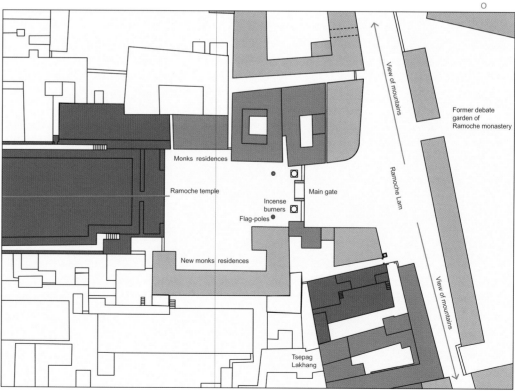

Buildings

INTRODUCTION

The old buildings of Lhasa inside the Lingkor once numbered more than a thousand. They lined the narrow lanes in a pattern that had evolved over centuries and which retained its traditional appearance until the 1950s. Each house was special, differing from all others in shape and size and yet connected by a simple, shared way of building. It was hardly possible to tell whether a building was ten years old or a hundred. Rebuilding and repair went on continually and certainly changed the town, but in such a slow way as to render these changes hardly noticeable.

This has all changed. Most of the old buildings – nearly two out of three – have gone. Vehicular traffic cuts through the old town and new, tall, often alien buildings make it difficult to find the old ones that remain. At the start of the LHCA study in 1994, demolition had almost reached its peak, as every year more than ten mostly fine buildings came down. Little attention was given to the old buildings[1] and there appeared to be even less documentation. The entire fabric of the old secular buildings was in danger of disappearing before 2005. On the brighter side, the demolitions seemed haphazard, with little planning. Buildings came down one by one and left the general image of the old town intact.

In Lhasa most of the lanes remain extant, giving a certain hope that the old town can survive. This survival, however, depends on official action based on detailed knowledge of the buildings in the old town and how best to protect, repair and upgrade them. The LHCA survey intended to contribute towards providing that information.

A survey of buildings in a townscape sets out to measure and establish shapes and physical relationships between existing elements. The undertaking at hand aimed to go further, by collecting physical information together with other types of data with which to describe in a simple, straightforward way the character, history, role and condition of each building.

The revered Danish architectural historian, Steen Eiler Rasmussen, began one of his many books on towns and buildings by stating that a remarkable building in a street is always noticed, while a clear picture of an entire street is only rarely grasped: 'Because as easy as it is to notice a detail, it is equally difficult to see or comprehend a simple united whole.'[2] An individual building, such as the monumental Jokhang on the Barkor, is experienced both as an individual building and as a strong architectural component that greatly influences the townscape around it. The Lhasa streetscape is composed of many individual volumes, both simple and monumental, which together form a visually integrated whole. When viewed as part of the townscape, a single building may have a different, often greater value than when it is viewed on its own. This dichotomy should be interpreted creatively and constructively in analysing both building and townscape. The understanding that results helps a great deal with the essential issue of protection.

A survey of physical objects in Lhasa must begin with the visual vocabulary of the town. This compiling and interpretation reflects on those who do the survey, and the story that results depends on the particular aspects of the environment on which they focus. The story often changes during the period of work, and the thousands of decisions made in this process clearly make the maps presented here subjective interpretations of Lhasa.

A Western-style map focuses on spatial relationships that define each object and the distances between objects. This is quite different from Tibetan traditions of visual representation, where buildings or elements geographically quite distant from each other may be juxtaposed in the same picture. The maps in this book are tools with which to grasp the spatial distribution of buildings and monuments in the townscape and to locate them in their correct proportions within this large space.

An architectural survey of a building is also a map of the building. It can take many forms. A quick five-minute sketch can convey a wealth of information, while a painstakingly elaborate registration may contain information that only a few will be able to appreciate. The appropriate level of detail for a survey depends on many factors, such as the intended use of the information, the audience, the physical context and accessibility of the survey area and resource availability.

At the outset, the *Danish City Atlases*, developed since the late-1980s with the so-called SAVE method and used to survey almost 100 Nordic towns, provided a model for the Lhasa survey. The overall goal of a Lhasa atlas is to support the town in increasing its concern for indigenous architectural resources. This survey collected visual and factual information of a number of categories, and at a level of detail one would have to describe as 'Emergency Registration'. The traditional method for

Potala Palace seen from Chakpori Medical College. F. Spencer Chapman, 1937. This remarkable photo shows a number of the buildings described in this chapter. The most striking feature is the clarity of relationships between buildings and landscape. The buildings are seen as distinct types in groups or 'patterns', with clear borders in between them. The Potala stands out as a strong, monumental form on top of Marpori, with perimeter walls, watchtowers and guarded gates that enclose the village of Shöl below. Inside Shöl several characteristic buildings can be seen clearly. Outer Shöl is mostly made up of tenement buildings and clustered housing, leaving a triangular space open around the West Gate. This entranceway to Lhasa, on the valley floor between the two hills, is made up of three stupas. Close to the West Gate, on the ridge of Chakpori's northern outcrop, appear the clear contours of another 'pattern', the dwellings for doctors of the Chakpori Medical College. The pond outside the West Gate is partially dried up, and inside the gate the road to Lhasa town, 1.5 km away, passes two small pavilions with old steles. The countryside is open; only two or three small buildings can be made out in the far distance.

architectural surveys is very different. Usually, considerable resources, trained staff and long periods on site are needed. Most surveys in the architectural and archaeological field are carried out in this manner, often resulting in wonderful detailed drawings. But the LHCA project found itself in a situation where limited resources and urban development pressures dramatically forced the pace of surveying and investigation. Lhasa old town is changing so fast that our 'Emergency Registration' survey method was the only way to secure at least outline information and documentation on the historical buildings and the townscape.

To survey Lhasa's historical buildings introduced special problems. Apart from the challenges of logistics, permits and access to information, modern base-maps and cadastral information were very difficult to find. At the same time, it was distressing to witness the speed with which the old buildings came down, replaced with poor structures of outsize proportions.

Surveying

The buildings described as 'historical' are those that pre-date 1950. All 292 historical buildings extant at the start of registration work in 1995 were visited and surveyed in outline. Sixty categories of information were collected for each building in the LHCA project database, and all buildings were photographed, many of them several times as part of periodic checks on changes in townscape and buildings. Where access was possible, building interiors were also photographed. The survey work, carried out by one or two small teams, took place over several seasons. The authorities provided permits to enter all the old buildings in Lhasa; only one, owned by the military command, was off limits. Some buildings had to be investigated from the roof because of furious guard dogs. In such cases, only the general arrangement or geometry could be determined. Other buildings were difficult to enter because of new extensions or additions. For these, the survey relied on estimates and details seen with sufficient clarity only in photographs. The work provided many Lhasa-based team members with their first introduction to the field of architectural surveys.

Maps

Individual buildings are identified in maps that cover an area named after its major monument, such as the Potala-Shöl area, the Jokhang area, and so forth. These areas are not official city districts but rather chosen to illustrate the distribution of historical buildings within the townscape at the largest possible common scale. When deciding on the scale, a main concern was to assure an optimal amount of detail while maintaining

suitability for publication. The main road, Beijing Shar Lam, divides the old town into northern and southern sections, much as the ancient track through this area always has. This made it logical to present the Jokhang Area as one map, with the areas north of Beijing Shar Lam as another, here called the Ramoche Area. To the west, Marpori (with the Potala and Shöl) makes a natural map area, with the northern and southern parts of Chakpori shown separately.

As a general rule, only extant and surveyed historical buildings are shown on the maps. By the end of 1999, a total of 70 old buildings shown in the old town no longer existed. Each building is represented on the map by its roof plan, with changes in floor levels shown as outlines. Dotted lines represent covered areas, entrances or galleries. Following each area map is a section with detailed descriptions of selected buildings.

Identification of buildings

Lhasa buildings were traditionally identified by name only. Here, the main sources for identification have been the maps by Aufschnaiter and Taring, municipal maps of the 1980s and aerial photographs, in addition to direct observation and interviews. Aufschnaiter identified all buildings in the old town by name and district, introducing a system of numbers and letter prefixes that represented the buildings and districts. With nothing better to hand, Aufschnaiter's numbering system from 1948 proved invaluable for the LHCA survey work.

To identify each extant building in the large survey area, a new numbering system was introduced that reflects the order in which the buildings were surveyed. This explains why the Jokhang is identified as number 313 and the Potala as number 316. Buildings are identified throughout by their Building Registration Form numbers. An Appendix is included to provide key information on all registered buildings (see pp. 165–170). All areas inside the Lingkor were covered in the survey. Street names are not used when identifying buildings, nor are they used in daily life in Lhasa. Written street names are hard to find even today – no official map with them seems obtainable – and therefore the names presented here may not be entirely correct.

Presentation of buildings

Each building was selected for presentation when sufficient materials became available for its adequate presentation. It also needed to fulfil one or more of the following criteria:
- an important building;
- an important element in its immediate townscape;

- an example of an important building type.

Of the buildings presented here, about one-half are secular. Most of the larger religious buildings are included, many of for the first time.

A major concern of the survey was to document traditional Lhasa architecture that tends to disappear more quickly and easily than well-known monuments. It is these anonymous buildings in the townscape that are most exposed to change. Building selections do not suggest any protection priority. In fact, so few historical buildings remain in Lhasa old town that every one of them should be protected and saved from demolition. One early intention was to present all extant monastic and secular historical buildings in Lhasa, but this has not been possible.

Describing selected buildings

The descriptions of the Potala Palace and Jokhang Temple may seem brief compared to their overwhelming cultural importance.[3] Most of the extant historical buildings can be adequately shown in drawings at a scale of 1 : 500. To illustrate and discuss the Potala or Jokhang in a similar manner would require a major undertaking. The building descriptions are kept at a level where they may be simply grasped; the emphasis is on the overall architectural character of each building and its relationship to the surroundings.

Sources

Many sources contributed to the architectural drawings: Chinese publications, publications from the Tibet Heritage Fund[4] and the LHCA surveys.[5] All line drawings included are amended and redrawn by the authors to ensure unity of graphics and information.

Assessing architectural values

All extant traditional buildings inside the Lingkor were investigated and assessed based on these criteria:

- Architectural value: expressed in terms of proportions, harmony of composition, character of design of the whole or particular parts of the buildings, or being a work by an outstanding architect or master builder;

- Cultural and historical value: evidence of a role in the cultural and historical life of the community, town or nation, or evidence of particular qualities in terms of craftsmanship or technology;

- Environmental value: the degree of environmental, visual, or social importance, and harmony between the building and its surroundings;

- Originality: the degree to which the original building still exists, and the degree to which repairs necessary to safeguard a relevant level of authenticity are considered possible;

- Technical condition: whether original components can be repaired or replaced in an acceptable manner.

Architectural value and cultural-historical value were given more weight than the other criteria. A concluding protection value was determined for each building, based on individual assessments and evaluating each building as being of high, medium or low protection value, as shown colour-coded on the map. A building considered to be of low protection value on its own was sometimes assessed differently as part of a larger townscape. In Lhasa, the reduced number of traditional buildings warrants full protection for all historical structures and townscape pre-dating 1960.

The main purpose of *The Lhasa Atlas* is to present a relevant sample of the most important historical and extant buildings and building types in Lhasa, as part of an overall description of the architectural and townscape qualities of the old town.

Illustrations

In this study, two independent assessments are made which do not always reach the same conclusion. One assessment focuses on individual buildings, the other on townscape. To illustrate

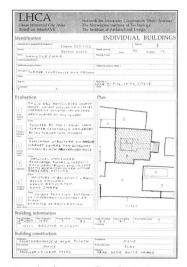

Sample of a survey form for single buildings; front page.
Categories of information:
   Identification
   Evaluation
   Plan in scale 1 : 400
   Building information
   Construction information
   Building materials and elements

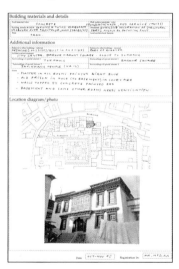

Sample of a survey form for single buildings; back page.
Categories of information:
   Architectural environment
   Notes
   Location plan in scale 1 : 2 000
   Photo

LHCA *survey team at work, on a rooftop, 1996. German architect Moritz Wermelskirch is holding the survey form while a Tibetan interpreter helps with the measuring tape.*

Buildings. Potala-Shöl area.
Scale 1 : 3 000. This map shows
Marpori hill with the Potala Palace and
its administrative village of Shöl located
below. North of the Potala lies a large
artificial pond with the small Lukhang
chapel on an island, and the Elephant
House (Langkhang) at the edge of the
pond. All buildings shown still exist
except for the Elephant House, which
was unexpectedly demolished in 1997
before being surveyed.[6]

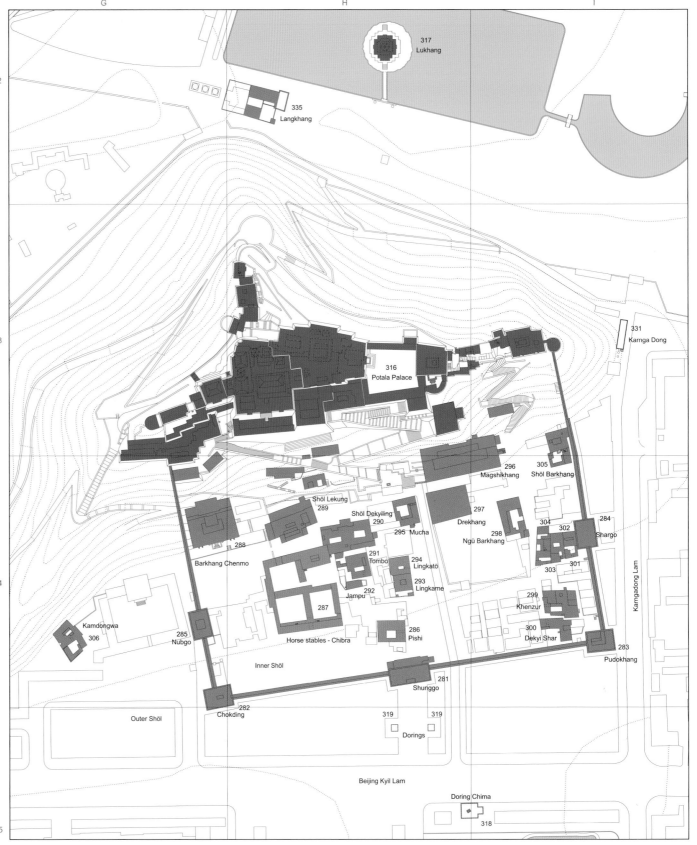

Key to Buildings maps

Building or - complex with national protection

Building with high protection value

Building with medium protection value

Building with low protection value

the conclusions from each assessment, we use two sets of colour codes, each using the same colours. In the 'townscape' maps, the colours signal important religious and secular buildings in relation to urban space. In the 'buildings' maps, the colours signal different degrees of protection value.

Buildings important in the townscape do not necessarily have a high protection value in themselves. Therefore there may theoretically be cases where a building is marked important in a 'townscape' map, but has no colour marking in a 'buildings' map. The reverse case may also appear.

Some information is entered by number codes which refer to a code list worked out especially for this study.

The buildings presented in this chapter are distributed across the old town inside the Lingkor, from Chakpori and Bhamari in the west to the eastern part of the old town. They appear in maps of the six main areas described in Townscape.

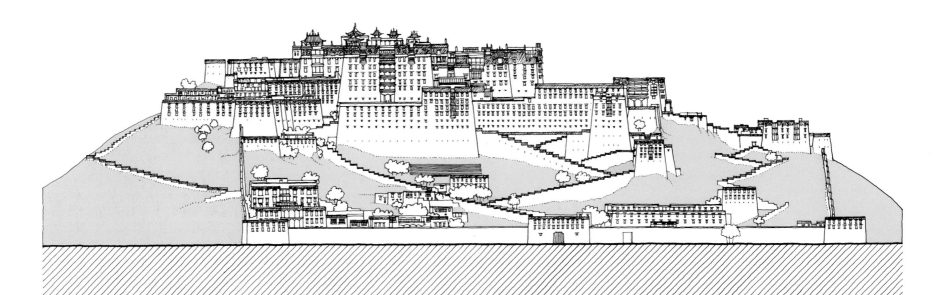

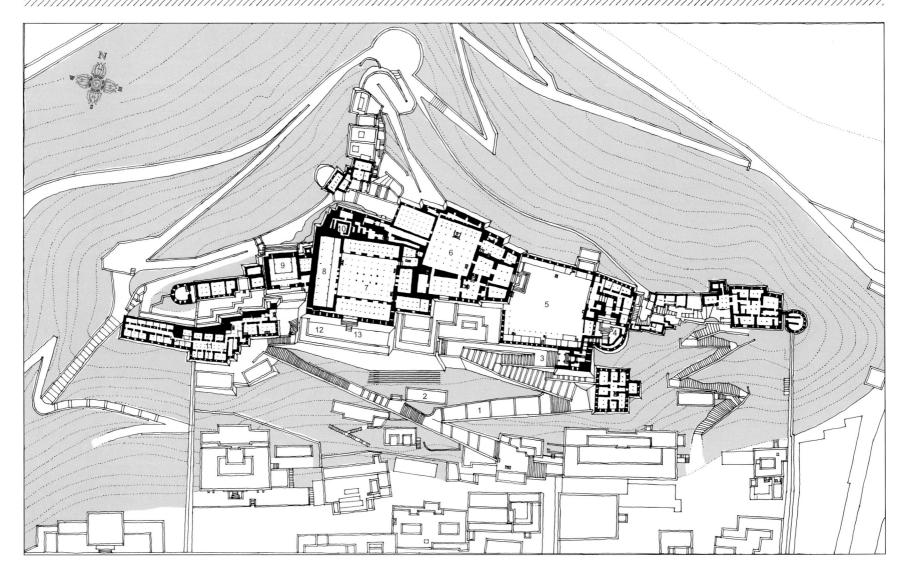

POTALA—SHÖL AREA

Potala Palace (316), monumental official building, 1645.

Named after holy Mt Potala in South India,[7] the Potala is among the world's great architectural masterpieces. It represents a culmination of Tibetan material culture that developed over more than a millennium. The many fine structures and overwhelming interiors display the rich building and decorative traditions of its master artisans. In spite of the limitations of building materials and methods, the Potala nevertheless exudes a unique presence. In its grand spaces, carved and decorated timber constructions, fine wall paintings and mass of richly executed objects and details, the Potala reaches unusual levels of architectural and artistic quality. A walk through becomes a series of revelations about the incredible inventiveness in the use of simple materials. Architectural motifs and artistic creativity are juxtaposed in endless and delightful variations.

The Potala in its present form was built during the reign of the 5th Dalai Lama to serve as his main residence, as the burial place of past and future Dalai Lamas, and to accommodate his personal Namgyal monastery.

Lhasa became the capital for the rule of the Dalai Lama after his major consolidation of Gelukpa power. Marpori was chosen for the palace-fort because of its dominant position over the Kyichu valley and its symbolic role as the mountain residence of Avalokiteshvara, main bodhisattva and Buddhist protector of Tibet; each Dalai Lama was considered the earthly incarnation of this being. Construction began on Marpori in 1645 and in 1648 Potrang Karpo, the White Palace, was completed. Potrang Marpo, the Red Palace, was built by Tibet's regent to honour the 5th Dalai Lama, who died in 1682; news of the death was kept secret until the Red Palace was completed in 1694.

Potala, front ramps, 1987. Visitors follow a more or less set route through the complex. The walk through Shöl from a gate in the perimeter wall brings one into direct relationship with the towering mass of buildings that otherwise seem majestic and awe-inspiring from a distance. The climb up four long flights of stepped ramps, with increasingly widening views of the valley, brings one to an enormous porch and gate in an attached tower (continued p. 104).

(continued p. 104).

Opposite, top: Potala Palace and Shöl village. South elevation. Scale 1 : 2 000.

Opposite, below: Potala Palace. Plan. Scale 1 : 2 000.
Key to plan:
1. *Outer stepped ramps*
2. *Storage building for giant thangkas*
3. *Main public entrance*
4. *Southern bastion*
5. *White Palace outer courtyard*
6. *White Palace assembly hall*
7. *Red Palace main assembly hall*
8. *Funeral chapel of the 5th Dalai Lama*
9. *Funeral chapel of the 13th Dalai Lama*
10. *Cave of Songtsen Gampo*
11. *Quarters of the Namgyal monastery monks*
12. *Red Palace outer courtyard*
13. *Red Palace entrance*

Potala with snow mountains, 1998. The Potala seen from the old town at sunrise.

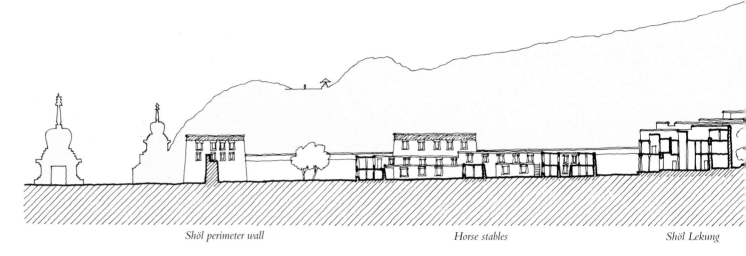

Shöl perimeter wall *Horse stables* *Shöl Lekung*

As an architectural composition the Potala appears as a series of massive tower buildings that grow together to form groups of volumes of different height and shape, all tied together with powerful horizontal bands. The seemingly floating golden roofs are ethereal forms in contrast to their solid substructure; they in fact cover the tombs, or 'dwellings', of the deceased Dalai Lamas. The contrasts and rhythms of different materials, of solids and voids, of heavy and light, of monochrome and intense colour are startling, subtle and pleasing at the same time. Whether there existed firm rules to govern proportions and groupings of masses in a building like the Potala remains to be ascertained. The impression is that this has not been the case. Creating a building complex of the size, complexity and architectural quality of the Potala Palace demanded the participation of large numbers of highly skilled and experienced craftsmen, builders and engineer-architects. The chief master-builder, probably a senior monk or lama, was certainly

one of the great architects of all time. Records tell of the building activity on Marpori, with thousands of labourers, craftsmen and artists drafted and invited from all parts of Tibet and beyond to participate in this extraordinary project.

General building practice – and with it the detailing of wooden members and use of colour – was guided by rules based on experience and spiritual-cultural traditions. Creating large and free compositions like the Potala could only be possible with a huge bank of practical experience, the involvement of the best builders, and the strong guiding hand of a brilliant, creative individual.

The use of colour constitutes a strong part of the visual and artistic drama. On the Potala roof, where complementary colours, red and orange, stand out against the sky with an almost unearthly intensity, one seems to float above the severe landscape of the valley. Up here the forms and colours combine into a symphony of powerful yet human force: heavy

Potala Palace

volumes, floating roofs, stone walls, textiles waving in the breeze, rounded forms, pointed forms, advancing and receding planes, open and closed spaces, golden forms, black forms and transcendent colours. It is not necessary to be a Tibetan or to know the whole cultural vocabulary of meaning in order to experience extraordinary beauty on the roof of the Potala.

An attempt to describe this wondrous building complex in a restricted space is nearly hopeless. After all, the mythical 'one thousand rooms' actually do exist; the interior is labyrinthine.

In the north-west corner of the Red Palace, on the third floor, a small cave and a chapel above it are believed to be the only remaining 7th-century parts of the original palace, supposedly built by King Songtsen Gampo. Both spaces, considered the most sacred on Marpori, are filled with images, statues, thangkas and holy objects.

The Potala is today a museum. After five years of repair and restoration by the Chinese government, it was in 1994 included on the UNESCO World Heritage List, and parts reopened for the public.[8]

Potala, turret and bastion, 1995. Hovering above the city, the large turret adjacent to the Shöl perimeter wall terminates the building complex towards the east. The round rim of the southern bastion is seen to the left.

Potala Palace, outer courtyard, 1995. The White Palace's outer courtyard; here the Dalai Lama watched ceremonies and performances from the balcony over the stairs. Access to the roof and the Red Palace is through this impressive building.

Potala, main assembly hall. Watercolour by Kanwal Krishna, 23 February 1940. The second day of the enthronement ceremony for the young 14th Dalai Lama took place deep inside the Potala. The closely spaced loadbearing timber columns are clad with colourful textiles. Sunlight filters down through layers of overhead constructions.

Potala Palace, 1995. The central space over the main assembly hall in the Red Palace. Textile curtains screen the open galleries, and the golden roof covers the funerary chapel of the 5th Dalai Lama.

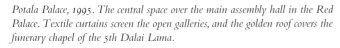

Potala Palace, from the White Palace roof, 1995. The entire vocabulary of 'classical' Tibetan architecture is in action here. The benma frieze is particularly prominent; the Red Palace with golden roofs in the background.

Barkhang Chenmo, interior. The large, main printing hall.

Barkhang Chenmo. Section. Scale 1 : 500.

Below right: Barkhang Chenmo. Plan. Scale 1 : 500. The printing hall is probably the largest indoor space in old Lhasa, a good deal larger than the Potala's main assembly hall. The expression 'forest of pillars' is here obviously justified. The building had mixed religious and secular functions.

Below: Shöl exterior and Barkhang Chenmo, 1998. Barkhang Chenmo sits just below the Potala's Namgyal monastery, near the Shöl perimeter wall. Stairs outside the wall connect the printing house with the western entrance to the monastery.

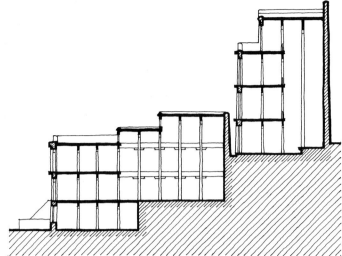

Barkhang Chenmo (288), monumental official building, 1926.

Situated between Shöl Lekung and the western Shöl perimeter wall (built almost against the wall), Barkhang Chenmo is a symmetrical terraced building of monumental proportions. It consists of two volumes, a broad volume with three floors in front and a slender, slab-like volume with four floors behind it. As the terrain rises steeply towards the Potala, the third floor of the front part corresponds with the ground floor of the back (upper) building.

The ground floor of the front part is divided into rooms that can only be entered from the small external open stairs. Some printing of religious and official books was probably done there, but the main printing was more likely performed on the first floor, a single space 22 metres deep. A Maitreya (Future Buddha) chapel along the rear wall of the front part is lit only from a large skylight. The images have been removed and the room is now used to store tens of thousands of wood printing blocks. The upper building contains a protector temple over

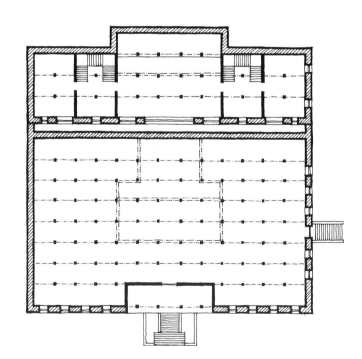

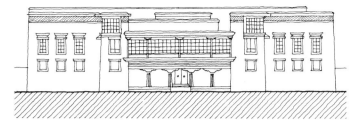

South façade

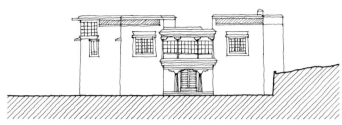

East façade

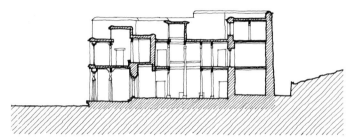

South–north cross-section

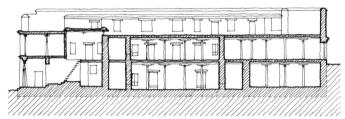

East–west cross-section

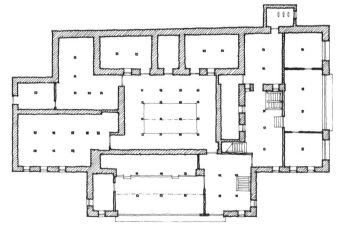

Plan of first floor

Right: Shöl Lekung. The architectural style of Shöl Lekung dates it to the start of the 20th century. Its characteristic bold corner windows suggest a connection to the Norbulingka summer palace of the 13th Dalai Lama, and it brings associations parallel motifs in early Western modernist architecture.

three storeys with galleries; all statues were demolished during the Cultural Revolution. The great number of wall paintings of very high quality in this building are well preserved. Barkhang Chenmo also contains the tomb of the 31st Ganden Tripa.[9] Although the building appears in good condition, it is seriously threatened by unstable foundations that are causing large cracks in the floors and roofs.

The TAR Archives Office, a regional institution, owns the building, which is protected at the regional level, as are the other main buildings close to the Potala inside Shöl.

Shöl Lekung (289), official building, c. 1900.

This government office, directly below the Potala Red Palace where the steep hill meets the plain, is unusual in that it addresses two directions and has two main entrances. The east entrance gives access to office areas on the first floor and the south entrance leads to a tall chapel, naturally lit from above, on the ground level. Shöl Lekung is a fine example of the use of traditional Tibetan architectural vocabulary to produce an independent building of great harmony and charm.

Shöl Lekung. East elevation. Up to 1950 the building housed government offices. Today it is the office of the Potala branch of the TAR Cultural Relics Administration.

Right above and below: Lukhang chapel. Plan and section. Scale 1 : 500. The mandala-like building plan has entrances at the four cardinal directions on the ground floor. Otherwise, Lukhang is clearly oriented towards the south, with a southern outer platform on the first floor. It is covered with a Chinese-style hexagonal roof. The chapel was rebuilt in 1791 by the 8th Dalai Lama and restored by the 13th Dalai Lama, who also used it as a retreat.

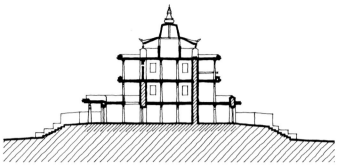

Lukhang and bridge, 1994. Lukhang chapel on its island, surrounded by old trees. One small kora follows the perimeter of the island, with another on the first floor. The bridge is a later construction.

Lukhang chapel (317), temple, 1690s.

The chapel, built in the time of the 6th Dalai Lama, sits on a small artificial island (40 m in diameter) in a lake behind the Potala. The cavity of the lake came from excavations of earth to build the great palace. According to legend, Regent Desi Sanggye Gyatso made a pact with Luyi Gyalpo, the Naga King (snake or dragon-like water spirit), in order to make use of the earth for building works. In exchange, the regent promised to build a shrine to honour the Naga King. The 6th Dalai Lama fulfilled this promise around 1695 by building this delightful three-storey pavilion. Lukhang was extensively reconstructed in 1984, but unfortunately the whole structure was encased in reinforced concrete, leaving only the inner walls untouched. The wall paintings inside are considered unique; they depict tantric practices, medicine and anatomy, famous spiritual masters and images that come from the *Tibetan Book of the Dead*. Sadly, these precious paintings have been seriously damaged due to penetration of water. An international field of art historians has tried to receive permission to attempt to protect the wall paintings before they deteriorate beyond rescue.

Lukhang chapel, 1994. Lukhang chapel; ground floor looking towards entrance and bridge.

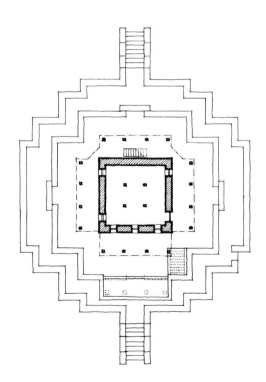

Shöl Dekyiling, from Potala roof, 1995. The view brings to mind the 14th Dalai Lama's observations of prisoners, watched from the top of the Potala through his binoculars.

Shöl Dekyiling (290), official building, c.1650.

This is the Shöl prison, situated below the Potala close to the foot of Marpori, opposite Shöl Lekung. In contrast to the old prison, Nangtseshar (8), on Barkor North, Shöl Dekyiling is not representative of traditional Tibetan buildings – it appears as a single-storey windowless perimeter wall enclosing a rectangular open courtyard. On the courtyard floor, two light wells allow sunlight to reach further small courtyards on the floor below, around which are grouped small dark cells – these cells are thus underground.

Shöl Dekyiling is protected at the regional level. It was repaired in traditional manner as part of the upgrading related to the Potala's nomination on the World Heritage List.

Shöl Barkhang (305), official building, c.1690.

This printing house lies at the foot of the hill just below the Potala's eastern bastion, against the Shöl perimeter wall. It was built at the same time as the White Palace in the 17th century.

A large square room (14 by 16 metres) on the ground floor was the printing hall, wither rooms used for storing the printing blocks. Tsetrung, the executive secretary, had his quarters here along with official rooms and stables.[10] The only natural light in the printing hall comes through small windows from the courtyard. The second floor, used apparently for domestic functions, was reached by an open stairway and a roof. With many sets of printing blocks seriously worn out, the 13th Dalai Lama in 1926 built a new and much larger printing house in the western part of Shöl.[11]

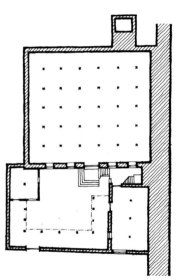

Shöl Barkhang, printing house. Ground floor plan. Scale 1 : 500.

Left: Shöl Dekyiling. Plan. Scale 1 : 500. The two isolated areas around open courtyards (with windowless cells) are underground.

Right: Shöl Barkhang. The printing house looks like an ordinary residential building with an attractive forecourt, stables and a roof terrace. Few would suspect that this was probably the main printing workshop in Lhasa if not all of Central Tibet for more than two hundred years.

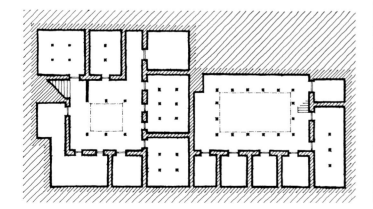

Chibra (287), outbuilding, 17th century and 1995. This large, two-storey building of former horse stables in the centre of Shöl was also a cowshed. It is popularly known as the 'Swastika-building' due to its plan shape (the swastika is an ancient Buddhist symbol of good fortune). Chibra was extensively reconstructed around 1956, but today is in poor condition. It is used for housing.

Magshikhang (296), monumental official building, 17th century and 1998. The former army headquarters, located against the slope below the Potala and believed built during the 5th Dalai Lama's reign, is a long, large building in two sections. These sections, one three storeys tall and the other five, are divided by a long, raised courtyard. Only the lower floors are old; the upper three floors were reconstructed in the 1990s. No original features or details remain in the building, today used for housing.

Lingkame (293), clustered housing, 19th century and 1996. Located in the middle of Shöl between the entrance gate and the steps leading towards the Potala, Lingkame is a modest single-storey residential building in mud brick, with a square layout of small rooms around a tiny inner courtyard. A small outer courtyard has two sheds for domestic animals. Lingkame, part of a cluster of similar houses, is typical of the many modest but decent traditional buildings for servants and lower staff that were built in Shöl and in the old town.

Ngü Barkhang (298), official building, c.1850 and 1996. Standing diagonally across the lane from Shöl Barkhang, this insignificant two-storey courtyard building has no features that separate it from other domestic buildings, apart from its very substantial entrance door and lack of windows towards the street. Tibet's paper money was printed inside Ngü Barkhang when this task was taken back from the Nepalese, who for several centuries had supplied the paper currency. Architectural style and craftsmanship place Ngü Barkhang around 1850; today it is in rather poor condition.

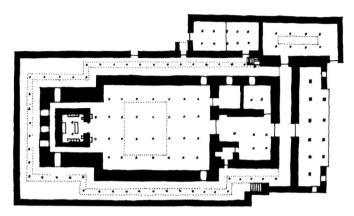

Left: Ramoche Temple. Plan. Scale 1 : 1 000.

JOKHANG AND RAMOCHE AREAS

Ramoche Temple (266), temple complex, c.640.

This temple complex is believed to be as old as the Jokhang, and is Lhasa's second largest temple and second in historical importance. It stands at the Lingkor's northern perimeter at the end of Ramoche Lam.

Legend says that in 641 a royal carriage got stuck in the sands at this place while transporting the sacred Jowo Buddha statue, a wedding present from Princess Wen Cheng to her future husband, King Songtsen Gampo. She took this as an auspicious sign and commissioned local and Chinese craftsmen to build the Ramoche temple here. In contrast to the Jokhang, also being constructed around that time, Ramoche's style was entirely Chinese. Its orientation is east–west with the entrance from the east, in contrast with Jokhang, where the entrance is from the west. Over the centuries, Ramoche was expanded, and after repeated fires and reconstruction it has today a more Tibetan architectural character.

While the Jokhang developed within a mandala-like spatial concept, Ramoche grew into a basilica-like structure, uncommon in the local context. The temple is described as having gone through four major stages of construction.[12] The first temple consisted only of the Tsankhang (choir) and Nangkor (inner kora). In the second stage (10th–13th centuries) the Dukhang (assembly hall) was added. The third stage (15th–16th centuries) saw the addition of the Drubkhang (protector chapels) and in the final stage (17th–18th centuries) the entrance portico, Khorlam (circuit corridor with prayer wheels) and outer kora were built.

In 1474, a second-generation disciple of Tsongkhapa turned Ramoche into the main teaching centre for the Upper Tantric

Ramoche Temple, roof, 1994. The golden roof over the second most important Buddha image in Tibet. The temple is situated at the northern edge of the old town, almost in the longitudinal axis of the Potala, visible in the distance.

College, with up to 500 monks from the three main Gelukpa monasteries (Ganden, Sera, Drepung) living and studying here. Their quarters were situated across Ramoche Lam but are now replaced with modern domestic buildings. Ramoche suffered considerable damage during the Cultural Revolution and was not reopened until 1985. A few monks have returned and religious functions have resumed to a certain degree. New smaller monks' quarters have been built in recent years around the entrance square.

Ramoche Temple, front, 1994. The temple faces a small entrance square and Ramoche Lam, the old street that connects it to the centre of town and the Jokhang.

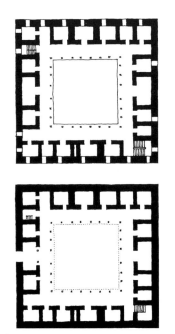

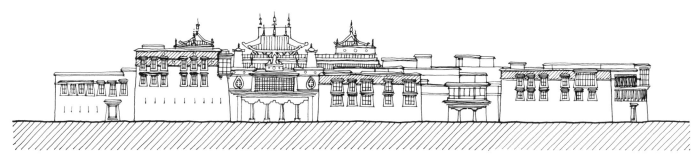

First Jokhang Temple, c.640.[13] Ground floor and first floor plans.
Scale 1 : 1 000. This first temple still forms the core of the present Jokhang. Models for the original design are believed to be Indian temples, among them the square Cave Temple No. 11 at Ajanta in India.

Above right: Jokhang Temple. West elevation. Scale 1 : 750.

Jokhang (Tsuglhakhang) (313), temple, 7th century and later.

Located within the heart of the Barkor, the Jokhang is the first and most sacred temple in Tibet, and also the building around which Lhasa developed. Tibetans know the entire Jokhang building complex, with its courtyards, monks' quarters, offices, kitchens and temple buildings as *Tsuglhakhang,* the Cathedral. It has been built in many stages from the 7th century onwards, with major rebuilding and extension in the 17th–18th centuries.

Its buildings, up to four storeys high, are made in traditional construction with raised roofs covered in gilded copper.

Founded by King Songtsen Gampo, the Jokhang was constructed with much trouble in the midst of marshes around 640. Legend tells that the temple was placed in this special location to subdue and pin down a gigantic demoness whose body spread across Tibet; the Jokhang stood directly above her heart.

As the Jokhang was built either at the initiative of, or as a present to Bhrikuti, Songtsen Gampo's Nepalese queen,

Jokhang Temple. Ground-floor plan.
Scale 1 : 1 000.
Key to architectural drawings:[14]
1. *Main entrance*
2. *Main open courtyard*
3. *Nangkor – the inner kora*
4. *Main assembly hall*
5. *Jowo chapel*
6. *Large open courtyard with well*
7. *Monks' quarters*
8. *Main kitchen*
9. *Outdoor assembly square*
10. *Enclosures with steles*
11. *Secondary entrances*

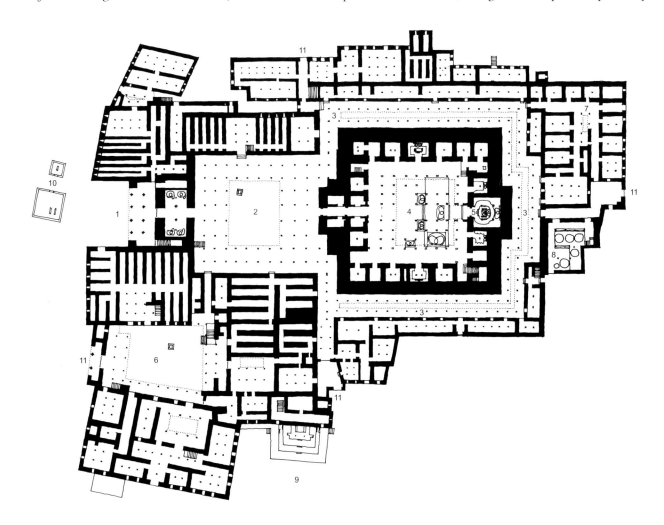

Jokhang Temple. East-west section.
Scale 1 : 750.

craftsmen from Nepal were commissioned to design and construct the temple. The king himself is attributed with the design as well, and he may have been an accomplished sculptor and painter.[15] The Jokhang originally housed the Mikyo Jowo (Little Lord) statue of the Buddha, brought from Nepal as part of the queen's dowry. Later, after the death of Songtsen Gampo, the Jowo image from Ramoche replaced it.

Through the centuries, additions caused the temple to become by far the largest building complex in the old town, with a length of 100 metres and a width of 150 metres. The major expansions took place in four stages.[16] First, the Jowo chapel, established for the sacred Buddha image, was extended eastward and upward into a first floor to double its volume. Second, the Nangkor inner kora was added between the 10th–13th centuries. Third, during the 13th–14th centuries, the inner courtyard became an assembly hall, a third floor was added and three of the four gilded, raised copper roofs constructed. Finally, in the 17th–18th centuries, the Jokhang was completed with two outer courtyards, four new entrances, a new main entrance porch and an outdoor assembly square.

Jokhang Temple, main entrance, 1987.
The main entrance, which faces towards
the new square constructed in 1985.
Enclosures with steles and incense
burners stand at front.

From an early time, the name *Jokhang* is said to have referred only to the Jowo chapel, but gradually it came to mean the whole temple. The name *Lhasa* is believed to have referred originally only to the Jokhang, but later it gave its name to the town.

Jowo, the most sacred image in Tibetan Buddhism, established the Jokhang as the prime site and destination for pilgrims from Tibet and surrounding Buddhist countries. Even during long periods when Lhasa lost its central role, the Jokhang held its elevated position among Tibet's holy places. After the 5th Dalai Lama's government recognized the temple as a national shrine, the governing body (Kashag) installed itself in the upper floors of the Jokhang.[17]

With its combination of restrained monumentality, long history, wonderful details and invaluable wall paintings, the Jokhang has an atmosphere and depth of quality of the highest order.[18] In 2000, the UNESCO World Heritage inscription of the Potala Palace was extended to include the Jokhang and central parts of the Barkor.

The Jokhang was built much in the manner of a *vihara* (square, cloistered courtyard; 18 metres by 18 metres) with small

chapels or monks' cells around. The entrance was from the west (towards Nepal) and the main chapel for the sacred Buddha image, brought by Bhrikuti, was located where the axis cuts the eastern wing (exactly east-west). Four other chapels, two flanking the main chapel and one each in the centre of the north and south wings, held other sacred images brought by the queen. Other rooms on the ground floor, originally used for monks' cells and storage, over time evolved into chapels. The first floor is practically identical in plan to the ground floor, apart from its windows.

Jokhang Temple, painting, 2000. A testimony to the overwhelming richness of delicate and decorative art found throughout the Jokhang are hundreds of tiny Taras (goddesses of compassion) painted between the beams of the golden roofs, and hardly noticed by anybody.

Jokhang Temple, assembly hall, 1987. The assembly hall was originally an open courtyard and is still 'open', although covered by a new roof. View from the north-east corner.

Jokhang Temple, roof, 2000. The roof of the Jokhang, with its multitude of forms, materials and colours, in the 'classical' Tibetan style. The Potala Palace rises in the distance .

Immediately east of the Jokhang, inside the Barkor, Meru Nyingba has parts believed to date from the 7th century. The greater complex, though, was built by the abbot of Nechung monastery around 1900. Meru Nyingba has a classical layout, with monks' residences originally in narrow buildings to three sides of the central, narrow courtyard and a main hall along the north side. All of these elements are reminiscent of Chödegang monastery in Tsethang, south-east of Lhasa.[19]

Thönmi Sambhota, a minister of Songtsen Gampo, is said to have finalized the creation of the Tibetan script while at Meru Nyingba in the 7th century. Around 820, Ralpachen built six protector chapels around the Jokhang. One, Zambala Lhakhang, a tiny chapel with its own inner kora, today forms part of Meru Nyingba's western wing. The 5th Dalai Lama enlarged the monastery to its present form in the 17th century to provide a town residence for the Nechung State Oracle. During the Great Prayer Festival, Nechung monks would perform ceremonies in the old protector chapel. Because of the high status of the oracle, Meru Nyingba was jointly administered by the Nyingmapa, Gelukpa and Sakyapa schools of Tibetan Buddhism.[20]

The main entrance into the courtyard was originally from the south but was later moved to the north-west corner.[21] Three wings surrounding the courtyard all have two floors and are today used for public housing. The main hall of four storeys contains a chanting hall up a flight of central external stairs, with storage areas to both sides. An inner chapel is raised about one metre above the level of the chanting hall. Meru was renovated by the Tibet Heritage Fund in 1999, in cooperation with the Lhasa government.

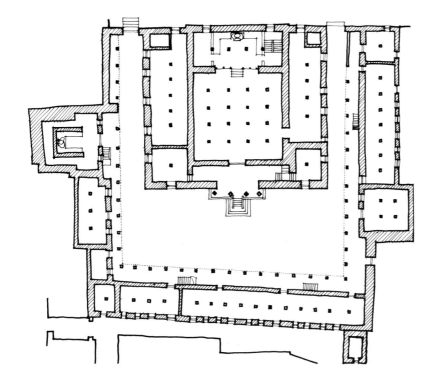

Shatra (143), mansion, c.1800.

This is one of the largest and best preserved urban mansions extant in Lhasa. It belonged to a former Tibetan prime minister, but the authorities confiscated the house when the Shatra family fled Lhasa in 1959. Today the family retains a few storage rooms in the western wing of the outbuildings.

Shatra was one of the few buildings surveyed in detail by the LHCA project. It contains many general features of major residential buildings: a classical layout, outward simplicity and fine details and workmanship. The mansion, large, well proportioned and reasonably well preserved, today accommodates many families.

A 'walk' through Shatra will explain important characteristics of a Tibetan house. The large three-storey main building, built in stone, was for the family. South of this, a large courtyard surrounded by outbuildings on two floors provided storage areas, sheds, stables and accommodation for servants. A main north-south axis, running from the gate through the main building, organizes the symmetrical layout of Shatra. The gate entrance comes in from the narrow lane called Barkor Rabsal Sanglam, which branches off Barkor South. This lane appears to be part of the kora system around the Jokhang, as seen in several early murals. The ground floor areas in the outbuildings, facing the lane, are mostly small shops. Only the rooms next to the main entrance have access from the courtyard and were probably rooms for servants who controlled the gate and courtyard.

The street gates are heavy and made in wood, with an opening wide enough for a carriage or car to enter. The large, nearly square courtyard (21 metres by 24 metres) has a water well surrounded by carved stone slabs and an adjacent carved stone cube that helps people get on their horses. Around the courtyard runs a gallery giving access to the upper level of the outbuildings.

Shatra, view from roof, 1996.

Directly in front is the symmetrical façade of the main building, with its large, central 'sun-windows'. Shatra's generous private chapel in the left wing, with access from a slightly raised porch, occupies the full height of the wing and has a number of windows towards a small outer square and one window on the second floor towards the gallery itself. Inside, twelve columns support two long beams that carry the flat roof. Between the beams a raised 2×3-column section of the roof forms a skylight and defines the altar space with its statues.[22]

Most remaining second floor areas in the outbuildings are servants quarters, largely in one- or two-pillar rooms. Above the raised main gate area is a small room with a large window. To the east the gallery leads to a pit latrine in a separate toilet-tower that can be emptied from the street.[23] The gallery is further linked via a side entrance to the central circulation space of the main building.

Shatra lacks fireplaces and chimneys, as do nearly all Tibetan buildings. There are simply no fixed hearths or fireplaces for heating the rooms, only simple coal and dung burners. At Shatra, the two rooms on the ground floor, each with two squares in the middle, were the kitchens, one for the family and one for the servants.[24] Scarce firewood required Tibetans to use dried yak dung as a supplementary fuel for cooking. Clay ovens for cooking were often built on a covered gallery or in the courtyard under a side gallery.

At ground level of the main building, the side entrance and two minor entrances on the south façade give access to the

Left: Shatra, main entrance from lane, showing small shops, 1998.

Opposite left top: Meru Nyingba. Section. Scale 1 : 500.

Opposite left middle: Meru Nyingba, newly upgraded courtyard, looking west.

Opposite left bottom: Meru Nyingba. Plan. Scale 1 : 500.

Opposite right: Meru Nyingba, newly upgraded courtyard, looking east.

main storage rooms. Also on the ground level, towards the narrowest alley to the Barkor, are three connected spaces – workshops for hire – with access only from the outside.

On entering the main building a small two-pillar room leads via a steep staircase to a long central space on the first floor that provides access to the major rooms. Two large rooms (16 and 24 pillars), lit only by large skylights, are the formal reception and living rooms. Other large rooms on the two sides are for domestic use: library, dining room, office etc. The smaller rooms with large windows towards the courtyard, on the first and second floors, were the main living areas for family members.

On the second floor in a long open courtyard the gallery leads to secondary smaller courtyards, from which one can enter other rooms. These extremely pleasing private courtyards receive plenty of sunshine and are shaded against the wind. The central open area in the main building allows views down into the formal rooms on the first floor, and here also is access to the roof and two latrines. The outbuilding roof serves as a working area for domestic activities and as a playing area, as does the main roof to a degree. An open latrine on the roof is a common feature in Tibetan buildings.

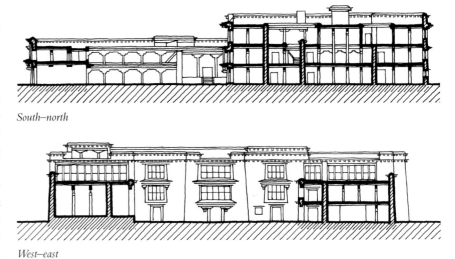

South–north

West–east

Shatra. Sections. Scale 1 : 500.

Shatra. Plans. Scale 1 : 500.
Left: Ground floor. Right: First floor.

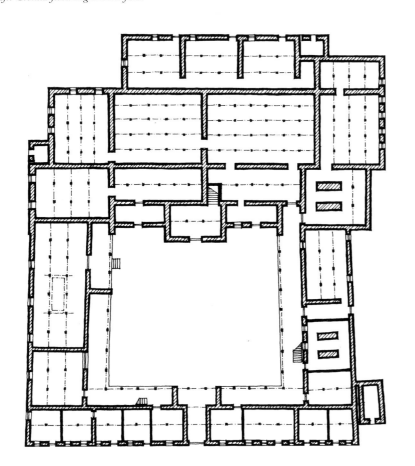

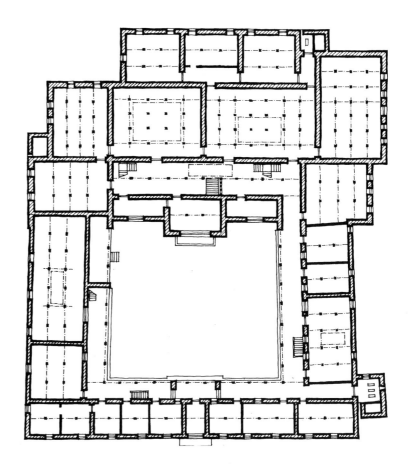

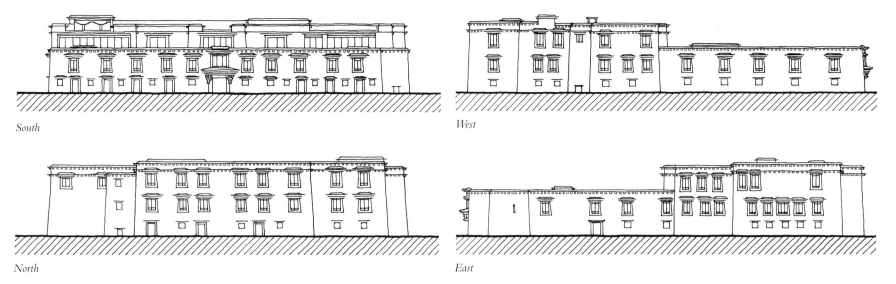

South

West

North

East

Shatra. Façades. Scale 1 : 500.

Shatra. Plans. Scale 1 : 500.
Left: Second floor. Right: Third floor.

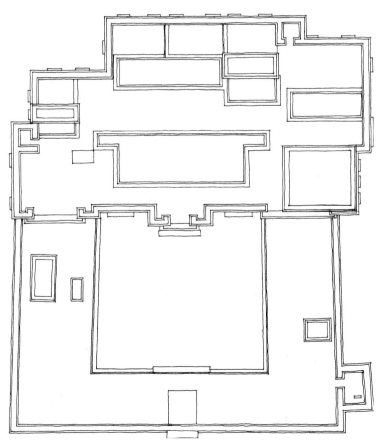

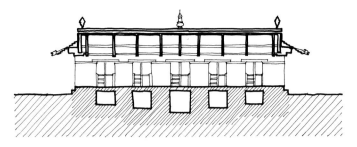

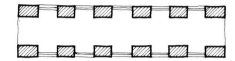

Yuthok Zampa. Plan and section. Scale 1 : 500.

Yuthok Zampa (63), bridge, 7th century, 1750 and 1993.

Sometimes called Turquoise Bridge because of the turquoise tiles of its raised roof, this 28-meter-long bridge of local stone retains parts thought to date from the 7th century. Five flow-through openings in its base correspond to five openings in the upper structure, now fitted with wooden railings. Its elaborate wooden Chinese-style roof construction dates to 1750. In 1993 the bridge was dismantled and rebuilt as a 'replica' of the original; the ancient foundations were reinforced with concrete and the wood constructions renewed. The bridge is today part of a modern restaurant. Despite this questionable role, Yuthok bridge acts as an important buffer in the no-man's-land between old Lhasa and the expanding new city.

Yuthok Zampa. F. Spencer Chapman, 1936. Yutok Zampa, once located in open marshland, linked the old town with the Potala-Shöl area. It also provided early photographers in Lhasa with a picturesque and popular subject.

khang and Barkor. It
gs shown on the map

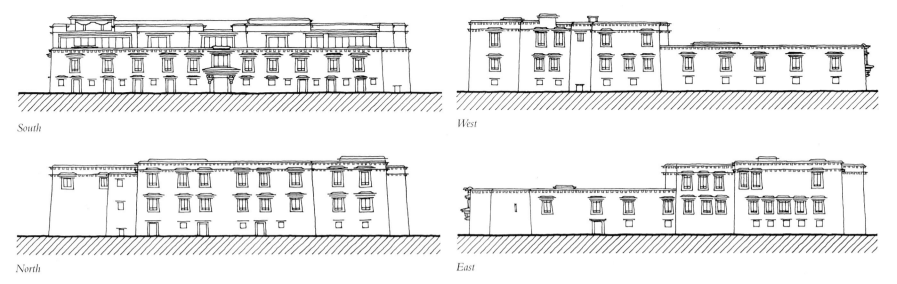

South

West

North

East

Shatra. Façades. Scale 1 : 500.

Shatra. Plans. Scale 1 : 500.
Left: Second floor. Right: Third floor.

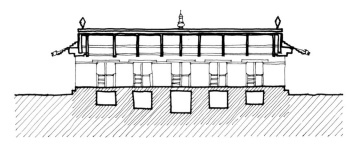

Yuthok Zampa. Plan and section. Scale 1 : 500.

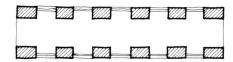

Yuthok Zampa (63), bridge, 7th century, 1750 and 1993.

Sometimes called Turquoise Bridge because of the turquoise tiles of its raised roof, this 28-meter-long bridge of local stone retains parts thought to date from the 7th century. Five flow-through openings in its base correspond to five openings in the upper structure, now fitted with wooden railings. Its elaborate wooden Chinese-style roof construction dates to 1750. In 1993 the bridge was dismantled and rebuilt as a 'replica' of the original; the ancient foundations were reinforced with concrete and the wood constructions renewed. The bridge is today part of a modern restaurant. Despite this questionable role, Yuthok bridge acts as an important buffer in the no-man's-land between old Lhasa and the expanding new city.

Yuthok Zampa. F. Spencer Chapman, 1936. Yutok Zampa, once located in open marshland, linked the old town with the Potala-Shöl area. It also provided early photographers in Lhasa with a picturesque and popular subject.

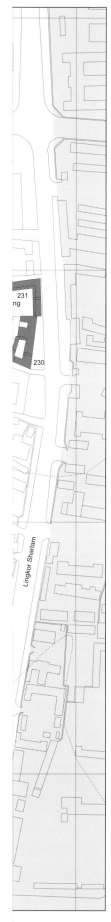

khang and Barkor. It
gs shown on the map

Right
Left

2

3

4

5

Nangtseshar (8), administration building, c.1650.

The old prison, situated on Barkor North almost adjacent to the perimeter wall of the Jokhang, has fine proportions and large windows which disguise the fact that it was a place of severe punishment. Hard criminals were kept in a windowless dungeon on the ground floor, accessible only through a hole in the floor of the raised courtyard. Lesser criminals and women were kept on the upper floor. Public executions took place on a platform on top of the external stairs. Nangtseshar is an old, well-articulated courtyard house, with a flight of unique exterior main stairs and an impressive symmetrical façade, distinguished with two 'towers'. The building is a dominant structure on the market square of Barkor North, although somewhat hidden behind a new prayer wheel house. The building was repaired in 1995 and serves as a reasonable example of restoration. There are plans to use Nangtseshar as a museum.

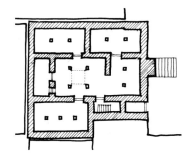

*Nangtseshar. Plan of first floor.
Scale 1 : 500. The photograph on p. 92
shows the building seen from the Barkor
market.*

Nangtseshar, façade towards the Barkor, 1996.

Gorkha Nyingba (183), mansion, 17th century.

This old mansion across the street from Shatra in Barkor Rabsal Sanglam is a unique variation of the building type in the Lhasa context. Built around 1650 during the reign of the 5th Dalai Lama, it served as the embassy of Nepal from at least 1750 onwards.

The site, located on a main lane, has a modest two-storey building facing the street and a three-storey detached main building. It is Lhasa's only known example of a detached three-storey main building surrounded on all four sides by two-storey outbuildings. A reason for this special layout could be that the enclosed site has in-and-out access only from the lane along its northern perimeter. To give the main building a quiet well-lit courtyard facing south – free of animals – stables and primary storage areas were located as close to the lane as possible.

The main building has superb craftsmanship, pleasant proportions and fine detailing. Its surrounding outbuildings, in fairly good condition, have the traditional low ceilings often found in such buildings. Two mature trees shade the beautiful courtyard. With its modest dimensions and intimacy, Gorkha Nyingba must be judged the most attractive of all remaining mansions.

Gorkha Nyingba constitutes a building ensemble of exceptional architectural quality and should be among the highest class of protected buildings in the old town. It is being rebuilt as a hotel and, sadly, most of the outbuildings have already been demolished.[25]

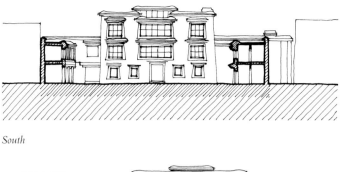

South

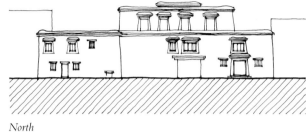

North

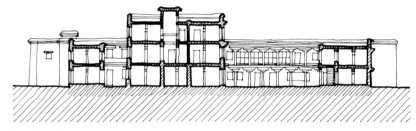

North–south

Above right: Gorkha Nyingba. Façades and section. Scale 1 : 500.

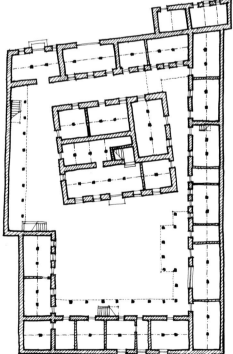

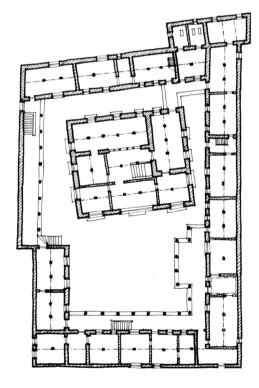

Gorkha Nyingba. Plans. Scale 1 : 500.
Left: Ground floor. Right: First floor.
Opposite left: Second floor.

Jamkhang (9), temple, 15th century.

Jamkhang , one of Lhasa's really old temples, rests on the Barkor adjacent to the Jokhang's north-east corner and forms the south-west corner of Barkor North's square. The temple was sponsored by Lo monastery in the Upper Kyichu valley and contains a two-storey-tall Buddha statue called Jampa Tromsik, the Maitreya watching over the marketplace. Its external walls washed in ochre, white and red give the temple a special appearance.

From the outside, the building looks symmetrical but the interior spaces show the geometry to be very different. The

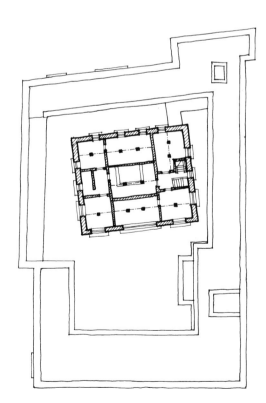

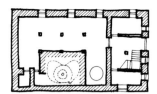

Buddha statue sits looking towards the square with its back towards the Jokhang's wall, which forms the side wall of the temple. This arrangement might indicate that the statue existed on the square before the building was erected over it. Architecturally, the important arrangement is the statue relating to the larger external space, not the usual interior space. Jamkhang is richly decorated outside and inside, but without the usual carvings on pillars or beams. The interior is lit from a large raised skylight. Regrettably, the benma frieze, as is so often the case with new 'traditional' constructions, has been replaced by a plaster imitation. The temple was stripped in 1959 and reopened in 1992.

Tarajhang (314), shrine, 7th century and 1913.

This tiny chapel-shrine near Barkor East's south-east corner was spared when the Surkhang house, enclosing it on three sides, was demolished in 1993 to make way for a department store. Tarajhang is associated with Palden Lhamo, Lhasa's female protector. According to old sources,[26] the shrine contains a very old stone figure of the goddess, which once guarded the Jokhang's entrance but was moved to Tarajhang to prevent floods. The shrine has two small windows but no door. Its front is decorated with many devotional stone tablets and a large incense burner stands nearby. Tarajhang is rectangular in plan but askew, indicating that it perhaps was not a freestanding building but built to fit in with earlier construction.

Far left: Gorkha Nyingba, main building from courtyard, 2000.

Left: Jamkhang Temple. Plan. Scale 1 : 500.

Tarajhang on the Barkor, 1987.

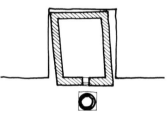

Tarajhang. Plan. Scale 1 : 500.

Left: Jamkhang Temple, 1996. The temple's purpose on a corner of Barkor North square was especially to facilitate the supervision of religious and secular activities in the market area.

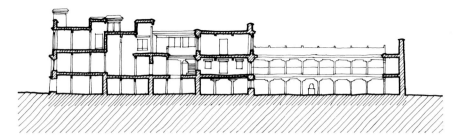

Pomdatsang. Section. Scale 1 : 500.

Far right: Pomdatsang, the large house built by Tsarong on an important Barkor corner.

Pomdatsang (141), mansion, c.1914.

Pomdatsang is located at the intersection of Barkor South and Barkor East. This is an important corner where the Barkor branches off into a narrow alleyway earlier used for religious processions. The building was entirely rebuilt after severe damage in the violent ousting of the Chinese garrison in 1912. This was undertaken by Pomdatsang's owner, Tsarong, the main reformer during the reign of the 13th Dalai Lama. In 1923, Tsarong decided that the town was too crowded and moved to a big new house near the Kyichu river, at that time well outside Lhasa. The Barkor residence was sold to the very successful East Tibetan trader, Pomdatsang, whose name the building carries. He in turn sold the property to the new government in the 1950s.

Pomdatsang is a typical large mansion with dimensions and layout of spaces quite similar to those of nearby Shatra. The main building is one of the largest in Lhasa and contains a two-

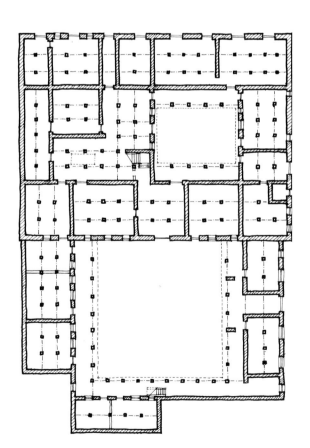
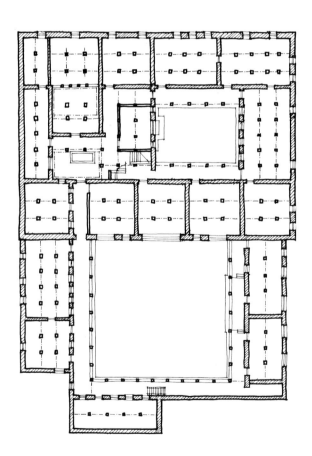

Pomdatsang. Plans. Scale 1 : 500.
Left: Ground floor. Right: First floor.

storey chapel. At its second level, Pomdatsang is connected to the gallery of the adjoining building, Kyakashar (142). The railings to the courtyard terraces are made of cast iron, a sure sign of modernity and progress.

The architectural format of Pomdatsang is one of spacious generosity. Along with its clear concept and beautiful detailing, it is this spaciousness which makes it so fine. At the time of the survey in 1996, the building complex was relatively well maintained, but not in particularly good condition.

Trapchishar (1), townhouse, 19th century.

Trapchishar stands immediately adjacent to the north wall of the Jokhang, at the start of Barkor North. It forms part of the Barkor's first important corner, and although an ordinary townhouse with shops and residential spaces, this location lends the building significance.

Trapchishar was owned by Sera monastery and used as a town dwelling for visiting monks. On the top floor was a lama's residence, and the lower floors were rented out to shopkeepers. The dwelling areas open out towards the cheerful inner courtyard. The odd, triangular shape of the Trapchisar site shows how traditional Tibetan building layout and construction may be used with great flexibility and ease. Trapchishar was repaired and upgraded by the Tibetan Heritage Fund in 1996 when under threat of demolition, and since then has housed a number of families. The building has interesting wall paintings, and both mobile and fixed clay ovens for cooking. Amidst the diminishing traditional townscape of the Barkor, Trapchishar's low-key architectural harmony, together with its location, make its protection essential.

Trapchishar. Plan. Scale 1 : 500.

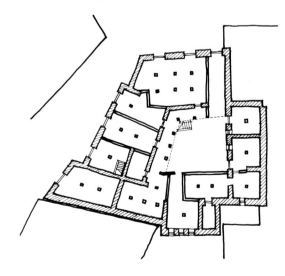

Trapchishar, view of courtyard from the roof, 1998.

Top and bottom: Delin Khangsar.
Façades: upper towards back street,
lower towards Barkor. Scale 1 : 250.

Delin Khangsar. Plans. Scale 1 : 500.
Left: Ground floor. Right: First floor.

Delin Khangsar (106), residential yard, c.1900.

Located on Barkor East, Delin Khangsar was one of the largest courtyard structures on the Barkor. It was owned by Shigatse's Tashilhunpo monastery and seems to have been built as a mixed commercial-residential complex where shops with upstairs dwelling spaces – some 24 units – were rented out to provide income for the monastery. Shops facing the Barkor

and Tsonak Lam enclosed two small courtyards in this two-storey building. The roof area saw a range of uses, from local craft production to games. The only gate is towards Tsonak Lam, all other doors leading to shops.

Detailed drawings illustrate the common shop-dwelling unit in Lhasa and the standard one-pillar room with practical furnishings. Access from the street to the dwelling area above was only through the shop, by way of a steep ladder in the rear

storage room. For such dwellings, access to the courtyard was only by ladder, through the skylight and over the roof. The rear dwelling room is shown used as a kitchen with a stove, shelves, a small table, and a kang for a child. The front room, with a large window towards the street, had two kangs for sitting and sleeping, a low table, cupboards and shelves. The pillars and beams were painted in bright colours, and under the ceiling, sheets of cotton cloth were stretched to collect dust and clay falling from the roof.

Delin Khangsar can be said to have formed a uniform row or terrace of streethouses, and its low height preserved important vistas of the surrounding mountains from Barkor East. This and its cultural- historical past made the building important in the townscape. At the time of survey in 1996, Delin Khangsar housed 36 families.[27] It was demolished in 1998.

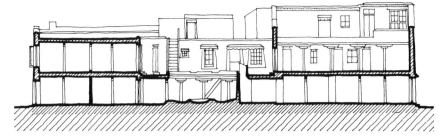

Delin Khangsar. Section.
Scale 1 : 500.

Delin Khangsar. Living room with local inhabitants and a Western student,
1994.

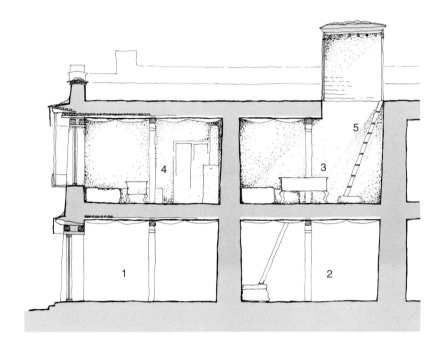

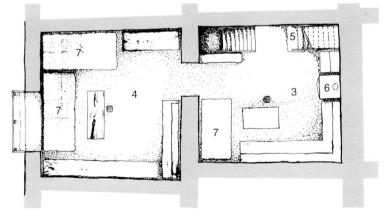

Delin Khangsar, typical shop-dwelling.   3. *Kitchen*
Plan and section. Scale 1 : 100.   4. *Living room*
Key: 5. *Access to roof, water tap and latrine*
1. *Shop*   6. *Stove*
2. *Storage*   7. *Plinths for sitting and sleeping*

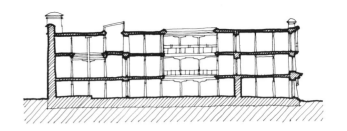

Labrang Nyingba. Section. Scale 1 : 500.

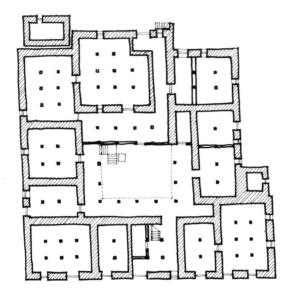

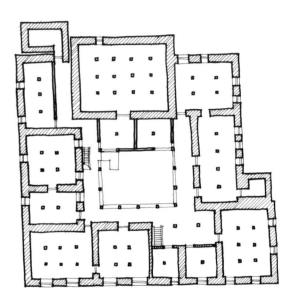

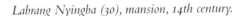

Labrang Nyingba. Plans. Scale 1 : 500.
Left: Ground floor. Right: First floor.

Labrang Nyingba (30), mansion, 14th century.

This mansion, the only remaining old building on the northern side of Barkor South, is the finest residential building on the Barkor. It has a long, rich history. Tsongkhapa maintained his residence here when in Lhasa. Also, the 5th Dalai Lama used Labrang Nyingba as his town residence until he moved into a new apartment in the Jokhang. Later it became the seat of the noble Tönba family, descendants of Songtsen Gampo's famous minister, Tönmi Sambhota.[28]

The three-storey stone building has a simple layout with a very pleasant and well-lit central courtyard. Labrang Nyingba is solidly built, with a high quality of craftsmanship and decoration visible throughout the building. The street façade is well proportioned and has an interesting rhythm of windows. The main gate has a small roof or overhang with cantilevered brackets. A quite spacious but dark and crooked corridor leads into the building and the courtyard, and from this corridor well-made timber stairs lead up to the first floor. Handsome stone steps in the corner of the courtyard provide access to the gallery that surrounds the courtyard on three sides.

Shops on the ground floor open towards Barkor South. Stables and storage rooms occupy the remainder of the lower level. The 12-pillar, two-storey-high formal reception room, with a gallery on the first floor, is impressive and rich in decorative details. The family living room was a four-pillar room with a large sun-window, located on the second floor towards the street, above the main gate. A common feature of these buildings is the incense burner on the roof; at Labrang Nyingba it is designed and built with particular care. Also of note is the roof shrine.

The mansion appears set back from the street, but this is mainly a result of the geometry of Surkhang department store, which was built next to it in the early 1990s on the foundations of the old Surkhang mansion. This recessed position becomes a pleasant minor space in the rather monotonous streetscape of Barkor South – an important reminder of the earlier more noticeable north-south orientation of major buildings around the Barkor, now broken with the continuous street-façades.

The benma frieze along the eaves shows that this is a building with links to the monastic community. Most murals were

Labrang Nyingba. Elevation towards the Barkor. Composite photo, 1994.

painted over during the Cultural Revolution. No modern extensions or additions were built at Labrang Nyingba, though the building was altered in 1900 and thoroughly repaired and upgraded by the Lhasa government in 1999–2000. Today it provides housing for many families.

Labrang Nyingba before upgrading, 1994.

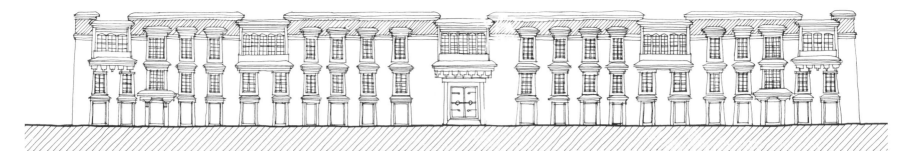

Tromsikhang. Elevation towards the Barkor. Scale 1 : 300.

Tromsikhang, from the Barkor.
Tromsikhang with its long façade
overlooking the Barkor market.

Tromsikhang Palace (71), government palace, c.1700.

Located on Barkor North facing the square from the north side, Tromsikhang was built during the reign of the 6th Dalai Lama and is perhaps the most prominent example of a monumental official building in Lhasa. It functioned as a major administrative and residential building. The Chinese Ambans, representatives of the Qing emperor, and various government officials lived in the three-storey building, which was also the scene of violent historical events.

The symmetrical layout of the whole building complex covered an area of 60 metres by 40 metres and probably had only one large courtyard originally. The building facing the Barkor had shops on the ground floor with dwelling units on the two floors above, connected by interior stairs. The top floor was richly decorated with carvings on wooden balconies and interior supporting structures. The main façade, beautifully proportioned, had a fine architectural rhythm. Supporting its overall balance were several minor symmetrical sections to be found in the façade; these worked as sub-themes in the larger architectural concept.

After 1959, parts of the building fell into disuse, though Tromsikhang was later officially protected at the regional level, confirmed in the 1992 Barkor Conservation Plan. At the time of the survey in 1996, sections of Tromsikhang were dilapidating but mostly the building was sound enough to justify conservation through repair and upgrading. Despite its status, the major part of the complex was demolished in 1997 – only the front section along the Barkor remains. Behind the old front building, four-storey residential blocks constructed in 1998 replaced the old wings and courtyard areas, making Tromsikhang a modern housing complex. The old front building facing the Barkor has been repaired and upgraded for housing by the Lhasa government.

Tromsikhang. Plan. Scale 1 : 500.

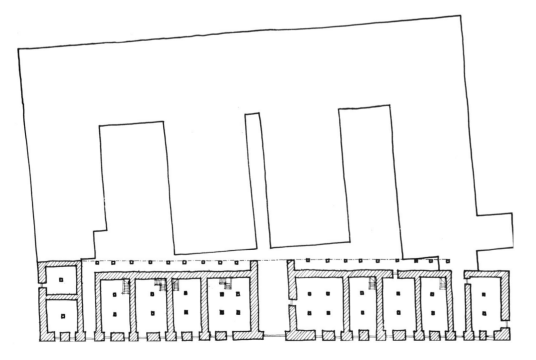

Numa (17), mansion, 1920.

On Barkor East, this fine three-storey house is an example of how a typical rural noble house may be adapted for the setting of Lhasa. Limited space and a different lifestyle help account for the disappearance of separate secondary buildings, so essential in a rural context. The house, always owned by the noble Numa family, constitutes together with a few adjoining buildings a small, traditional, intact townscape. Towards the Barkor are four two-storey shops and living units. A small, well maintained internal courtyard has galleries on three sides. The family living rooms on the top floor have wonderfully decorated and well preserved interiors.

The three-storey stone building was extensively altered in 1965; its eastern part was rebuilt after 1977. Although generally in good condition, Numa at the time of the survey in 1995 revealed leaking roofs in need of repair. At that time the site comprised six dwelling units. Recent excavation work to lower the ground level outside exposed the shallow stone foundations; this caused stones to drop out and the foundations to weaken. Numa has an almost closed façade towards the narrow alleyway that leads up to the east entrance of the Jokhang. The only element of relief is an impressive courtyard entrance gate with considerable visual character, in contrast to the lively Barkor façade. In terms of its type and age, Numa must be considered a highly important building to protect. In addition, this building is an essential component of the extant townscape of Barkor East.

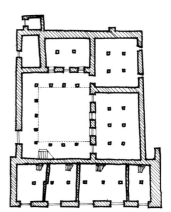

Numa. Plan. Scale 1 : 500.

Top left: Tromsikhang, close-up of façade towards the Barkor, 1997.

Middle left: Tromsiklang, from the courtyard, 1996.

Far left: Numa from the Barkor, 1996. Numa stands on a small corner site with a fairly small volume; it is architecturally very well formed.

Numa, courtyard, 1997.

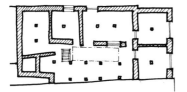

Kame Tara. Plan. Scale 1 : 500.

Right: Kame Tara on the Barkor, 1996. The building forms an integral part of the traditional and special Barkor East façade. Surfaces and details are simple but of good quality.

Far right: Phala from courtyard,1998. Phala is today totally enclosed on all sides at the end of a narrow lane.

The main building is in stonework of good standard but clearly not as fine as older examples. Timber work and details are generally of quite low standard, and craftsmanship of the outbuildings is also poor. The original windows were enlarged with the arrival of glass. The building is in some structural danger, as the eastern wing is separating from the main structure, yet the overall standard and condition is relatively high considering age and lack of maintenance.

Left: Karmashar from square, 1994. Karmashar, a small, old temple with fine ochre stone walls sits in the corner of a square. On the ground floor, towards the square, a workshop is occupied by a silversmith.

Karmashar's overall symmetrical layout has an entrance from the south that leads via an external flight of steps up to a temple room occupying the entire first floor. The building is clearly rebuilt and altered from the original, though the extent of these changes are not known. The temple faces a small triangular public square and is an important element in the neighbourhood.

Right: Sumdona Khangsar (40), mansion, 1920s and 1997. This mansion exemplifies the early modernization of traditional architecture. Steel beams were used to create interior space without the traditional timber pillars that constitute the interior structural support.

Kame Tara (20), former outbuilding, 7th century.

Located on Barkor East, this anonymous two-story townhouse is believed to have been used as stables for Songtsen Gampo. Parts of the building might indeed go back to the 7th century. Alterations were made in 1954 and again in 1993. Kame Tara was part of a Tibetan Heritage Fund-initiated townscape upgrading project and is today a house with shops on the ground floor facing the Barkor.

Karmashar (112), small temple, c.700.

This handsome temple on Ongdu Shingka Lam, some 200 metres east of the Barkor, was home to the Karmashar oracle, one of Lhasa's best known mediums. The building is owned by Sera monastery and used as a temple and accommodation for monks. It is one of only a few ochre-coloured buildings in

Lhasa; a local informant claims this colour indicates that a buildings is at least 200 years old.

Phala (234), mansion, c.1750.

Phala has considerable cultural and historical importance. It was one of Lhasa's original mansions, built for the Phala noble family who came to Lhasa from Gyantse and Sikkim. The house was owned by three brothers, the oldest of whom was the highest monastic official under the 13th Dalai Lama. Phala was again extensively altered in 1992.

Phala was so heavily altered at the start of the 20th century, it appears as a building from that time. Only a few parts of the original complex exist today, and they are largely obscured by newer buildings and later extensions.

Yamyang (38), tenement, c.1860.

Yamyang is located on Jamyangshar Sanglam almost immediately north-west of the Jokhang. It stands as one of the old town's largest tenement buildings, with six courtyards of varying size and a three-storey series of combined stone and mud brick buildings. Yamyang forms part of one of the last few remaining traditional clusters of buildings in Lhasa.

Ongdu Khangsar (44), townhouse, 1870s and 1996.

It stands less than 100 metres north of the Jokhang and was once owned by Sera monastery. The building dominates several alleyways and is architecturally prominent with its two special corners on the main alley. This outstanding streethouse with an irregular floor plan is an excellent example of this building type. The craftsmanship is clearly of a high standard, although the building has few ornate decorations.

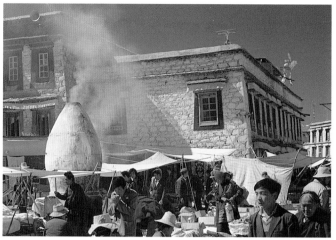

Shamo Karpo (7), streethouse, c.1910.

Shamo Karpo on Barkor North is a good example of the small streethouse on a site too small to allow for a courtyard. The two floors receive light only from the street. Such small buildings were often situated on corners, thus able to enjoy a longer window-façade than most other street buildings.

Pode Khangsar (173), temple c.1670 and 1998.

This small protector chapel, located in a hidden courtyard south of the Jokhang, was built during the reign of the 5th Dalai Lama. A number of its murals were destroyed during the Cultural Revolution, but many fine architectural details remain.

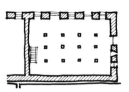

Above: Shamo Karpo. Plan. Scale 1 : 500. Shamo Karpo appears in the 1987 photograph on p. 93.

Above left: Shamo Karpo, façade towards the Barkor, 1996. Shamo Karpo was known for its Nepalese shops, and the building plays an important role here where the Barkor widens from a street to become an urban space. It looks original, with the exception of recent roof structures, and despite minor damage the building is generally in good condition.

Shamo Karpo is modest although built in pleasant proportions. The external stonework displays high quality craftsmanship; the stone walls seem to grow together with those of the adjacent building (No. 5), which indicates they were built at the same time.

Above centre: Yamyang, seen from roof, 1996. Yamyang, with the Jokhang's golden roofs in the background.

Fairly low standards of materials and workmanship mark the building, which is considered original. One wing was demolished in 1992. Official government upgrading and reconstruction of the building complex was ongoing in the summer of 2000.

Left: Uneven geometry and unusually large windows distinguish Ongdu Khangsar. Three separate courtyards each has its own entrance and external walls of the upper floor are built in mud brick. At the time of the survey in 1996, Ongdu Khangsar showed few recent additions or extensions, suffered from a low standard of interior repair and maintenance and had a south-east corner in danger of collapsing. Alterations were made in 1920.

Right: Pode Khangsar, almost the same size as Karmashar, is symmetrical with a mandala-like layout and approximate north–south axis; the entrance faces south.

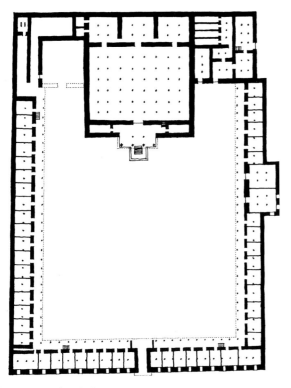

Shide monastery. Plan. Scale 1 : 1 000.

Shide, 1994. The fine main hall has collapsed. Traces of wall paintings and decorations reveal that Shide once had outstanding artistic qualities. Its present dilapidated state allows one to analyse traditional building methods.

Shide Dratsang (268), monastery, 14th century.

Located just off the north side of Beijing Shar Lam and west of Ramoche Lam, Shide Dratsang is traditionally considered one of the six protector chapels built by King Tri Ralpachen around the Jokhang in the 9th century. At that time much smaller, and created for only four monks, it was given the appropriate name Shide (*shi* means 'four' in Tibetan). Shide was destroyed in the mid-9th century and later rebuilt for 20 monks between 1239–50. It took its form in the middle of the 14th century as a dependency of Reting monastery and was the seat and residence in Lhasa of the Reting Tulku (incarnate lama), with more than ten Reting incarnations being abbots here. The 9th Reting Tulku expanded the building complex considerably, and in 1816 Shide reached its present size and layout. In 1862, it was again destroyed. Shide was extensively repaired again in 1935, and apart from the obviously recent additions and extensions inside the courtyard, the main structures are considered to be original.

Shide, 1994. Shide has the largest courtyard of any building complex in old Lhasa (50 m by 60 m). The three-storey main hall stands on the northern side, and two-storey monks' quarters make up the other sides (now informal housing).

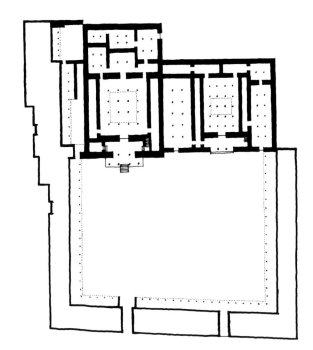

Tsomonling Dratsang. Plan. Scale
1 : 1 000.

Tsomonling Dratsang (308), monastery, 18th century.

Close to Shide on the lane Beijing Sharlam Sanglam Sumpa, Tsomonling has a traditional courtyard layout, but is unusual in having two large temple halls built at different times. Two-storey buildings with monks' quarters surround the courtyard in front of the main halls. The monastery originally also had two primary entrances into the courtyard, one to each hall.

Tsomonling, one of the four 'Ling' temples, belonged to Loseling college of Drepung monastery. It is the main seat of the Tsemö incarnations, two of whom became regent, one under the 8th Dalai Lama, the other under the 10th and 11th Dalai Lamas.

The architectural and artistic ambitions of the western hall are greater than those of earlier construction. Tsomonling is, despite the changes, still a traditional courtyard compound of great architectural quality and charm.

Tsomonling Dratsang monastery, 1998. The western hall, Marpo Podrang, was built by the 2nd Tsemö incarnation around the start of the 19th century. Behind the main hall, formerly with two stupa-tombs, were a prayer chapel and two protector chapels. Today, the hall is an active temple with a few guardian monks. Kitchen and storage rooms flank the main hall. The former monks' quarters are now used for public housing and workshops. The third floor of Tsomonling's main building was destroyed and totally removed during the Cultural Revolution. Some extensions and informal structures are located in the large courtyard.

Tsomonling Dratsang, 1998. The first Tsemö incarnation built the eastern hall, Karpo Podrang, in 1777, while he was regent. The main assembly hall, with original decorated pillars on the ground floor, contains six chapels and two one-storey-high silver stupas that contain the remains of the 2nd and 3rd Tsemö incarnates. On the second floor was the protector chapel (gonkhang) and on the third were the abbot's quarters.

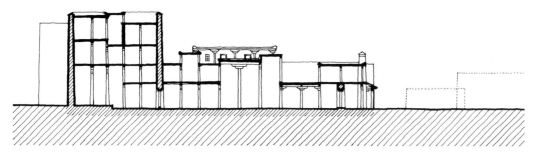

Gyume Dratsang. Section. Scale 1 : 500.

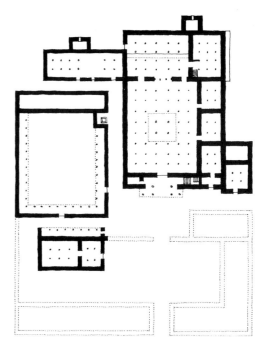

Gyume Dratsang. Plan. Scale 1 : 1 000.

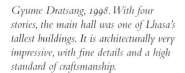

Gyume Dratsang, 1998. With four stories, the main hall was one of Lhasa's tallest buildings. It is architecturally very impressive, with fine details and a high standard of craftsmanship.

Gyume Dratsang (269), monastery, 15th century.

Next to Meru on Beijing Shar Lam, Gyume is also hidden from the street. Gyume has been active as a religious institution since the middle of the 15th century. The Tantric colleges were founded in the 15th century by one of Tsongkhapa's famous disciples in order to train novices. Gyume Dratsang became a major religious institution in Lhasa ranked only after Ganden, Drepung, and Sera, and only monks from these monasteries were admitted. In the 1940s, Gyume Dratsang housed 500 monks and owned 28 estates, six small monasteries and five sub-colleges. Its summer retreat was located 200 kilometres from Lhasa.

Apart from isolated smaller parts, the oldest buildings at Gyume Dratsang are believed to be from the 18th century and of these, only the main hall and a secondary wing are left; all others are quite recent constructions. An open court for debate still lies west of the main hall. Inside the hall are well crafted and decorated pillars. Much of the original decoration in metal and wood, as well as wall paintings, were removed or destroyed during the Cultural Revolution. Since then, the courtyard structure has also been changed, with buildings demolished and replaced. The old buildings of Gyume Dratsang are generally in sound condition but suffer from lack of maintenance and repair.

Meru, 1998. Meru monastery's minor and only functioning temple.

Meru Dratsang (270), monastery, 9th century; 1864.

Located at the eastern end of Beijing Shar Lam, Meru is believed to have been founded by King Tri Ralpachen in the 9th century and later destroyed.[29] It became one of the largest Gelukpa monasteries in Lhasa and the Meru abbot was at one time also the abbot of Shide Dratsang. The two colleges separated after 1684, with the Meru abbot remaining a powerful contender for the seat of regent. Meru became one of the four royal monasteries when Tengyeling ceased this function in 1912.

Meru's large, rectangular courtyard (40 by 50 metres) is entered from the south through an impressive three-storey gate-building. Opposite and facing south is the main temple hall, and next to it on the left a small chapel. To the right of the main hall stands a building with large common rooms. Along the other sides of the courtyard are monks' cells on two storeys. The west wing has an unusual double row of monks' cells separated by a very narrow open light well.

Though Meru was rebuilt in 1864, the present buildings date mostly from the turn of the 20th century, built by Sakya Ngape, the abbot of Nechung monastery during the reign of the 13th Dalai Lama.[30] Architecturally, the extant buildings reflect the trends of the latter part of the 19th century. Two large new extensions today fill much of the courtyard. The main buildings show an outstanding quality of materials and craftsmanship, and the whole complex is architecturally very impressive. Many of the buildings are now used for housing. At the time of the survey in 1996, parts of the complex were dilapidated. It is strongly hoped that despite such drastic adaptive re-use, this superb building complex can be adequately protected.

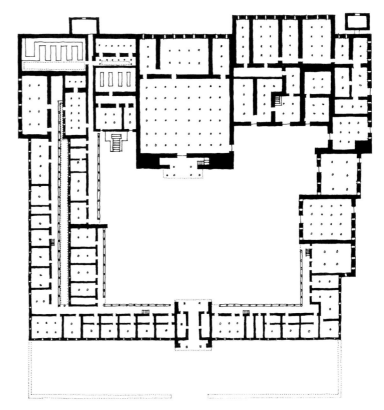

Meru monastery. Plan. Scale 1 : 1 000.

Meru, 1998. The main building from the roof of the monastery.

Bonshö (265), mansion, c.1920.

This mansion located on Ramoche Dozam Sanglam, about 200 m east of Ramoche Lam, is perhaps the most elaborate expression of the noble lifestyle. Bonshö has the typical three-storey stone building and attached two-storey outbuildings embracing a courtyard. Rooms in the outbuildings were rented out and used for storage and stables.

The main Bonshö building is of conventional size, but the courtyard is relatively small, perhaps a consequence of the site being squeezed between a narrow lane to the south and the earlier Lingkor route to the north. This resulted in a higher than normal degree of intimacy between private family areas, servants' quarters and storage areas, a situation probably compensated for by locating additional outbuildings east of the main courtyard compound. Bonshö thus illustrates a standard building layout being adapted at the time of its construction (around 1920) to an existing, confined urban site. The lane to the south has further forced the main entrance out of the normal central axis towards the east wing. The southern wing holds a row of shops that face the lane. The main building's central courtyard is on the first floor, with two minor courtyards on the second floor. To the west of Bonshö, until 1997, was a private vegetable plot and gardener's home; to the east, stables and additional servants' quarters.

Bonshö's main building, totally shielded from the outside, had a chapel with wall paintings (destroyed during the Cultural Revolution); the site was used as a school from 1959–81, with the government renting it out since then. At the date of survey in 1996, about 30 families lived in Bonshö. In 1990, half of the building was given back to relatives of the family who owned it in 1959. When surveyed, it was terribly dilapidated, with serious wall damage and a collapsed roof. The latrine-tower at the south-west corner, in awful condition, was demolished in 1998. During its heyday, the dimensions, architectural quality and craftsmanship of Bonshö were apparently so admired that the house became a popular model for subsequent construction in the old town.

Tsomonling Drokhang (252), summerhouse, c.1945.

This summerhouse, built around 1945, stands at the back of Ramoche Temple surrounded by modern buildings, yet it can be experienced as a small oasis, with a pleasing garden and old trees. Its park-like grounds once belonged to Tsomonling monastery (until 1966) and extended about 200 m from the monastery up to the old Lingkor. The grounds were 120 m wide, with the summerhouse in the middle; this two-storey stone building, with excellent workmanship and fine details, has a symmetrical layout around an open terrace connected to the garden by monumental stone stairs. A secondary entrance is located in the north-east corner. Architecturally, the summerhouse has associations to the style of the latest building at Norbulingka. A small, one-storey building containing storerooms is located adjacent on a 1.5-m-high platform. Tsomonling Drokhang is now used for housing.

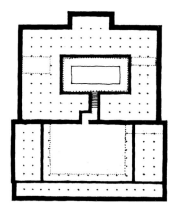

Bonshö. Plan. Scale 1 : 1 000.

Right: Bonshö, 1996. Bonshö's south façade with shops towards the narrow lane.

Bonshö, 1996. Bonshö's south façade of the main building, facing the courtyard.

Shide Drokhang, exterior, 1998.

Shide Drokhang (253), summerhouse, 1935.

Shide summerhouse is located immediately north of Shide monastery but can be reached only after a long walk from Dosenge Lam, the nearest main street west of the old town. The two-storey stone building has since 1966 been used for government housing. At that time, a new building was put up in gardens that formerly served as the link between the summerhouse and the monastery. The symmetrical layout is planned around an interior east-west axis starting at the entrance in the eastern gable wall. Quarters of the abbot of Shide were upstairs, with servants' quarters on the ground level. The Reting Rinpoche (Tulku) lived here as well; he was a powerful figure from Reting monastery and Tibet's regent on and off in the 1930s and 40s. The house has characteristic building elements associated with monasteries, such as the benma frieze at the top of the walls. The workmanship at Shide Drokhang is excellent, and the interiors are extremely well preserved. Several wall paintings are in good condition and the wooden floor in the studio is a rare detail.

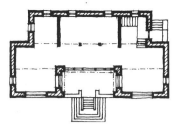

Above: Tsomonling Drokhang. Plan. Scale 1 : 500.

Top left: Tsomonling Drokhang, The summerhouse seen from the garden.

Left: Tsomonling Drokhang, interior, 1998.

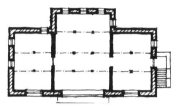

Shide Drokhang. Plan. Scale 1 : 500.

Shide Drokhang, interior, 1998.

Shide Drokhang. F. Spencer Chapman, 1936. The house from the roof of Shide monastery.

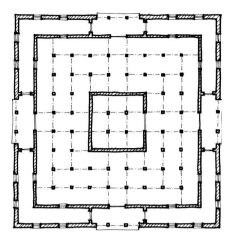

Jebumgang. Plan. Scale 1 : 500.

Jebumgang Lhakhang (321), chapel, 17th century.

This square, bilaterally symmetrical detached building sits close to the intersection of Beijing Shar Lam and Ramoche Lam, hidden from view by the street façades. Jebumgang has a classical vihara-like layout that is rarely seen in the Lhasa valley. It perhaps was built in the 17th century, although local sources consider it an 11th century foundation. The chapel was dedicated to Tsongkhapa. Jebumgang has four entrances – located on the two axes and two surrounding galleries – to a square, 4-pillar space lit from above. The central space has only one entrance, from the east.

The building is well built in stone and structurally sound. Its walls and most other elements of construction are covered with paintings and decorations, though now severely worn. During the Cultural Revolution, the chapel was used to store grain and today it is part of a tsampa factory.

Ganden Khangsar (274), residential yard, 1930s and 1996. Located just south of Ramoche, this is the largest shared residence, or tenement building, in old Lhasa with nine courtyards, some quite large. Ganden Khangsar replaced a 300-year-old, four-storey mansion known by the same name and demolished in 1930. Although of average workmanship and architectural quality, Ganden Khangsar is a very important building complex to protect in view of its building type and general arrangement.

Lhading (37), residential yard, c.1900 and 1996. This residential yard, built around 1900 for several government families, was located adjacent to Tsomonling monastery west of Ramoche Lam . Each unit had its own small courtyard and sun-gallery. Although ordinary and anonymous in design and execution, Lhading was important as part of a cluster of traditional residential buildings that gave this part of the Ramoche area considerable character. Demolished in 1997, the building had two storeys in a combination of stone and mud brick.

Jebumgang, exterior, 1996. Jebumgang seen from a neighbouring roof.

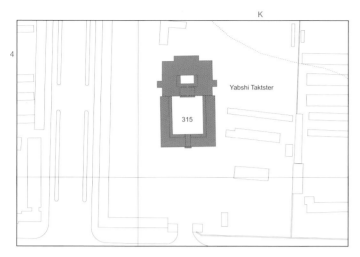

Buildings. Yabshi Taktster area. Scale 1 : 3 000.

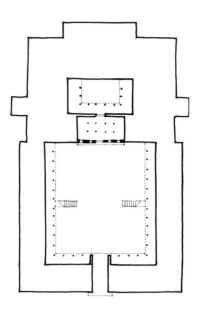

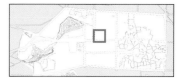

Yabshi Taktster. Plan. Scale 1 : 1 000.

YABSHI TAKTSTER AREA

The area is given its name from the Taktster mansion, the only pre-1950s building here. It originally stood in extensive gardens east of Marpori on the north side of Beijing Shar Lam.

Yabshi Taktster (315), mansion, 1940s.

This residence of the 14th Dalai Lama's family is found inside a large compound off Beijing Shar Lam between the old town and the Potala. It was perhaps built on the example of an ex-

isting mansion. Although large and generous, Yabshi Taktster lacks the traditional standards of craftsmanship and character of older residential buildings. It now houses a large number of families and, hidden inside a compound, is difficult to notice in the growing townscape.

Yabshi Taktster, exterior with Potala, 1998. This large mansion with traditional courtyard layout and symmetrical design is one of two remaining 'Yabshis', a term for the residence of the Dalai Lama's family (the other is Yabshi Phünkhang in the centre of the old town). The name Taktster refers to the village in north-east Tibet (Amdo), from where the family originated before moving to Lhasa in 1939.

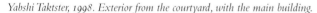

Yabshi Taktster, 1998. Exterior from the courtyard, with the main building.

Left: Buildings. Kundeling area. Scale 1 : 3 000. The map shows Bhamari hill with the small Chinese-style Gesar Lhakhang and the location of Kundeling monastery (now demolished).

Right: Gesar Lhakhang . Plan. Scale 1 : 500.

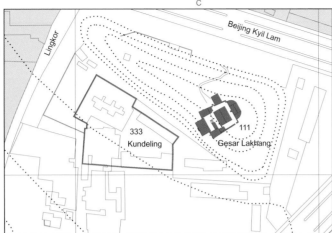

KUNDELING AREA

Kundeling (333), monastery, 18th century.

One of Lhasa's four royal monasteries, Kundeling is located below sacred Bhamari, about 400 metres west of the West Gate. The four Lings, all Gelukpa institutions decreed by the 5th Dalai Lama, were Tsemchok Ling across the Kyichu River, Tengye Ling and Tsomonling in the old town, and Kundeling. Their abbots were often elected as regents. Kundeling's large complex had several chapels which stood in a pleasant, wooded garden. The main four-storey building housed an assembly hall that stretched up through all floors.

Gesar Lhakhang (111), temple, 1792.

This small temple complex on top of Bhamari, under the jurisdiction of Kundeling, consists of the main temple (in Chinese style on an upper level), a small chapel almost hidden in the wall behind, and a lower part built into the south-western slope. The present temple, erected in 1792 by the Chinese Ambans after victory over the Nepalese Gorkhas, was dedicated to Guan Di, the Chinese god of war and justice. Guan Di became identified with the Tibetan folk hero Ling Gesar, a legendary warrior king, and so the site became known as Gesar Lhakhang. A stele in Chinese with descriptions of the battle still stands to the left of the central stairs. Gesar Lhakhang is enclosed by a high perimeter-wall and lies along a symmetrical axis turned north-east to south-west. A flight of stone steps leads to a lower courtyard, which is flanked by two-storey Tibetan-style buildings with monks' quarters and offices. An elaborate porch with a monumental staircase once closed off the complex towards the south. Formerly, two large bells adorned the gate, with two carved horses facing the courtyard. Today, access to the main hall is by a small side door on the top level.

Left: Kundeling. F. Spencer Chapman, 1937. Kundeling had a special quality in its local landscape, sitting comfortably below the southern slope of Bhamari. It was totally destroyed during the Cultural Revolution; in recent years some rebuilding has taken place, but no old remains can be seen.

Right: Gesar Lhakhang, 1996. As early as the 8th century, King Trisong Detsen built a simple structure here and Padmasambhava (Guru Rinpoche), famous Indian spiritual master and Buddhist missionary, was said to come to Bhamari. The temple, now in very poor condition, sits on a site that could be turned into a fine ensemble.

CHAKPORI SOUTH-WEST AREA

Sanjia Gudong, 'the Picture Rock' (332), rock carvings and chapel, 7th century and later.

This outstanding rocky outcropping forms the western tip of Chakpori. The Lingkor passes by here just before turning north towards Kundeling. Chakpori and Marpori have been adorned with religious images and mantras carved and painted on the rock face since the 7th century. Today more than 5000 such images in different styles, sizes and states of preservation can be found on Chakpori alone, with some 1000 here at Sanjia Gudong. They were painted in bright colours and although the colour has faded, the carvings are generally intact. The more accessible and popular of the carvings are regularly repainted, and some are newly carved.

Below: Buildings Chakpori South-west area. Scale 1 : 3 000. The map shows the most important site of rock carvings at Chakpori's south-western limit; the Lingkor passes close by.

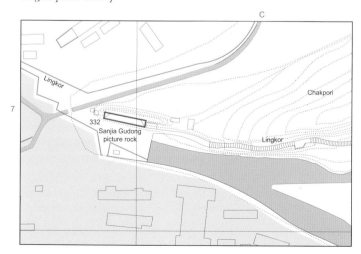

Above: Sanjia Gudong, Chakpori, 1997. This natural slab of rock, 50 m wide, 27 m high and c.5 m thick, is like a huge painting set in the middle of a once sublime landscape, but today surrounded by residential compounds. The rock face is protected by an open roof structure supported on tall pillars that makes it into a large outdoor chapel. Small shrines flank the rock, and raised podiums for prostration are located on the flat surface in front of it.

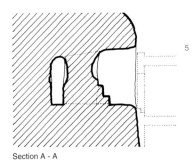

Section A - A

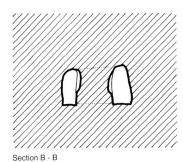

Section B - B

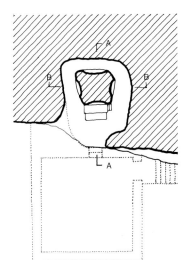

Plan

Above, left and right: Palha Lupuk, 1999. The cave (4.5 m by 5.5 m) faces east and consists of a narrow oval path (0.75m wide by 1.75m high) around its central rock pillar.

CHAKPORI NORTH-EAST AREA

Palha Lupuk (323), chapel, 640s.

As early as in the 640s this cave on Chakpori is believed to have become a Buddhist site and may have been used as a retreat by King Songtsen Gampo. It stands 20 metres above the

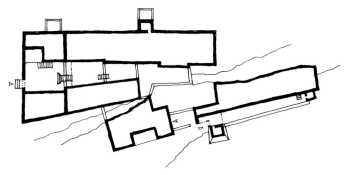

Palha Lupuk. Plan and sections. Scale 1 : 200.

Left: Buildings. Chakpori North-east area. Scale 1 : 3 000. This map shows the West Gate and the small group of buildings on the northern tip of Chakpori hill. The small doctors' residences are a unique type of structure in Lhasa, adapted to the steep slopes and highly worthy of protection. The adjacent nunnery and caves are historical landmarks of great importance.

Clustered houses on Chakpori, 1997.

Caves, nunnery and houses seen from road, 1994. A new chapel gives access to Palha Lupuk. The nunnery and some of the housing on the side of Chakpori are seen to the right.

ground and contains many images of Buddhas, bodhisattvas and saints cut into its rock face. In the 7th century Newari artists from Nepal embellished the cave by adding about 70 images in high relief on the three walls. A nearby cave, reached via a new temple building, is said to have been used by Bhrikuti, Songtsen Gampo's Nepalese queen. This cave, too, has interesting rock carvings.

Clustered houses (277–280).

At the northern end of Chakpori numerous houses were built for the doctors of the Medical College. The buildings, adapted to the landscape with high foundations, have a spectacular monumentality in spite of their otherwise modest dimensions. The topography of their setting makes these buildings atypical for Lhasa, though the type of structure is otherwise well known from settlements and small village clusters spread throughout the rocky terrain surrounding the Lhasa valley. Old

photographs show that similar houses (now demolished) also existed on the higher ridge of Chakpori. It is said that one house (280), from which the view is particularly splendid, contained monks' meditation rooms.

Bargo Kani (334), city gate, 17th century (?) and 1995.

The West Gate of Lhasa (Bargo Kani) is made up of three stupas that close the gap between Marpori and Chakpori. Outer stupas stand at the foot of each hill and the central, much larger one stands on the narrow valley floor. The original gate constructions were demolished with the upgrading of roads in 1968 – the new gate structures were built in 1995 as part of a government project to upgrade the Potala. Traffic now passes to each side of the central stupa. The West Gate remains a popular and potent symbol, in spite of its rebuilding and modern use.

Bargo Kani, old West Gate. Watercolour by Kanwal Krishna, 1940. The entrance gate itself was fitted into the original central stupa, and the space between the stupas was filled with secondary construction. These stupas (date unknown) quite possibly replaced an even earlier gate; it is assumed that the stupas were part of the great building activity under the 5th Dalai Lama (17th century).

The Conservation and Future of Lhasa

This book is concerned with the physical environment of Lhasa – townscape, buildings and spaces. Architecture and townscape will always reflect social, economic and cultural conditions, embodying the needs and aspirations of society, through time, for structures within the limits of available resources. Recently, though, the modern state introduced with the incorporation of Tibet into the Chines State in the 1950s created profound changes in the life of Lhasa that had dramatic consequences for Tibetan society.

The Lhasa valley, known historically as a Buddhist holy land, saw a build-up through the centuries of more than 200 cultural sites and monuments which today spread over the seven counties and one urban district that constitute Lhasa. In 1961, the State Council of the People's Republic of China protected the Potala Palace and Jokhang Temple as national monuments, yet despite a limited policy of protection, vast numbers of invaluable sites and buildings were destroyed throughout Tibet between 1959–1976.

Contemporary Lhasa is a result of numerous plans and efforts by many people, but its recent development can be summed up in the phrase 'official policies, market forces and room to manoeuvre'. Lhasa to a large extent evolved from plans formulated ten and twenty years ago. In the 1990s, an increasingly active private sector adapting to the market economy probably shaped the townscape more than urban policy.

The government of the 1950s and 60s set about to create a contemporary city. Large areas of land surrounding the old town were quickly developed as office and housing compounds, especially south of Marpori where the government clearly distanced itself from the old symbols of power. Lhasa's new physical and administrative structure steadily eroded or relocated functions central to the life and vitality of the old town. As a result, the old town became marginalized, with most activities important to the economic and administrative and cultural life of Lhasa now shifting to the new urban areas. This trend has continued to the present day. Still, the old town remains the cultural heart of Lhasa, albeit mostly for the Tibetan population.

Small businesses, always the economic lifeline of the old town, are currently expanding in number, though they probably cater mainly to people in the old sections.

Lhasa's population exploded from about 30,000 people in 1950 to around 400,000 in 2000. The average rate of increase compares with a middle-to-high expansion rate in other parts of the world. This rapid and steady increase must be seen as very considerable, particularly when noting Lhasa's isolation and small, contained valley area. One can only conclude, therefore, that such growth has resulted from direct policies that encourage migration into Tibet from other parts of China. Tibetans in Lhasa today are a minority in their hometown.

During the next 20 years, Lhasa must prepare for a major expansion of its urban areas. The population might double in this time – reaching close to one million people and making the past two decades of growth seem insignificant. Such a large population will seriously affect the environment through loss of land and damage to fragile natural resources.

The urban environment of Lhasa is a synthesis of its urban structure and urban life, two aspects that are in fact inseparable. Physical Lhasa, made up of monuments, streets, buildings, external spaces and public works, generally changes little from year to year, though even these physical and functional divisions are increasingly under the stress of development. In contrast, urban life – mobile, changeable and particularly influenced by money – transforms itself rapidly. All these material, spiritual and intellectual changes have taken Lhasa from a pre-modern traditional society to a modern regional urban environment in just 50 years.

Lhasa City may accommodate more than half of its incoming population over the next 20 years by using present low-density urban blocks for higher-density and low-height housing. Urban blocks surrounding old Lhasa could in this way perhaps relieve the old town of half its present population, or 40,000 people.

Alternatively, a more constructive long-term scenario might see the blocks around the old town used to create a low-density buffer zone. Combined green areas and townscape would then stretch from Norbulingka to the old town and contribute to the protection of Lhasa's historical character.

A wise development strategy for Lhasa City might be to build new and separated clusters of townscape in the larger landscape of the extended Lhasa valley, away from the city centre. This would allow natural surroundings to interact with a growing townscape and reduce environmental stress.

The natural ecosystems in the Lhasa valley are under strain and seem to be headed towards real trouble. Lhasa each year absorbs land from agriculture, pasturage and the traditional

Opposite: Demolition of Tromsikhang, June 1997. Tromsikhang, one of the oldest secular buildings on the Barkor and with the longest, finest façade in town, once functioned as a government palace. This site of historical importance was unexpectedly demolished in 1997; unexpected because it was a protected building. When we arrived to commence a detailed survey we were shocked to find people being moving out of the building in preparation for demolition. The Lhasa City Construction Committee, with whom we had a written agreement of collaboration, assured us Tromsikhang was protected. We conferred immediately with the national cultural heritage management authority, but in the end were merely able to record the destruction. Only the narrow building facing the Barkor was left standing, its façade upgraded. Today, Tromsikhang has been replaced by four-storey concrete residential blocks behind the old façade. This loss, along with the Barkor's Surkhang corner, is among the most regrettable in the old town.

Upper left: The western courtyard before demolition. Though common space is dilapidated due to neglect, the buildings seem robust and in good condition. The architectural style of the main building is remarkable for its rhythm and forceful detailing.

Upper right: Inhabitants have started emptying their flats. To the left is the rear side of the front building, which in the end was reconstructed. At front is part of the fine side wing that was demolished.

Lower left: The north-west corner of Tromsikhang during demolition of a neighbouring street house. The beautiful stonework in perfect condition and the rare benma frieze of the western wing are clear signs of an important, high-quality building.

Lower right: The western courtyard of Tromsikhang during demolition. Former inhabitants search for the last useful items.

Opposite: Surveyed, protected and demolished buildings in old Lhasa, 1994–1999. Scale 1 : 6 000. The coloured buildings, with a few exceptions, were built before 1950 and represent those surveyed by the LHCA project. Buildings without colour were all built after 1950. The buildings coloured yellow were demolished in the five-year period between 1994–99, and those coloured red are protected buildings. The level of protection is shown in the Appendix (p. 165).

The number of buildings actually destroyed during this period is larger than shown here, because the surveys did not keep pace with the demolitions. These demolitions were quite evenly spaced out across the old town; the LHCA survey revealed only one case of an entire street being destroyed. The fact that traditional buildings remain in all parts of the town has helped preserve the net of old lands and alleyways. An old building is always demolished to make way for a new one, and in every case a new building goes up in a few months. This speed of construction usually results in poor design, poor workmanship and overall poor quality. The new buildings are always taller and bulkier than their neighbours and accommodate many more people; after one year they often look ten years old. Protected buildings have a special colour coding. The demolitions, quite evenly spread out, revealed only one case of an entire street being demolished. The fact that old buildings remain in all parts of the old town has helped preserve the net of old lanes and alleyways. An old building is always demolished to make way for a new building, and in every case a new building goes up in a few months. This speed of construction usually results in poor quality, poor design and poor workmanship. The new buildings are always taller and bulkier than their neighbours and accommodate many more people; after one year they often look ten years old.

flood expansion areas.[1] Waterlogged areas have always been important reservoirs for regulating the valley's entire water system, but increased construction of all types may drastically affect this. Water consumption now exceeds traditional capacities – that is, the Lhasa of 40 years ago – by up to ten times. The old town may already be sitting atop saturated masses of stagnant surface spill and sewage water, thus polluting groundwater and altering the ground conditions of traditional buildings.

Shifts from traditional agriculture to industry, trade and tourism increase pollution and the demand for land. The slow degradation of the valley's natural environment may be unstoppable and seems to parallel the loss of cultural heritage. Consumption of resources in Lhasa probably surpasses all estimates and constitutes a long-term limiting factor to the future of Lhasa itself. The city only recently passed from a stable ecological state into the 'unstable' condition of a modern city with hugely increased resource demands. Little is yet known about the 'balancing' needed to sustain a complex city, and for Lhasa such balancing of natural resources was probably upset decades ago. The greatest challenge facing Lhasa will be to ensure the provision of new resources while slowing down the depletion and destruction of its natural and cultural heritage. Tourism as well as the health of the city depends on these factors. If even limited levels of 'sustainability' are to be reached, Tibetans and Chinese must develop the concepts, skills and socio-economic vision to save their city.

The Chinese government abolished private ownership in the 1950s, and the state turned most private residential properties into housing for government work units or subsidized housing for people in need. By the mid-1980s, the city government began returning properties to the original owners, though not in proportion to what was originally appropriated. Even with this policy, the LHCA survey has shown that most traditional buildings inside the Lingkor are still owned by the authorities.

Traditional private ownership normally means that owners and tenants regularly repair and maintain buildings and their surroundings – all the time making small but steady investments in time and money. Community ownership in Lhasa has meant that the authorities assume responsibility for building maintenance and repair, but they have had few resources to do this. In contrast to much modern construction, the traditional buildings in Lhasa require very regular upkeep because of their 'soft' materials (sun-baked bricks, clay surfaces etc), and the lack of such upkeep in the old town is a consequence of several factors: ownership and tenure rights, planning policies and availability of resources. Due to these and

other conditions, most traditional Lhasa buildings, into the late-1990s, were allowed to slip into neglect and dilapidation, a state both difficult and expensive to counteract.[2] As a result, the old town appears as a low-standard 'ghetto' area with a population of approximately 80,000, compared to a population of 25,000 before 1960.

Beginning around 1990, many traditional buildings were demolished in the old town every year. As a result the total number of historical structures in the old town in 1999 has been reduced by about 70 buildings or building complexes, from some 330 when the LHCA survey started in 1994. Many selected for demolition in the 1990s were admittedly dilapidated and had low ceiling heights; all lacked modern facilities. Despite this, most were fit for rescue and upgrading as good quality housing. Most of the demolished structures disappeared without any detailed investigation because officials were in a rush to renew the building stock in the old town.

A slowdown or even a halt to the demolition of Lhasa's traditional buildings could allow a proper review of the overarching conservation policy for the old town as well as other valuable sites in the TAR. Lhasa Old Town Protection Working Group was established in 1998 with a broad mandate to coordinate repairs and conservation in the old town, to implement projects and to consider new measures for heritage administration. As part of this activity, the working group was supposed to have drafted and made public new conservation guidelines for the old town in 1999.

Today, old buildings no longer offer generous single-family or low-density occupancy, but rather have been transformed into cramped multi-family accommodation. With water and sanitation services of low standard and numerous new informal additions, the buildings themselves are changing into hybrids of their original building types. This is not a problem in itself, as every society must use the buildings it has to meet the real needs of people. Problems arise only when essential assets – in this case unique townscape and historical buildings – are allowed to change without control and with little chance to reverse the process.

The market economy that arrived in Lhasa in the mid-1990s fundamentally altered the availability and cost of housing, largely making obsolete the municipal housing authority, which up until then had administered the city's housing. As elsewhere in China, subsidized housing in Lhasa has been phased out,[3] with the population increasingly turning to the open market. The cost of renting space in Lhasa suddenly jumped, with prices in 2000 often 50 or even 100 times higher than before 1995.[4] Such dramatic changes have contributed to the increase of informal housing in the old town, and particularly to additions

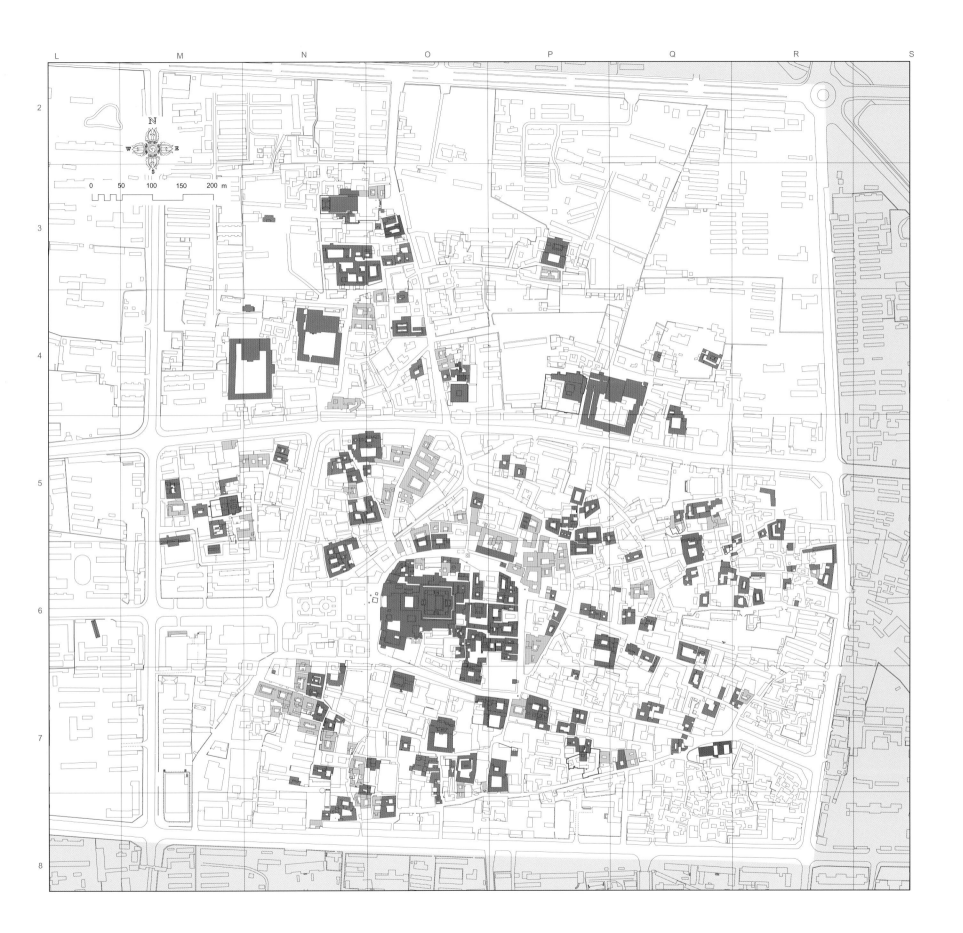

Informal building extensions, 1997.
A mansion in the old town contains a
courtyard filled up with informal
extensions.

and extensions, often built of impermanent materials, in order to create affordable housing. The larger old buildings particularly are being transformed beyond recognition. As an urban area under fewer controls, and as a priority area for housing, the old town is being allowed by the authorities to grow and increase its density 'naturally', far beyond the carrying capacity of the fragile, dysfunctional townscape.

In the 1990s, large investments were made in new buildings for the old town, with few funds going towards water supply, sanitation or roads. Investment needs today may radically exceed the total accumulated investment in new housing in the last ten years. The result is a situation that may very well isolate the old town as an under-serviced area for the urban poor.

Conservation, urban planning and development are exercised within the urban plan framework. In the early 1980s, policies were adopted to replace traditional housing in Lhasa with modern, higher density accommodation. The old town was designated as a major housing zone for the city and several traditional areas were quickly redeveloped. Lhasa's need to

expand, combined with an improved economy, ushered in the municipal housing programme in 1995. Much of the new housing, built with modern methods to simple standards, allows far higher densities than before, though with a corresponding reduction of external public space. Developers have been able to turn projects around rapidly to offer the market large quantities of housing.

Public-sector housing projects account for the vast majority of construction volume in Lhasa old town; there are few private housing projects. One main intention of the public projects is to encourage 'original' tenants to move into the new housing, but the vastly increased costs make it impossible for many to afford such a move. This situation only increases the urban population in need of housing subsidies, and with it the volume of informal, low-standard construction in the old town increases.

In 1983, the State Council in Beijing approved the Lhasa Development Plan 1980–2000, which has proved decisive for the city's urban development. The plan defines protection of cultural heritage as a priority concern, but today, after almost 20 years, it is fair to say that new construction has won over traditional townscape in a major way.[5] In 1994 administrators revised the plan to better match the needs and potentials of the city,[6] with the result that most building, road construction and other improvements were completed by 2000.

To improve links across the Kyichu river, four new bridges have been proposed beyond the single one now existing near the eastern end of the city. A planned railway line, approved by the State Council, will connect Lhasa with the rest of China through the north-east; the line is expected to enter the city on the south side of the Kyichu, then cross a railway bridge to end at a station about 2 kilometres west of Norbulingka. Some station buildings have already been built. The railway, when completed, will bring huge new changes to Lhasa.

New bridges across the Kyichu could open up the southern and eastern riverbanks for urban development, potentially relieving pressure from the heavily developed central areas. Bridges and an expanded road network might dramatically alter the old town, but if planned correctly they could also protect it from being overrun. Likely consequences, however, will be increased development pressure surrounding the old town. At the local level, widening Beijing Shar Lam could mean demolition of the last few traditional buildings there and a

devastating loss of Yabshi Phünkhang, former home of the Dalai Lama's family.

Today, sections of the riverbank have been hardened and strengthened to reduce flooding. The development of Thieves' Island (Gumo Lingka) is part of this flood control plan and coincides with the island's growth as an entertainment area, with restaurants, clubs, hotels and housing. All of this has radically changed the riverfront and its relationship with the town, to the detriment of Lhasa; the loss of this green historical recreation area on the river is sad and irrevocable.

The Conservation Plan for the Historical City of Lhasa of 1990 defined conservation units and protection zones, with the historical areas divided into three categories of protection. The plan also provided guidelines for urban development inside and outside the zones. In 1994, the State Council took the initiative to formulate the Overall Plan of Lhasa City.[7]

The Barkor Conservation Plan[8] attempted to describe and analyse each area of the old town in terms of conservation needs and development potential, but without presenting an overall analysis. This may have caused the authorities to view the old townscape as segmented and lacking a wholeness. Consequently, the authorities' approach to the management of cultural heritage has suffered, and the plan only identifies a small number of buildings for future protection.[9] Despite good intentions,

Lhasa valley showing Thieves' Island (Gumo Lingka) with Chakpori behind, 2000. This popular picnic spot on a formerly serene island in the Kyichu river is fast becoming a new district of Lhasa. The island has been enlarged and reinforced.

The second island directly south of the old town has also been enlarged and reinforced, and has a concrete road along the entire waterfront. Only one institution stood there in 1999 and the intended use of the remaining area is not yet disclosed.

Yabshi Phünkhang, Beijing Shar Lam, 1994. This view from the street shows one of the two remaining Yabshis, houses for a Dalai Lama's family. The only surviving old building on Beijing Shar Lam, this is among the finest secular structures in Lhasa, with exceptionally fine proportions, interesting façade rhythms and richly decorated interiors. It stands on the southern side of the main street, formerly a lane that was widened, which resulted in the building sitting on the very edge of the thoroughfare. Eager planners might wish to see it removed in order to widen the street further, but this must definitely not happen – Yabshi Phünkhang should be protected by all available means.

Tromsikhang, a protected building and possibly the most important one on Barkor North, was demolished in 1997 and replaced with a four-storey residential complex. Only Tromsikhang's old street frontage – 6 metres deep – remains.

The Barkor plan presented two alternatives for the future of the old town. In the first, Barkor, with urban blocks enclosing it, was defined as a Grade One Conservation or Protection area[10] to include all buildings inside the Barkor and those outside to a depth of 30–100 metres, depending on the dimensions of each block. In the second alternative, the Grade One Conservation or Protection area was limited to the area circumscribed by the Barkor, with streetscape and buildings outside the Barkor only as part of a general Grade Three protection zone. The first alternative has the potential to protect the centre of the old town, yet the second alternative seems to be the one chosen, even though it appears to be only partially implemented.

The plan offered detailed guidelines for the use of architectural styles in the various parts of the old town,[11] with specific areas classified into four 'levels'.[12] A visitor to old Lhasa might have difficulty spotting the results of such apparently strict building design codes and controls. In this respect Lhasa

is a good example of the difficulties involved with building design and urban planning in a historical townscape that is also part of a dynamic, expanding city living through its first generation of real-estate development.

Today, most streets in the central old town have become market streets; economic opportunity has clearly expanding the commercial core beyond the expectation of planners back in the early 1990s. Before the recent bout of construction, quite large areas of open space existed between the clusters of buildings in the old town. Today, there are no such 'green' areas left. Vehicular traffic, controlled to acceptable volumes and limited to selected streets at present, will very soon be a large problem in the old town.

Despite a national policy to protect cultural heritage, Chinese and Tibetans destroyed an amazing number of cultural sites and buildings throughout Tibet before and during the Cultural Revolution. In 1982 Lhasa was confirmed as one of 24 historical towns in China; today 99 towns are included. The early 1980s saw proposals to protect Lhasa old town's secular architecture, but these were not adopted by regional and municipal authorities. In 1985, the Lhasa City Cultural Relics

Bureau proposed that all monastic sites and structures in Lhasa be protected, including inactive monasteries. Since 1991 six of these sites have become protected at the municipal level of Lhasa City.[13] Some religious buildings, despite official protection, have been damaged since then. In the late 1980s, the TAR Cultural Relics Bureau declared several sites in the Lhasa valley as 'regionally protected buildings', including Meru monastery, the Great Mosque (Gyal Lhakhang) and the Ani Tsangkung nunnery in the old town.

Since the early 1970s, the state has invested perhaps 300 million yuan (US$36 million) in repair and restoration of cultural property in Tibet. Of this, most has been spent on religious structures in or near Lhasa; 100–150 million yuan (US$12–18 million) alone has gone to the Potala and Jokhang in the last 15 years, largely to create the square in front of the Potala and to move two imperial steles back to their original positions. Also, three white stupas were reconstructed west of Potala Square to re-establish the West Gate, demolished in 1968. These considerable investments, modest when compared to the actual needs of cultural heritage in Tibet, do nevertheless indicate the extent of funding.

In 1997, a group of foreign professionals with Lhasa experience proposed to the municipality to protect secular and residential buildings in the old town, a proposal also brought to the attention of Beijing. In 1998, Lhasa City agreed to protect 76 secular buildings in the old town; these have now also been confirmed by the regional authorities. This represents a good change in policy and a step forward in the protection of anonymous architecture and traditional townscape. Recent efforts to enforce traditional building heights in the Barkor – no building should exceed the height of the Jokhang – and plans to tear down or reconstruct ugly modern structures there are also

Left: Yabshi Phünkhang, 1994. The western part of the main façade, towards the courtyard, exemplifies beautifully a common motif in Tibetan buildings: openings in the wall widen from the lower towards the upper floors. The technical condition of the building is excellent.

Right: Yabshi Phünkhang, 1994. The eastern part of the main façade, towards the courtyard, shows the main entrance with large 'sun-windows' on the first and second floors. The exterior also displays rich detailing. In Tibet, the function of entering a house is typically separated from major, architectural compositions, unlike in Western architecture. Here, the monumentality of the main façade is present in the overall composition, with vertical elements emphasized to such a degree as to architecturally identify them almost as interconnected towers.

New cinema building, Beijing Shar Lam East, 1997. This example of modern architecture, while conforming to the general height of traditional buildings, goes out of its way to use forms and materials that contrast as much as possible with these buildings. This tendency illustrates a lack of talent, or experience, with handling contemporary architectural forms. During a three-week stay in the Banak Shöl Hotel, the building to the left, the authors followed numerous attempts to fit an oval skylight on top of the circular form. Three years later the task was still not completed. There has been little will or control in modifying modern construction to the traditional forms and building materials of the old town. Architects who design buildings for Lhasa may be located elsewhere in China; they often try to emulate architectural images from international magazines. Construction workers in Lhasa remain inexperienced in handling new materials and building methods.

positive developments. Buildings and sites protected by the regional and municipal authorities are identified in the attached Appendix (p. 165).[14]

'Lhasa World Heritage Town' or, more officially, 'The Historic Ensemble of Potala Palace, Lhasa' is today the name by which the extended historical zone in Lhasa is identified by China and UNESCO. The Potala was inscribed on the UNESCO World Heritage List in 1994, with the acclamation of the World Heritage Committee.[15] As suggested by ICOMOS,[16] the committee 'requested the Chinese authorities to envisage … extending the site to include the historic village of Shöl, the Temple of Jokhang as well as the Chakpori Hill', hoping that the authorities would propose a larger historical area – including Shöl, Lukhang temple, park and lake, Chakpori, Norbulingka and the old town with the Jokhang and Barkor – for World Heritage protection. With the Potala inscription, the authorities upgraded the Potala buffer zone by establishing the new Potala Square, completed already in autumn 1995. This included the demolition of Outer Shöl, a cluster of traditional and old buildings outside the fortified walls of Shöl–Potala. As part of the same project, some old buildings inside Shöl were demolished and their residents relocated. Some of the Shöl buildings have been well rebuilt in a near-traditional style.

In 1999 the Chinese proposed to extend the Potala World Heritage listing to include the Jokhang Temple and central parts of the Barkor. The subsequent review made by ICOMOS for the World Heritage Committee states: 'The buildings and decorations of Jokhang reflect the high quality of Tibetan art

in the 7th century and again in the 15–16th centuries, and also demonstrate cultural exchange between Tibet and its neighbouring countries.' In 2000 the Jokhang, with central Barkor, was added to the UNESCO World Heritage List as an extension to the Potala nomination. Overall protection of Marpori with the Potala and Barkor with the Jokhang now seems possible.[17]

The Potala, Norbulingka and Lhasa old town together create an axis of history and culture through the fabric of the expanding modern city. In response to suggestions from the World Heritage Committee, China in 2000 proposed that Norbulingka be added as an extension to the Potala World Heritage inscription. This proposal will probably be recommended by ICOMOS and approved by the UNESCO World Heritage Committee during 2001.[18]

Recent losses to Lhasa's cultural heritage mean that the authorities must increase their efforts of protection over the next 10 to 15 years. Conservation of historical areas requires a clear, long-term strategy, and protection for Lhasa needs flexibility in the face of its changing urban structure, which surrounds the historical fabric.

Training of craftsmen at all levels is vital to preserve building traditions. Cultural heritage, traditional crafts and building methods, as well as tourism, can all provide jobs and income and may very well be areas of growth for Lhasa. In the past few years, Lhasa municipality has shown increased interest in the traditional townscape and its buildings, and urban conservation in China will perhaps influence planners in a positive way. Since 1997, efforts by the municipal authorities and others seem to have raised awareness among local communities of the value of the historical environment;[19] examples from many countries show that there is good potential for upgrading historical environments when such awareness grows.

In spite of the recent waves of monotonous construction and demolition, much of the grain of the traditional townscape seems intact; the charming, age-old web of streets, lanes and alleyways that criss-cross the intricate landscape of public and private spaces remains to be enjoyed. But protecting townscape demands vigilance.

Modern buildings go up in Lhasa with a speed and efficiency rarely seen in other towns. Such speed, economy and simple construction can make new housing appear dilapidated even before completion, and thus many buildings put up in the 1990s may be short-lived and expensive short-term investments for Lhasa. There are signs, however, that people want improved craftsmanship in parts of the old town.

New buildings in the old town are supposed to respect certain rules for architectural style and size, but in reality many projects slip through the net of conservation and planning.

Are townscape rules appropriate, or are they defined too openly, or administered too leniently? Important questions such as these remain.

Only in some parts of Lhasa does one get the sense of buildings and residents really 'belonging'. This notion may seem romantic, but it goes to the heart of what townscape means in all its sensual and functional complexity. As a rare and precious example, the old town still largely invokes that feeling of identity – of being a townscape with a population that truly belongs. In contrast to the character of the old town, the

New market hall, Barkor Sang Trom Sanglam, 2000. The market hall, built around 1990 and thus too recent to be featured in our maps, replaced an open vegetable market in the very heart of the old town, behind Tromsikhang. It represents another example of insensitive 'modern' architecture taking over. Fire damaged the market hall a few years ago, but unfortunately it was repaired rather than torn down. The building, though better than much new architecture in Lhasa, is utterly out of place in the old town. This is not to say that all modern architecture is alien to Lhasa's traditional townscape. Some modern buildings could work, but they would have to harmonize with and respect the existing architectural integrity in terms of scale, proportion and rhythm, and use of materials.

uniform language of contemporary urban culture taking over Lhasa makes most of the city look like anywhere else in China.

Traditional buildings possess unique qualities of design and special affinities with the landscape, in contrast to modern buildings. The traditional heavy construction remained cool in summer and relatively warm in winter, offering protection against Lhasa's extreme climate in a way not possible with contemporary construction.

The old town can no longer be enjoyed as an entity, hidden as it now is inside recent and incidental urban streetscape. A regular grid of wide, tree-lined streets, introduced in the 1960s, presses down its orthogonal geometry over the organic townscape of the old town. Some of these streets do really contribute positively to the new townscape, with alleys of mature trees along otherwise bleak urban blocks. Hardly any of the traditional townscape of Lhasa, however, is allowed to penetrate this uniform 'dress' of the modern city.

Outside the core area of the Barkor, the grain of traditional townscape is being wiped out, not by changing street patterns, but by new larger and taller buildings filling semi-urban meandering spaces – former gardens, marshy areas and incidental grazing land. Traditional open fringe areas are no longer anything but modern cityscape encroaching on old townscape.

Proposals to establish more paved squares in front of protected cultural sites in the old town are both positive and dangerous at the same time because traditional Tibetan townscape probably never had formal urban spaces like those now being introduced. Lhasa needs to adopt measures that are in character with its traditional townscape and not merely borrowings from other cultural-architectural contexts.

In traditional townscape, sight lines constitute a vital dimension of the rich visual environment. The premier landmarks of Lhasa are the Potala, Marpori, Chakpori, the Jokhang and Ramoche, and of course the wonderful mountains to the north and south. The taller and bulkier townscape of modern Lhasa threatens all traditional sight lines, of which the essential ones to protect are included here in maps. The new townscape in the next few years will either preserve a future for Lhasa's

Top: Vacant site, Beijing Shar Lam East, 1997. A traditional old house on this site was suddenly gone before we could survey it. The site is adjacent to the fine, old Meru monastery, whose massive buildings are seen to the left.

Below: New building, Beijing Shar Lam East, 1997. Four months later, the vacant site was occupied by a four-storey narrow block that dwarfed everything around it. The building was not just built in four stories – they were gigantic, making the structure unreasonably tall. It is a relief to remember that the 'rotation' of new generations of buildings on the same site is quite fast in Lhasa.

historical character or forever marginalize it into charming but isolated small pockets within a featureless modern city – a serious scenario indeed.

The Kyichu river, canals, marshy green areas and gardens (*lingkas*) contribute to Lhasa's inestimable qualities. Although almost gone from the old town, some of these elements are still there in controlled form and could be revived to improve the townscape. Lingkas and external grasslands once characterized Lhasa, so tree planting in the valley and inside the old town might rejuvenate the environment and help to prevent a complete expansion of the grey contemporary urban landscape. The marshes in the northern part of the Lhasa valley are probably the region's most successfully protected landscape corridor, and from them one retains the wonderful silhouette of traditional Lhasa. The area from the foothills between Drepung and Sera monasteries down to the recent urban blocks north of Marpori forms a protected natural landscape, with an almost intact ecosystem, that still manages to halt urban development.

Sustainable, meaningful tourism for Lhasa will depend on the city protecting the old town's historical and cultural environment, repairing townscape and buildings, adding new infrastructure and creatively using fragments of early history in the Lhasa valley to present a more complete picture of life and culture in Central Tibet (the Qugong village ruins are one example). Unless the people of Lhasa increase their skills and experience from the present tourist situation, future earnings from tourism may remain limited. Such skills and education can promote and protect the historical environment while simultaneously meeting the requirements of foreign visitors and tourists. Recent transformations of the traditional townscape have already reduced the value of Lhasa, and its earning potential could easily be prejudiced further. For Lhasa to keep its unique character and quality for the future, it must hold onto all that remains of old buildings and townscape.

The Potala Palace was largely constructed under the 5th Dalai Lama in the 17th century and extensively reshaped Marpori, but little is known of earlier structures on the site. The Jokhang Temple has by virtue of its central role in the religious life of Tibet been altered, extended and restored

Potala, seen from the north-west, 1999. The large marshy area north-west of Lhasa forms a protected natural landscape with an almost intact ecosystem. This broad zone still provides a necessary barrier to urban development and affords outstanding views of the Potala.

almost continually over 13 centuries. The Barkor achieved its present character of historical townscape through piecemeal development over some 300 years, with most of its current character coming from Lhasa's expansion during the first half of the 20th century. Succeeding decades of urban change, before and after the 1950s, profoundly altered the townscape. Such continuous agglomeration of monuments and townscape over many centuries makes it difficult to discuss the authenticity of these structures within conventional international terms, as these are identified in international charters and declarations.[20] Their unquestionable importance in representing Tibetan culture rests on many points. A major and indisputable claim to Lhasa's authenticity may be its role in the religious and cultural life of Buddhist Tibet over more than a thousand years.

The official principle for managing cultural heritage in Lhasa – 'conservation in development and development in conservation' – is based on legislation at regional and national levels.[21] Authorities in Lhasa realize the need to respect and support the natural and cultural landscape, and they intend initially to fund repairs and restorations of sites, with these in time becoming economically viable on their own. To assure that Lhasa's sites and monuments survive financially, turning them over to an aggressive form of tourism management seems to be the only solution, however unappetizing and unrealistic that may seem.

This dilemma goes to the heart of international conservation, namely, how to afford 'initial heritage' with sufficient funds to begin generating further income within the local community. A number of towns in China are struggling with this question and Lhasa may benefit from their experience.

The protection of Lhasa old town began late and only recently have authorities and society in general realized the great value of Lhasa's cultural heritage. Sustainable conservation in Lhasa must build on local community participation, while adapting and extending existing technical, institutional and legal practices. Cultural resource protection, in Lhasa as elsewhere, requires the maintenance of environmental resources, such as the repair of valuable buildings and heritage, and the improvement of living conditions. Cultural heritage can provide jobs and money, too, through training schemes for craftsmen, the development of traditional arts and crafts and tourism.

Upgrading buildings and townscape in the old town started in 1997 as a partnership between municipal authorities and external private interests. The positive results of this work came about in spite of immature and weak institutional tools, and the question remains how Lhasa can continue to improve the management of its cultural heritage effectively on its own as foreign support – funds and expertise – could be diminishing. All considered, the municipal authorities seem active and committed to conservation work in the old town, though at their own pace.

Social and economic changes during the last 30 years allow fewer opportunities to make a living from traditional crafts. In many historical towns, old and experienced craftsmen generally find work in other fields or simply stop working entirely, thus making it difficult to establish training schemes to take care of traditional townscape and buildings. Lhasa, fortunately, has competent and experienced groups of craftsmen who still build and repair in traditional ways. These men and women, essential for ensuring the future of traditional habitat, hold the potential to train apprentices and younger craftsmen.

Practical conservation work must embrace an understanding of how old and new can be integrated, with mutual respect for the value of each. The best way to achieve this is to educate a first generation of Tibetan architects and planners who understand architectural traditions and who truly desire to work with them. In short, architectural education does not yet exist in Tibet and needs to get started.

In 1994, Norway proposed to fund conservation studies in Lhasa[22] to enable international and Chinese experts to present academic and field-based education in areas such as architectural conservation, architectural engineering, building studies, repair of historical structures, and restoration of wall paintings. The proposal was rejected by the Chinese authorities.

As stated, the future of the urban environment in Lhasa and other Tibetan towns depends on adequate education being quickly established. Highly competent local experts already exist, and their skills can be supplemented by visiting foreign experts. Lhasa is fertile ground for academic studies that focus on conservation within a vibrant historical and modern city.

Cultural Centre, New Potala Square, 1997. This building on the left side of the large new square, directly facing the central fountain in front of the Potala, is an example of the architectural style adopted for Lhasa's new development. Its style and aesthetic are certainly not of Tibetan origin. The building stands within the 'Zone of restricted construction' established around the Potala in connection with its inclusion on the UNESCO *World Heritage List in 1994.*

Over the years, we have had close contact with only one trained Tibetan architect in Lhasa, a man of unusual experience who also contributed towards our detailed surveys. One experienced professional can achieve a lot, but Tibet needs many more such people. The current negative situation cries out for help and amelioration: population growth and influx of migrant labour, demolition of traditional buildings, construction of alien and inappropriate buildings, destruction of townscape, uncontrolled growth and pollution. It is plain for all to see that serious challenges must be faced straightaway. We therefore conclude here by strongly encouraging the authorities to continue strengthening its protection of cultural heritage and to this end establish education in architecture, building conservation and traditional crafts in Lhasa.

Yamyang, 2000. Yamyang, a large residential yard or tenement with several courtyards, located north-west of and fairly near the Jokhang's main entrance, was in poor shape and in danger of demolition. In the summer of 2000, the City Government Traditional Construction Team was well under way repairing and upgrading the site, a clear sign that the protection of 76 secular houses in the old town is being followed up by action. In 1999, the same team finished upgrading at least two other large buildings, Labrang Nyingba and Sampo, both on the Barkor. The Tibet Heritage Fund, a Western organization, also worked to restore several of the 76 protected buildings in the old town. The photo shows reconstruction work in progress in one of the courtyards. The walls of the upper floor were originally made with sun-dried clay blocks, which are now substituted with stonework, as with the two lower floors. The fine stonework with its layers of small stone flakes between the granite blocks indicates the high quality of workmanship in the new walls.

Historical buildings in Lhasa
Inside the Lingkor and standing in 1994

Building number is the number given each building in the survey and as recorded in the maps in the Buildings chapter. Some building numbers are not included because although given survey numbers, the structures turned out to be very recent constructions, or demolished before an adequate survey could take place.

Name of building is the Tibetan name that the building is known by. The name of a religious building is shown in *italics*. Sources for names are partly the maps by Aufschnaiter and Taring, and partly local information.

Building type refers to the following listing of building types:
Religious buildings:
  A. Large temple complex or compound
  B. Temple or chapel
  C. Monastery
Secular buildings:
  D. Monumental official building
  E. Other official building
  F. Mansion
  G. Townhouse
  H. Streethouse
  I. Tenement or Residential yard
  J. Clustered housing
  K. Summerhouse
  L. Outbuilding

Area refers to the area-map on which the building is identified.

Map coordinates refers to the 200 × 200 metre-square grid shown on the maps. The red letters and numbers appear at the top and left side of each map.

Date of construction / date of demolition, according to the following key:
  ( )   uncertainty concerning the exact date
  ?/   date of construction not known
  /-   no change reported
  /p   preceding a date means that part of the building has been demolished
Correct dates cannot be ascertained for all buildings, and therefore the accuracy of information varies. The LHCA survey database in a number of cases provides further information concerning dates.

Because a number of buildings were already replaced by new construction when the survey started, or they were in the process of being demolished, this list does not identify all demolished historical buildings inside the survey area.

Construction type refers to the following categories:
  1. Three-storey stone building
  2. Three-storey stone/mud brick building
  3. Two-storey stone building
  4. Two-storey stone/mud brick building
  5. Single-storey stone building
  6. Single-storey stone/mud brick building

Plan type refers to building layout:
  1. Mansion
  2. Courtyard structure
  3. Massive structure

Protection level refers to the level at which the building may be protected:
  N. National level
  R. Regional level
  M. Municipal level

Bldg No.	Name	Bldg type	Area	Map coord.	Date of construction/ demolition	Constru. type	Plan type	Protn. level
1	Trapchishar	G	Jokhang	O 6	(1850) / –	1	2	M
2	Chötri Kangnub	G	Jokhang	O 6	1910 / –	3	2	M
3	Chötri Kangnub	G	Jokhang	O 6	1910 / –	1	2	
4	Chötri Kangshar	G	Jokhang	O 6	1920 / 1996	3	3	
5	Changling	G	Jokhang	O 6	1910 / –	3	2	
6	Changlingbo	G	Jokhang	O 6	1910 / 1996	3	2	
7	Shamo Karpo	G	Jokhang	O 6	(1910) / –	3	3	M
8	Nangtseshar	E	Jokhang	O 6	1650 / –	1	2	
9	*Jamkhang*	B	Jokhang	O 6	15 c / –	1	3	
10	Gangkarshar	G	Jokhang	O 6	1920 / –	4	2	M
11	Lubumshar	G	Jokhang	P 6	1900 / –	4	2	M
12	Dochang, Zhongkhang Sapa	H	Jokhang	P 6	1900 / –	4	3	M
13	Dochang, Zhongkhang Sapa	H	Jokhang	P 6	1900 / –	2	2	M
14	Tsethang Khangsar	H	Jokhang	P 6	1900 / –	2	2	M
15	Kabgyenub	G	Jokhang	O 6	1890 / –	2	2	M
16	Kabgyeshar	G	Jokhang	P 6	1925 / –	4	2	M
17	Numa	F	Jokhang	P 6	1920 / –	2	2	M
18	*Meru Nyingba*	B, C	Jokhang	O 6	7 c / –	1	3	R
19	Gotashar	G	Jokhang	P 6	800 / –	4	2	M
20	Kame Tara	G	Jokhang	P 6	7 c / –	4	2	M
21	Nangmamo	G	Jokhang	P 6	? / –	2	2	M
22	Tadongshar	G	Jokhang	P 6	1250 / –	2	2	M
23	Dokyilzur	G	Jokhang	P 6	1850 / –	2	2	M
24	Rongdra	G	Jokhang	O 6	1650 / –	1	2	M
25	Nyanang Tsongkhang	G	Jokhang	P 6	1935 / –	4	2	M
26	Nagtsejang	G	Jokhang	P 6	? / –	1	2	M
27	Gotri Tsongkhang	G	Jokhang	P 6	1890 / –	4	2	M
29	Chünpa	G	Jokhang	O 6	1790 / –	4	3	M
30	Labrang Nyingba	F	Jokhang	O 7	14 c / –	1	2	M
31	Janglashar	G	Jokhang	O 6	? / –	4	2	M
32	Tengkhangsar	G	Jokhang	O 6	? / –	4	2	M
33	Lanyinggyap	E	Jokhang	O 6	1890 / –	4	2	M
34	Ratö Khangtsen	G	Jokhang	O 6	1935 / –	2	2	M
35	*Shitro Lhakhang*	B	Ramoche	O 4	1920 / –	3	2	
36	Khardonub	G	Ramoche	O 4	1900 / 1997	4	2	
37	Lhading	G	Ramoche	N 4	1900 / 1997	4	2	M
38	Yamyang	I	Jokhang	N 6	19 c / –	2	2	M
39	Padru Khangsar	G	Jokhang	O 5	? / 1996	4	2	
40	Sumdona Khangsar	F	Jokhang	O 5	1920s / 1996	3	2	
41	Changlochen	G	Jokhang	O 5	? / 1997	3	1	
42	Yabshi Phünkhang	F	Jokhang	O 5	1843 / –	1	1	M
43	Tsuymo Khangsar	G	Jokhang	O 5	1947 / –	4	2	M
44	Ongdu Khangsar	I	Jokhang	O 5	1870s / –	1	1	M
45	Ganden Gowa Khangtsen	G	Jokhang	O 6	(8 c) / –	2	2	M

Bldg No.	Name	Bldg type	Area	Map coord.	Date of construction/ demolition	Constru. type	Plan type	Protn. level
46	Deleg Khangsar	G	Jokhang	N 5	1845 / –	1	2	M
47	Samding Khangsar	G	Jokhang	N 5	1900 / –	1	2	M
48	Singma Khangchung	G	Jokhang	N 5	1920 / 1996	4	2	M
49	Chinggurlho	G	Jokhang	N 5	? / 1997	4	2	M
51	Trompachang	G	Jokhang	N 5	1940 / –	4	2	
53	Demo Labrang	G	Jokhang	M 5	1958 / 1998	1	1	
54	Demo Labrang Khangkhung	G	Jokhang	M 5	1956, 1990 / –	3	3	
56	Drakhang (Old post office)	E	Jokhang	M 6	1925 / –	–	3	M
57	Nedrönshar	G	Jokhang	M 5	1945 / –	4	2	
58	Tenling Khangkhung	G	Jokhang	N 5	1954 / 1998	4	2	
59	*Tengyeling*	A, C	Jokhang	M 5	1770 / p 1996	1	2	
60	Simzur	G	Jokhang	M 5	1945 / –	3	2	M
61	Karmaykhang	G	Jokhang	M 5	1945 / 1996	4	2	
62	Mentsikhang	E	Jokhang	M 5	1016 / –	3	3	
63	Yuthok Zampa	–	Jokhang	L 6	(7 c) /–	–	3	
64	Lhalu Podrang	G	Jokhang	M 5	1954 / –	3	1	
66	Yulkhangchang	G	Jokhang	O 5	1946 / p 1997	2	2	M
67	Sonam Tsongkhang	G	Jokhang	O 5	1950 / –	4	2	M
69	Chumignub	G	Jokhang	O 5	1949 / 1997	4	2	
70	Shakapa	G	Jokhang	O 5	1926 / 1997	3	2	
71	Tromsikhang	D	Jokhang	P 6	(1700) / p1997	1	2	R
72	Songa Tsoba	G	Jokhang	O 5	1758 / –	3	2	
73	Gora Pentse	G	Jokhang	O 5	1840 / 1997	3	2	
74	Magang	G	Jokhang	P 6	1896 /1998	4	2	
75	Derabnub	G	Jokhang	P 6	? / 1998	3	2	
76	Derabshar	G	Jokhang	P 6	1889 / 1998	3	2	
77	Palunga	G	Jokhang	P 6	1898 /1998	4	2	
78	Yunan Tsongkhang	G	Jokhang	P 6	1936 / –	4	2	
79	Shikashar	G	Jokhang	P 6	1946 / 1996	4	2	
80	Darpoling	G	Jokhang	P 5	1650 / p 1996	1	2	
81	Shikanub	G	Jokhang	P 6	1953 / 1996	4	2	M
82	Pabongka Labrang	G	Jokhang	P 6	1954 / –	1	1	M
83	Kirey Dekyi Khangsar	G	Jokhang	P 5	? / –	4	2	Protn.
84	Kirey Labdra	G	Jokhang	P 5	1900 / –	4	2	M
85	Kirey Rabathil	G	Jokhang	P 5	1920, 1968 / –	4	2	M
86	Marlampa	G	Jokhang	P 5	1954 / –	1	2	
88	Changyap Khangsar	G	Jokhang	P 5	1946 / –	4	2	
90	Chati	G	Jokhang	P 5	1930 / –	4	2	
91	Dumra Tokhang	G	Jokhang	Q 6	? / –	4	2	
94	Tashi Khangsar Sarba	G	Jokhang	P 6	? / –	2	2	
95	Tashi Khangsar	G	Jokhang	P 6	1896 / –	2	2	
97	Tanshim Pangpe	G	Jokhang	Q 6	1896 / –	4	2	
98	Lukangpu	G	Jokhang	Q 6	1930 / –	4	2	
99	Shaglho	G	Jokhang	Q 6	1890 / 1997	4	1	

Bldg No.	Name	Bldg type	Area	Map coord.	Date of construction/ demolition	Constru. type	Plan type	Protn. level
100	Keding Khangsar	G	Jokhang	O 5	1906 / 1998	4	2	
102	Kedung	G	Jokhang	O 5	1934 / 1997	1	2	
103	Samdhu Poling	G	Jokhang	O 5	1936 / 1997	4	2	
104	Sechung	G	Jokhang	O 5	1952 / 1997	2	1	
106	Delin Khangsar	I	Jokhang	P 6	(1900) / 1998		2	
107	Dzeshimey	G	Jokhang	P 6	1906 / –	4	2	
108	Tashi Khangsar Nyingba	G	Jokhang	P 6	1950 / –	4	2	
110	Khongdong Bakhang	G	Jokhang	P 7	1940 / –	3	2	
111	*Gesar Lhakhang*	C	Kundeling	C 4	8c / –	4	–	
112	*Karmashar*	B	Jokhang	Q 6	(700) / –	4	3	R
113	Karma Sharchen	G	Jokhang	Q 6	1926 / –	4	2	
116	Namseling	G	Jokhang	Q 7	1920 / –	3	2	
118	Gegyapnub	G	Jokhang	Q 7	1920 / –	3	2	
119	Ragtsipa	G	Jokhang	Q 7	1953 / 1996	4	2	
121	*Shar Rigsum Lhakhang*	B	Jokhang	Q 7	8 c / 1910 / –	5	2	M
122	Rago Khangchung	G	Jokhang	Q 7	1954 / –	4	2	M
123	Chagtre	G	Jokhang	Q 7	1916 / 1998	4	2	
124	Khime	G	Jokhang	Q 7	? / –	3	2	M
125	Derge	G	Jokhang	P 7	1913 / 1997	3	2	
126	*Ani Tsangkung*	A, C	Jokhang	P 7	9 c / –	4	2	R
127	Kunsangtse	F	Jokhang	P 7	1907 / –	2	1	M
129	Benjoling	G	Jokhang	P 7	1916 / 1998	3	2	
130	Nyarongshar	G	Jokhang	P 7	1925 / –	4	2	M
131	Yunggongsha	G	Jokhang	P 7	1937 / –	4	2	M
132	Tagosha	G	Jokhang	P 7	1890 / –	4	2	
133	*Rabsel Tsenkhang*	B	Jokhang	P 7	? / –	1	1	
135	Sonam Lekung	G	Jokhang	P 7	1916 / –	4	2	M
136	Minkyiling	G	Jokhang	P 7	1932 / –	4	2	M
137	Gyatso Tashi	G	Jokhang	P 7	1958 / –	4	2	M
139	Abu Satsang	H	Jokhang	Q 7	? / –	4	3	
140	Ramoche Chokhang	G	Ramoche	O 3	1920 / –	4	2	
141	Pomdatsang	F	Jokhang	P 7	(1914) / –	1	1	M
142	Kyakashar	H	Jokhang	O 7	1945 / –	1	2	
143	Shatra	F	Jokhang	O 7	(1800) / –	1	1	M
144	Samdrup Podrang	G	Jokhang	O 7	1880 / –	1	1	M
145	Podrang Sarba	G	Jokhang	N 7	1925 / –	1	1	M
146	Chungsang Labrang	G	Jokhang	N 7	1890 / 1997	2	2	
147	Nyare Khangtsen	G	Jokhang	N 7	? / 1997	2	2	
148	Lingtsang	G	Jokhang	N 7	1938 / –	1	1	M
149	Lingtsang Gora Rense	G	Jokhang	N 7	1890 / –	4	2	
150	Lubu Liushar	G, I	Jokhang	N 7	1937 / 1997	1	2	
151	Paldenchang	G	Jokhang	N 7	1900, 1955 / 1997	4	2	
152	Dzomora	G	Jokhang	N 7	1930, 1959 / 1997	4	2	
153	Lubu Gowa Khangsar	G	Jokhang	N 7	1600 / –	2	2	M

Bldg No.	Name	Bldg type	Area	Map coord.	Date of construction/ demolition	Constru. type	Plan type	Protn. level
154	Petse	G	Jokhang	N 7	? / 1997	4	2	
155	Labrang Gora	G	Jokhang	N 7	? / 1997	2	2	
157	Ganden Gyalrong Khangkhung	G	Jokhang	N 7	1865 / 1997	4	2	
158	Pomzur	H	Jokhang	N 7	1945 / 1998	2	1	
159	Yuthok Khangchung	G	Jokhang	N 7	? / –	4	2	
160	Thangkhar, Gyaldrong Nangtso	G	Jokhang	N 7	1957 / –	4	1	M
161	Shamdzokhang	G	Jokhang	N 7	1880 / 1998	4	2	
163	Kyikya Pari	G	Jokhang	N 7	? / 1998	2	2	
164	Chongye Bumthang	G	Jokhang	N 7	1930 / –	3	1	M
165	Punthang	H	Jokhang	N 8	1870 / 1996	4	3	M
166	Liushar	G	Jokhang	N 8	1700 / –	4	2	
168	Dagshum	I	Jokhang	N 7	1790 / 1998	1	1	
169	Lanying Taptsang	L	Jokhang	O 6	(1890) / –	4	2	M
170	Liushar Dzomora	L	Jokhang	N 8	1860 / 1997	4	2	M
171	Kharden	G	Jokhang	O 7	1890 / –	4	2	M
172	Nakyid	H	Jokhang	N 8	1890 / 1997	4	2	
173	*Pode Khangsar*	B	Jokhang	O 7	(1670) / –	3	3	M
174	Dzomora	L	Jokhang	O 8	1954 / 1997	4	2	M
175	Trijang Labrang	F	Jokhang	O 8	940 / –	1	1	M
176	Tentrikang	F	Jokhang	Q 6	1890 / –	4	2	
177	Powo Dago	G	Jokhang	O 7	1890 / –	4	2	
178	Rampa	G	Jokhang	O 7	1900 / –	2	1	
180	*Lho Rigsum Lhakhang*	B	Jokhang	O 8	7 c (680) / –	4	2	M
181	Manithang	G	Jokhang	O 7	1900 / –	1	1	M
182	Shungso Rabden Khangsar	G	Jokhang	O 7	1900 / –	6	2	
183	Gorkha Nyingba	F	Jokhang	O 7	17 c / –	1	1	M
184	Rame Tsenkhang	B, G	Jokhang	O 7	1900 / –	4	2	
186	Shalho Menkhang	G	Jokhang	Q 6	1905 / –	1	2	
187	Thentong	F	Jokhang	Q 6	1912 / –	3	1	M
188	Shongka Tsenkhangnub	G	Jokhang	Q 6	1870 / 1996	4	3	
189	Yulgang Chopatsang	H	Jokhang	Q 5	1955 / 1996	6	3	
190	Yunying Khangchung	G	Jokhang	Q 5	1954 / 1996	4	2	
191	Tsewang Khangchungnub	G	Jokhang	Q 5	1950 / –	4	2	
192	Tsewang Khangchungshar	G	Jokhang	Q 5	1890 / –	4	2	
193	Yartsho Khangchung	G	Jokhang	Q 5	1946 / 1998	2	2	
194	Lakyil	G	Jokhang	Q 5	? / –	4	2	
197	Pulung Khangsar	G	Jokhang	R 5	1954 / –	4	2	
198	Kyele Khangchung	G	Jokhang	Q 6	1954 / –	4	2	M
200	Tashikyil	G	Jokhang	Q 6	? / –	4	3	
201	Gyatso Tashi	G	Jokhang	Q 6	1940 / –	4	2	M
202	Tronpashar Khangsar	G	Jokhang	Q 6	1916 / –	4	2	M
204	Lhakhangsar	G	Jokhang	R 6	1890 / –	4	2	
205	Döpatsang	H	Jokhang	R 6	? / –	6	3	
206	Kangsa	G	Jokhang	R 5	1900 / –	4	2	

Bldg No.	Name	Bldg type	Area	Map coord.	Date of construction/ demolition	Constru. type	Plan type	Protn. level
207	Cholhakhang	G	Jokhang	R 5	1947 / –	4	2	M
209	Norzin Khangsar	G	Jokhang	R 6	1936 / p 1996	4	2	
211	Sumo Khangchang	G	Jokhang	N 5	1876 / –	4	2	
212	*Dashöl Gyekhang*	B	Jokhang	R 6	1500 / –	5	3	
214	Lumo Khangchung	H	Jokhang	R 6	? / –	6	3	
215	Donwang	F	Ramoche	Q 5	1913 / –	1	1	M
216	Tashi Gödöchang	G	Jokhang	Q 6	1949 / –	4	2	
219	Tashi Gödöchang	G	Jokhang	Q 7	1953 / –	4	2	
220	Ragyab Tsenkhang	G	Jokhang	R 7	1920 / –	1	2	
221	Gutsang	G	Jokhang	R 7	1920 / 1997	4	2	
223	Gyal Lhakhang *(mosque)*	B	Jokhang	Q 7	1959 / –	–	2	R
224	Ngaritsang	G	Jokhang	R 6	1936 / –	6	2	
225	Yunying Khangchung	G	Jokhang	Q 5	1914 / –	4	2	
226	Rabdre Khangkhung	G	Jokhang	R 6	? / –	6	2	
227	Trombasha	F	Jokhang	R 6	1650 / –	4	2	M
228	Köjamdu	H	Jokhang	R 6	1846 / –	4	2	
229	Dara Kansha	H	Jokhang	R 6	1915 / –	4	2	
230		G	Jokhang	R 6	1936 / –	4	2	
231	Yangdungtsang	H	Jokhang	R 6	1954 / –	4	2	
233	Tashi Gödönub	G	Jokhang	Q6	1910 / –	3	2	
234	Phala	F	Jokhang	P 6	1750 / –	3	1	M
235	Dechen Rabden	G	Jokhang	P 6	1650 / 1995	4	2	
236	Horkhang	H	Jokhang	P7	1956 / –	3	2	
237	Chatsang	G	Jokhang	P7	1900 / –	4	2	
238	Chuminub	G	Jokhang	O 5	1916 / 1997	4	2	
239	*Mani Lhakhang*	B	Jokhang	P 6	1940 / –	3	3	
240	Tashi Khangsar	G	Jokhang	P 6	1896 / –	4	2	
242	Risurnub	G	Jokhang	P 5	1929 / –	3	2	M
243	Dechen Rabdenshar	I	Jokhang	P 6	1850 / 1998	3	2	
244	Lalung Surchi	F	Jokhang	P 5	1946 / –	4	2	
246	Gopön Nyempa	H	Jokhang	N 7	? / –	3	3	
247	*Jigje Lhakhang*	B	Jokhang	M 5	1800 / –	3	2	
248	Chindanub	G	Jokhang	O 7	1948 / 1999	3	1	
249	Kardo Labrang	G	Ramoche	O 4	1955 / –	3	1	
250	Gyalgodong	H	Ramoche	O 3	1850 / –	6	2	
251	Gyalgochang	G	Ramoche	O 3	1850 / 1997	4	2	
252	Tsomonling Drokhang	K	Ramoche	N 3	1945 / –	5	3	M
253	Shide Drokhang	K	Ramoche	N 4	1935 / –	5	3	
254	Dranangtsang	G	Ramoche	O 4	1880 / –	2	1	
255	Tsamkhang/Tara	G	Ramoche	N 3	1880 / –	4	2	
256	Khangchung Karpo	G	Ramoche	O 3	1880 / 1997	4	2	
257	Changra	F	Ramoche	N 3	1880 / 1997	4	1	
258	Drigung Labrang	G	Ramoche	P 3	1850 / 1997	3	2	
259	Kardo/Samthong	G	Ramoche	O 4	1920 / –	1	2	M

Bldg No.	Name	Bldg type	Area	Map coord.	Date of construction/ demolition	Constru. type	Plan type	Protn. level
260	Jebumgang Khenpotsang	G	Ramoche	O 4	1920 / 1997	1	2	
261	Donchodkhang Nyingba	G	Ramoche	O 4	1920 / 1997	1	2	
262	Rampa	G	Jokhang	N 8	1900 / –	4	3	
263	Chumi Dön	G	Jokhang	P 6	1918 / 1997	4	2	
264	Möndro	F	Ramoche	Q 4	1920 / –	1	1	
265	Bonshö	F	Ramoche	P 3	1920 / –	1	1	M
266	*Ramoche Temple*	A, C	Ramoche	N 3	(640) /–	1	2	R
267	Drepung Ashu Khangtsen	I	Ramoche	N 4	1947 / 1997	2	2	
268	*Shide Dratsang*	A, C	Ramoche	N 4	1350 / –	1	2	R
269	*Gyume Dratsang*	A, C	Ramoche	P 4	1450 / –	1	2	R
270	*Meru Dratsang*	A, C	Ramoche	P 4	9c / –	1	2	R
271	Lhamo	G	Ramoche	Q 4	1930 / –	4	2	
272	*Chang Rigsum Lhakhang*	B	Ramoche	O 4	1930 / –	6	3	M
273	Tsesum Pukhang	G	Ramoche	O 3	1650 / –	4	2	
274	Ganden Khangsar	I	Ramoche	N 3	1930 / –	4	2	M
275	Gyantsenub	G	Ramoche	O 3	1780 / –	4	2	
276	*Druptop Lhakhang*	B	Chakpori NE	F 6	1940 / –	4	2	M
277	Drekhang	J	Chakpori NE	F 6	1940 / –	6	2	M
278	Chapa	J	Chakpori NE	E 5	1900 / –	4	3	
279	Liushar	J	Chakpori NE	F 5	1930 / –	4	2	
280	Tsamkhang	J	Chakpori NE	F 5	1930 / –	4	2	
281	Shunggo	E	Potala – Shöl	H 4	1650 / –	1	3	
282	Chokding	E	Potala – Shöl	G 4	1650 / –	1	2	M
283	Pudokhang	E	Potala – Shöl	I 4	1650 / –	1	2	
284	Shargo	E	Potala – Shöl	I 4	1650 / –	1	3	
285	Nubgo	E	Potala – Shöl	G 4	1650 / –	1	2	
286	Pishi	G	Potala – Shöl	H 4	1850 / –	4	2	
287	Chibra	L	Potala – Shöl	H 4	1650 / –	4	2	
288	Barkhang Chenmo	D	Potala – Shöl	G 4	1926 / –	–	3	
289	Shöl Lekung	D	Potala – Shöl	H 4	(1910) / –	–	3	
290	Shöl Dekyiling	E	Potala – Shöl	H 4	1650 / –	–	2	
291	Tombo	G	Potala – Shöl	H 4	1750 / –	3	2	
292	Jampu	H	Potala – Shöl	H 4	1850 / –	4	3	
293	Lingkame	G	Potala – Shöl	H 4	1850 / –	6	2	
294	Lingkatö	I	Potala – Shöl	H 4	1850 / –	4	2	
295	Mucha	G	Potala – Shöl	H 4	1850 / –	4	2	
296	Magshikhang	D	Potala – Shöl	H 3	1650 / –	–	2	
297	Drekhang	D	Potala – Shöl	H 4	? / –	1	3	M
298	Ngü Barkhang	E	Potala – Shöl	I 4	1850 / –	3	2	
299	Khenzur	G	Potala – Shöl	I 4	1850 / –	4	2	
300	Dekyishar	G	Potala – Shöl	I 4	1800 / –	3	2	
301	Nyira Nechag	L, G	Potala – Shöl	I 4	1796 / –	4	2	
302	Gapo Nyingba	G	Potala – Shöl	I 4	1800 / –	4	2	
303	Nanglo	G	Potala – Shöl	I 4	1900 / –	6	2	

Bldg No.	Name	Bldg type	Area	Map coord.	Date of construction/demolition	Constru. type	Plan type	Protn. level
304	Phuntsok Rabden	G	Potala – Shöl	I 4	1850 / –	4	2	
305	Shöl Barkhang	E	Potala – Shöl	I 3	1690 / –	3	2	
306	Kamdongwa	G	Potala – Shöl	G 4	1900 / –	4	2	
307	*Tsheda Lhakhang*	B	Ramoche	O 3	? / –	2	2	M
308	*Tsomonling Dratsang*	A, C	Ramoche	N4	1750 / –	4	2	R
309	Trizur Nganor Labrang	G	Jokhang	N 5	1930 / –	4	2	M
310	Gyantseshar	G	Ramoche	O 3	1810 / 1998	3	2	
311	Tashi Khangsar	G	Ramoche	O 3	1900 / –	3	2	
312	Tentrikang	L	Ramoche	O 3	1890 / –	4	2	
313	*Jokhang Temple*	A/C	Jokhang	O 6	(7–8 c) / –	–	2	N
314	*Tarajhang*	B	Jokhang	P7	(7 c) / –	6	1	
315	Yabshi Taktster	F	Taktster	K 4	1940s / –	1	1	
316	*Potala Palace*	A/C	Potala – Shöl	H 3	1645, 1682 / –	–		N
317	*Lukhang chapel*	B	Potala – Shöl	H 2	1695 / –	–	3	R
321	*Jebumgang Lhakhang*	B	Ramoche	O 4	17c / –	5	3	
322	Ramoche Tsokhang	E	Ramoche	O 3	1900 / –		3	
323	*Palha Lupuk cave*	B	Chakpori NE	F 6	640s / –	5	–	
324	Sharsang	H	Ramoche	O 4	1900 / –		3	
325	Zomphud	G	Jokhang	O 7	1912 / –		2	
326	Namsekhang	G	Jokhang	P 5	1900 / –	4	2	M
327	Kirey Drokhang	G	Jokhang	P 5	1900 / –	2	2	M
328	*Nub Rigsum Lhakhang*	B	Jokhang	N 7	? / –	–	2	M
329	Hursur	H	Jokhang	Q 7	1720 / –	4	3	
330	*Ragyab Tsengang*	B	Jokhang	R 7	1900 / –	5	2	
332	*Sanjia Gudong picture rock*	–	Chakpori SW	B 7	7c / –	–	2	
333	*Kundeling*	C	Kundeling	C 4	18c / 1960s	3	1	M
334	Bargo Kani (West Gate)	E	Chakpori NE	F 5	17c, 1995 / –	–	1	
335	Langkhang (Elephant House)	E	Potala – Shöl	H 2	? / –	–	1	
336	Thangbön	G	Jokhang	N 5	1950 / –	–	2	

Notes

PREFACE

1   The Network for University Cooperation Tibet–Norway was established in 1994. Cooperating institutions in the Tibet Autonomous Region (TAR) are the Tibet Academy of Social Sciences (TASS), Tibet University, TAR Committee of Science and Technology, TAR Forestry Bureau and TAR Bureau of Meteorology, all based in Lhasa. Norwegian members of the Network are the universities of Oslo, Bergen, Trondheim and Tromsoe, and the Institute of Applied Social Science (FAFO) in Oslo. The Norwegian Foreign Office and the Norwegian Agency for Development Cooperation (NORAD) are also represented on the Network board.

2   The SAVE-method (Surveying Architectural Values in the Environment), as developed by the Danish Ministry of Environment and Energy in 1988. Relevant publications can be found on Web-address: http://www.sns.dk (look under 'Byer og bygninger', go on to 'SAVE-systemet' and finally to 'InterSAVE' English version).

3   The resulting LHCA photo archive has several thousand images, which we wish to make available to the Lhasa authorities.

4   The UNESCO World Heritage List was established in response to the Convention concerning the Protection of the World Cultural and Natural Heritage, adopted by the United Nations Educational, Scientific and Cultural Organization, at its General Conference, Paris, 16 November 1972. In 2000 there were 630 properties – 480 cultural, 128 natural and 22 mixed in 118 countries of the 158 State Parties that have ratified the World Heritage Convention.

5   The Norwegian Council of Universities' Committee for Development Research and Education

6   The following students from the Norwegian University of Science and Technology (NTNU) took part in studies in Old Lhasa and contributed to the LHCA project: Elisabeth Baekken, Bodil Fremstad, Hege Laegreid Gangstoe, Anne-Marie Loof, Cathrine Grande, Vidar Knutsen, Jacob Munkhammar, Hilde Therese Remoey, Bodil Angard Rian, Wibeke Riise and Oeystein Rognebakke.

INTRODUCTION

1   The map is entirely redrawn in AutoCad and Adobe Illustrator after the scanning of two sets of official maps: one set of six sheets of 1 : 1 000 scale maps by the Surveying Team no.1 of Guangxi Surveying Bureau, July 1985, and one set of six sheets of 1 : 5 000 (?) scale triangulated maps by Wuhan City Surveying Institute, May 1987. Amended and supplemented by the authors.

ARCHITECTURE

1   The term is also used by Fernand Meyer.

2   These complex issues are dealt with in many specialist publications on Tibetan religion and anthropology.

3   See Mario Bussagli, ed. 1973.

4   Ibid.

5   Note for instance the active play of architectural volumes in Hindu architecture and the extraordinary external decoration and resulting architectural fragmentation of its main volumes and motifs.

6   The Jokhang's innermost kora is inside the holy central chapel, just an arm's length from the Jowo image. The second kora is called the Nangkor – it surrounds the original inner temple, today inside the Tsuglakhang (the entire temple complex). The third kora, the Barkor, some 800 m in length, encircles the Jokhang complex. The fourth kora, the Lingkor, is 7.5 km long and encircles the entire old town, Marpori and Chakpori.

   Koras are not planned structures, but rather the result of religious practice. Yet there was also a highly planned, circular, mandala-like system of sacred protective buildings surrounding the Jokhang. The four Rigsum temples, named for the four cardinal directions, were situated on a circle with a radius of about 400 m. It is likely that they were once connected by a kora.

   These koras are thus among the oldest man-made structures in Lhasa. In addition to these circuits were roads radiating out from the centre (the Jokhang) to locations outside the town. The resulting net of paths formed a highly irregular pattern before the arrival, one by one, of most of the town's later religious and secular buildings. The radiating paths can be seen to serve the functional need of bringing goods and people in and out from the central temple area, and the circular koras primarily serve the spiritual purpose of bringing worshippers into a close, geometrical – almost physical – relationship with sacred sites and objects.

7   This has also been the all-governing rule of building orientation and layout in China from the earliest examples known until very recent times.

8   See Semple 1992, p. 111.

9   See Semple 1992.

10 See Gerner 1987, p. 89.

11 Information from Minyag Chökyi Gyaltsen, senior Lhasa architect.

TOWNSCAPE

1   See Bolling-Ladegaard 1996.

2   The terms and approach described and used are based on the SAVE method.

3   In old paintings, the prayer masts are more numerous. The Potala mural (p.62) reveals 13 prayer masts around the Jokhang.

4   Shöl has never been archaeologically investigated.

5   See Waddell 1894.

6   See Richardson 1993, pp. 72–73, 75 and 78.

7   See Richardson 1993, p. 76; this shows one of the pavilions next to Doring Chima.

8   See Batchelor 1987, p. 168.

9   See Yuthok 1990.

10 See Richardson 1993, p. 28; this shows Sungchöra during the New Year Festival.

BUILDINGS

1   An exception was 'The Lhasa Archive Project', an informal NGO from Europe that helped in practical ways with the LHCA surveys. 'The Lhasa Archive Project' (LAP) later developed into the Tibet Heritage Fund.

2   See Rasmussen 1991.

3   The Potala and Jokhang are described in many other publications, though these generally lack survey drawings, as provided here.

4   An international NGO working with repair and protection of physical cultural heritage in Lhasa and Central Tibet since about 1996; see above.

5   A few buildings were surveyed specially for the LHCA project by a senior Lhasa architect, Minyag Chökyi Gyaltsen. Some of these drawings will enable interested readers to study the spatial and structural design of a complete traditional building. Contrary to European surveying traditions, Chinese-style

surveys are usually somewhat 'idealized'. Angles that 'should be' 90 degrees are drawn as such even if in reality they clearly are not when surveyed. This inevitably leads to problems when interpreting and drawing exact measurements. One example of this is the Shatra mansion main building. Although it is obvious that the northern and southern façades are not parallel, the building survey shows them as parallel. Keeping this in mind, it is still possible to extract the basic information from the drawings.

6 The source of its plan is the official Chinese map of 1987.

7 See Batchelor 1987, p. 99.

8 See Phuntsok Namgyal et al, 1994. Other books describing the restoration process, with beautiful drawings of plans, sections, façades, constructions and details, are available in Chinese.

9 See *The History of the Cultural Relics of Lhasa* 1985. The Ganden 'throne holder', Jampa Chödrak, donated a large abount of money to the Tibetan government to establish statues in the new printing house; he was commemorated after death by having his tomb there. The 13th Dalai Lama named the printing house in his honour.

10 See *The History of the Cultural Relics of Lhasa* 1985, p. 77.

11 Ibid. Tibetan books (*pecha*) are printed from woodblocks – boards of a hard wood, such as walnut, engraved on both sides. A preserved catalogue of books printed at Shöl Barkhang (eastern printing house) gives an impression of the huge amount of work performed in these productions. (The number of woodblocks is in brackets.)
    1. Tsongkhapa: Collected works. 18 volumes (7589).
    2. Gyaltsab Darma Rinchen: Collected works. 8 volumes (3029).
    3. Khetrub Gelek Palsang: Collected works. 11 volumes (5903).
    4. The biography of Tsongkhapa (337); etc.
       Many of the old wood printing blocks were destroyed during the Cultural Revolution.

12 See *The History of the Cultural Relics of Lhasa* 1985, p. 75.

13 See Chan 1994, p. 62–96. This section gives a thorough description of the major parts of the Jokhang interiors.

14 Sources of the drawings are mainly from *The Jokhang Temple* 1985 and the Tibet Heritage Fund amendments of the same material.

15 Pommaret 1996 tells the story of Songtsen Gampo's temple.

16 See *The Jokhang Temple* 1985.

17 See Chan 1994, p. 68.

18 Ibid., p. 203.

19 See *The History of the Cultural Relics of Lhasa* 1985, p. 42.

20 See Chan 1994, p. 119.

21 Ibid., p.120.

22 The chapel is today occupied by a small business for washing used glass bottles. The painted wooden constructions and ceiling are extant.

23 Traditional latrines were usually emptied twice a year, the waste mixed and used by farmers as manure for the fields.

24 This coincides with the old Vedic tradition in which the fire is always in the south-eastern corner.

25 An adaptive re-use proposal for Gorkha Nyingba was the subject of an M.Sc. in Architecture by Wibeke Riise, at NTNU Trondheim, Norway.

26 See Alexander and Azevedo 1998, vol. 1, p. 64

27 Delin Khangsar was the subject of survey for a small group of Norwegian students of architecture in 1994. They provided the base material for the presentation.

28 The 5th Dalai Lama's 'Guide to the Temple' (1645), referred to in Alexander et al. 1999, vol. 2, p. 25.

29 Batchelor 1987, p. 169.

30 Chan 1994, p. 174.

THE CONSERVATION AND FUTURE OF LHASA

1 Agricultural land in the Lhasa valley may be disappearing at a rate close to that in Nepal's Kathmandu valley, where current population growth might consume all such land within 20 years from now.

2 In numerous historical towns in Asia, the Middle East and Africa we have observed that the disappearance of private ownership has led to a breakdown of traditional maintenance and repair of both buildings and external shared spaces. This appears to happen largely as a result of reduced responsibility and security.

3 This situation may indicate potential in Lhasa for establishing contemporary housing associations in which individual members share financial and operating responsibility within the safety and shared ownership of the association.

4 Rent levels in Lhasa were very low, often only US$2–5 per year for an average-sized flat.

5 By comparison, in the Nordic countries up to 1 per cent of total cultural heritage assets may be lost each year, due to urban change, dilapidation, fire and other damage.

6 The Lhasa Development Plan 1980–2000 has been available to us as a separate volume of plans; comments here are made on main elements that focus on overall development.

7 Main conservation and planning issues: appropriate protection areas should be defined to reflect the environment and conservation needs of each monument, site or area; traditional townscape areas should be defined as 'historical and cultural streets and areas' and declared as conservation areas; conservation of the historical city should be viewed as a whole, including the city's macro-environment; the above three elements should protect the historical city, its historical areas and traditional features, and develop its traditional culture.

8 The name of the plan document (translation from Chinese) is 'The future detailed construction plan for Barkor in the City of Lhasa', prepared in 1992 by the China Institute of Urban Planning and approved by the State Council in Beijing in 1996. A revised plan for Lhasa City should now be approved or already under implementation.

9 Only two buildings were proposed for protection at state level, two at regional level and six at municipal level. Another 11 buildings received general protection status.

10 The plan describes the architectural style to be used in the old town.

11 For 13 identified cultural sites or areas, 'traditional Tibetan architectural style' must be used. Style A in the plan designates 'monasteries, noble family houses and other buildings of high artistic value'. The townscape is designated for architectural styles A and B, where 'freedom for "Traditional Tibetan style and Normal local style Tibetan building design"' is permitted for designers and authorities. In fact, most old town areas today express a mixture of styles: 'C-Tibetan-style modern building', 'D-Modern-style building with Tibetan symbols' and 'E-Modern-style building'.

12 1st level: buildings lower than 8 m, up to 2 stories and close to prime cultural sites. 2nd level: buildings lower than 15 m; building patterns and colours near conservation areas and along roads to conservation areas should be in harmony with and respect the conservation units. 3rd level: buildings lower than 21 m, to build 6 stories; architectural design is not restricted to the traditional. 4th level: special control areas in the vicinity of main cultural sites; restricted measures apply to design, topography, landforms, vegetation, streets, water-levels etc.

13 They are Karmashar temple, the four Rigsum temples (of which only two exist today), and Meru Nyingba monastery.

14 Monuments inside Lhasa City protected as national monuments are the Potala Palace, Jokhang Temple, Norbulingka Summer Palace, Drepung monastery, Sera monastery and Ganden monastery. For regional level protection, the TAR Cultural Relics Bureau has since the mid-1990s included most monastic sites, whether active or not, inside Lhasa prefecture; this is a very positive achievement.

15 Presented in 1993 to the UNESCO World Heritage Committee by the State Bureau of Cultural Relics in Beijing (now State Administration for Cultural Heritage), on behalf of the PRC, the Potala Palace was approved and inscribed in 1994 as fulfilling the criteria for inclusion:
  - criterion (i): the Potala is an outstanding work of human imagination and creativity for its design, its decoration, and its harmonious setting within a dramatic landscape;

– criterion (iv): the scale and wealth of the Potala, which represents the apogee of Tibetan architecture, make it an outstanding example of theocratic architecture, of which it was the last surviving example in the modern world;

– criterion (vi): the Potala Palace is a potent and exceptional symbol of the integration of secular and religious authority into a single entity.

16   ICOMOS, International Council on Monuments and Sites, is one of three international NGOs appointed under the UNESCO Cultural Heritage Convention of 1972 as consultative bodies. The responsibility of ICOMOS is to advise on cultural sites.

17   The World Heritage inscription (December 2000): 'The Potala Palace and the Jokhang Temple Monastery (extension of the Potala Palace)'.

18   ICOMOS assessed this proposal in March 2001 as part of its annual review of new World Heritage nominations presented to the UNESCO World Heritage Committee.

19   An important pilot project was and continues to be carried out by the Lhasa City Cultural Relics Bureau. Earlier, the Tibet Heritage Fund, an international NGO, provided assistance and funding for the repair of Lhasa old town, but it was later stopped by the authorities and is presently inactive.

20   A growing literature is expanding the international discussion on authenticity. The Venice Charter and the Nara Conference on Authenticity are among the most important documents.

21   Regional legislation: 'Regulations of Tibet Autonomous Region on the Protection and Management of Cultural Relics', adopted at the 3rd meeting of the Fifth People's Congress of TAR on 31 May 1990. National legislation: 'Law of the People's Republic of China on the Protection of Cultural Relics' was adopted at the 25th meeting of the Standing Committee of the Fifth National People's Congress and promulgated by the Standing Committee of the National People's Congress on and effective as of November 19, 1982; 'Regulations on the Management of Sites of Religious Activities', adopted by the State Council of the People's Republic of China in 1984 and effective as of February 1, 1984.

22   Central and regional authorities in China and Norway developed the proposal in conjunction with UNESCO World Heritage Centre, Paris.

Bibliography

Alexander, André and Pimpim de Azevedo. 1998. *The Old City of Lhasa. Report from a conservation project*. Lhasa: Tibet Heritage Fund.

Alexander, André et al. 1999. *Lhasa Old City*, vol. 2. Lhasa: Tibet Heritage Fund.

Algreen-Ussing, Gregers, Grethe Silding and Allan de Waal. 1992. *Byens træk. Om by- og bygnings-bevaringssystemet SAVE*. Copenhagen: Miljøministeriet, Planstyrelsen.

Batchelor, Stephen. 1987. *The Tibet Guide*. London: Wisdom Publications.

Bech-Nielsen, Gert. 1998. *SAVE – Survey of Architectural Values in the Environment. En kritisk analyse*. Copenhagen: Miljø- og Energiministeriet, Skov- og Naturstyrelsen.

Bell, Charles. 1924. *Tibet, Past and Present*. Oxford: Clarendon Press.

Bernier, Ronald M. 1997. *Himalayan Architecture*. Cranbury NJ: Associated University Presses, Inc.

Bølling-Ladegaard, Erik. 1996. *Konsekvensvurdering i bymiljøet*. Copenhagen: Kunstakademiets arkitektskole.

Booz, Elisabeth B. 1994. *Tibet*. Hong Kong: The Guidebook Company.

Brauen, Martin. 1983. *Peter Aufschnaiter: Sein Leben in Tibet*. Berwang, Tirol: Steiger Verlag.

Bussagli, Mario. 1973. *Oriental Architecture*. New York: Harry N. Abrams.

Chan, Victor. 1994. *Tibet Handbook: A Pilgrimage Guide*. Chico: Moon Publications.

Chapman, F. Spencer. 1938. *Lhasa, The Holy City*. Reprint, New Delhi: Genesis Publishing, Cosmo Edition, 1989.

Choedon, Yeshi and Dawa Norbu. 1997. *Tibet*. New Delhi: Lustre Press.

Clarke, John. 1997. *Tibet, Caught in Time*. Reading: Garnet Publishing.

Danziger, Nick. 1987. *Danziger's Travels*. London: Flamingo, HarperCollins Publishers.

Das, Sarat Chandra. 1902. *Journey to Lhasa and Central Tibet*. London: John Murray.

David-Neel, Alexandra. 1927. *My Journey to Lhasa*. New York: Harper & Brothers Publishers.

Denwood, Philip. 1971. 'Forts and Castles: An aspect of Tibetan Architecture', in *Shambala, occasional papers of the Institute of Tibetan Studies*, N. 1, pp. 7–17. Tring.

——. 1975. 'Brackets in the Architecture of Buddhist Central Asia', in *Art and Archaeology Research Papers*, 7, June, pp. 56–63. London.

——. 1980. 'Introduction to Tibetan Architecture', in *Tibet News Review*, vol. 1, n. 2, pp. 3–12.

Essen, Gerd-Wolfgang and Tashi Thingo Tsering. 1989. *Die Götter des Himalaya, Buddhistische Kunst Tibets*. Munich: Prestel-Verlag.

Fisher, Robert E. 1993. *Buddhist Art and Architecture*, London: Thames and Hudson.

——. 1997. *Art of Tibet*. London: Thames and Hudson.

Francke, A. H. *Antiquities of Indian Tibet*, vols. 1 and 2. Calcutta and New Delhi: Asian Eduational Services.

——. 1995. *A history of western Tibet*. Dehli: Asian Educational Services.

Gerner, Manfred. 1987. *Architekturen im Himalaja*. Stuttgart: Deutsche Verlags-Anstalt.

Goldstein, Melvyn C. 1989. *A History of Modern Tibet, 1913–1951*. Berkeley: University of California Press.

Goldstein, Melvyn C., Willian Siebenschuh and Tashi Tsering. 1997. *The Struggle for Modern Tibet. The Autobiography of Tashi Tsering*. Armonk NY: M.E. Sharpe.

Grünwedel, A. 1919. *Die Tempel von Lhasa*. Heidelberg: Sitrungsberichte der Heidelberger Akademia der Wissenschaften.

Gyurme, Dorje. 1996. *Tibet Handbook*. Bath: Footprint Handbooks.

Harrer, Heinrich. 1954. *Seven Years in Tibet*. New York: E.P. Dutton.

——. 1980. *Ladakh: gods and mortals behind the Himalayas*. Innsbruck: Pinguin Verlag.

——. 1983. *Return to Tibet*. Hammondsworth: Penguin Books.

——. 1992. *Lost Lhasa, Heinrich Harrer's Tibet*. New York: Abrams and Summit Publications.

Hedin, Sven. 1954 (reprint). *Forunderlige Tibet*. Oslo: Familiens boksamling, Najonalförlaget AS.

Held, Suzanne. 1987–88. *The Monasteries of the Himalayas*. New Delhi: B I Publications.

Henss, Michael. 1981. *Tibet. Die Kulturdenkmaler*. Zürich:

Hicks, Roger. 1988. *Hidden Tibet, The Land and Its People*. Shaftsbury, Devon: Element Books.

Hummel, Siegbert. 1956. 'Wen Waren die Erbauer der Tibetischen Burgen?', in *Paideuma*, VI, 4, pp. 205–9.

——. 1960. 'Der Bauplatz der Kathedrale von Lhasa und seine Kosmologishe Bedeutung', in *Kairos*, pp. 240–44.

——. 1963–64. 'Tibetische Architektur', in *Bulletin der Schwizerischen Gesellschaft für Anthropologie und Ethnologie*, 40, pp. 62–95.

——. 1965. 'Die Kathedrale von Lhasa', in *Antaios*, VII, 3, pp. 289–90.

Kirkegaard, Jens, Allan Tønnesen and Knud Vaaben. 1993. *Vejledning. Kortlægning og registrering af byers og bygningers bevaringsværdier og udarbejdelse af kommuneatlas. SAVE*. Copenhagen: Miljøministeriet, Skov- og Naturstyrelsen.

Landon, Perceval. 1905. *Lhasa*, 2 vols., London: Hurst and Blackett Ltd.

Leckie, Scott. 1994. *Destruction by design: Housing rights violations in Tibet*. The Netherlands: Centre on Housing Rights and Evictions (COHRE).

Lhalungpa, Lobsang P. 1983. *Tibet: The Sacred Realm, Photographs 1880–1950*. New York: Aperture.

Müller, Claudius C. and Walter Raunig. 1982. *Der Weg zum Dach der Welt*. Innsbruck: Pinguin-Verlag.

Norbu, Jamyang and W.D Shakabpa. 1995. *Map and Index of Lhasa City*. Dharamsala: Amnye Machen Institute.

Pommaret, Françoise. 1996. *Lhassa, Lieu du Divin (La Capitale des Dalai Lama)*. Geneva: Editions Olizane.

Proceedings of 4th Seminar of the International Association of Tibetan Studies, Munich 1985. 1988. Munich: Tibetan Studies, Studia Tibetica.

Rajesh, M. N. and Thomas L. Kelly. *The Buddhist Monastery*. New Delhi: Lustre Press.

Rasmussen, Steen Eiler. 1991 (reprint). *Byer og bygninger II*. Aarhus: Aarhus arkitektskole.

Rhie, Marylin M. and Robert A. F. Thurman. 1991. *Wisdom and Compassion, The Sacred Art of Tibet*. London: Thames and Hudson.

Richardson, Hugh. 1993. *Ceremonies of the Lhasa Year*. London: Serindia Publications.

Rockhill, W. Woodville. 'Tibet' (2 articles). *Journal of the Royal Asiatic Society*, Jan and Apr, 1891. London.

Sandberg, S.L. Graham. 1901. *An Itinerary of the route from Sikkim to Lhasa*. Calcutta: Baptist Mission Press.

Semple, William. 1992. 'Symbolism and Ritual in Tibetan Architecture', in *Chö Yang: The Voice of Tibetan Religion and Culture*, no. 5. Dharamsala: Department of Religion and Culture, Gangchen Kyishong.

Shakabpa, W.D. 1967. *Tibet, A Political History*. Reprint, New York: Potala Publications, 1984.

Shakya, Tsering. 1999. *The Dragon in the Land of Snows*. London: Pimlico.

Sís, Vladimir and Josef Vanis. 1956. *Der Weg nach Lhasa*. Prague.

Snellgrove, David and Hugh Richardson. 1986. *A Cultural History of Tibet*. Boston: Shambhala.

Snellgrove, David and Tadeusz Skorupski. 1980. *The cultural heritage of Ladakh*, vols. 1 and 2. Warminster: Aris & Phillips.

Stein, Rolf A. 1972. *Tibetan Civilization*. London: Faber.

Stierlin, Henri and Michele Pirazzoli-t'Serstevens. *China, Architecture of the World*. Lausanne: Benedikt Taschen.

Stierlin, Henri and Andreas Volwahsen. *India, Architecture of the World*. Lausanne: Benedikt Taschen.

Sun, Jie, ed. 1990. *Tibet, Land of mystery*. Beijing: Morning Glory Publishers.

Thomas, Lowell. 1998 (reprint). *Out of this world, across the Himalayas to forbidden Tibet*. New Delhi: Cosmo Publications.

Thubten, L.G. 1979. *Gateway to the Temple. Manual of Tibetan Monastic Customs, Art, Building and Celebrations.* Kathmandu: Ratna Pustak Bhandar.

Tønnesen, Allan. 1995. *InterSAVE.* Copenhagen: Ministry of Environment and Energy, National Forest and Nature Agency.

Tu, Shungeng. 1983. 'Architecture in Tibet', in *China Building Selection*, pp. 1–10. Beijing.

Tucci, Giuseppe. 1967. *Tibet, Land of Snows*. London: Paul Elek Ltd.

——. 1973. *Transhimalaya*. Geneva: Nagel Publishers.

——. 1983. *To Lhasa and Beyond*. Ithaca: Snow Lion Publications.

Tung, Rosemary Jones. 1980. *A Portrait of Lost Tibet*. London: Thames and Hudson.

Vanis, Josef, Vladimir Sís, Josef Kolmas and Per Kvaerne. 1997. *Recalling Tibet*. Oslo: Institute for Comparative Research in Human Culture and Prague: Práh Press.

Vergara, Paola, Gilles Béguin et al. 1987. *Dimore Umane, Santuari Divini. Origini, sviluppo e diffusione dell'architettura tibetana. Demeures des Hommes, Sanctuaires des Dieux. Sources, développement et rayonnement de l'architecture tibétaine.* Rome: Università di Roma «La Sapienza», Dipartimento di Studi Orientali.

Vitali, Roberto. 1990. *Early Temples of Central Tibet*. Serindia Publications, London.

Waddell, L. Austine. 1894. *The Buddhism of Tibet*. Reprint, Cambridge: W. Heffer & Sons, 1934.

——. 1905. *Lhasa and Its Mysteries*. Reprint, New York: Dover Publications, Inc. 1988.

Walsh, E.H.C. 1938. 'The image of Buddha in the Jo-wo khang temple at Lhasa', in *Journal of the Royal Asiatic Society*. London.

Yeshe De Project. 1986. *Ancient Tibet*. Berkeley: Dharma Publishing.

Younghusband, Francis. 1910. *India and Tibet*. New Lonson: John Murray.

Yuthok, Dorje Yudon. 1990. *House of the Turquoise Roof.* Ithaca: Snow Lion Publications.

Zhang, Wenbin. 1999. *Jokhang Temple Monastery. The Potala Palace renominated as the Potala Palace and the Jokhang Temple Monastery for inscription on the World Heritage List*. Beijing: State Administration of Cultural Heritage.

Zwalf, Vladimir. 1981. *Heritage of Tibet*. London: British Museum Publications.

BOOKS IN CHINESE (ENGLISH TITLES)

Chinese Institute of Urban Planning. 1992–96. *The Barkor Conservation Plan*. Beijing.

Cultural Relics Management Committee of TAR. 1985. *The History of the Cultural Relics of Lhasa.* Lhasa.

Jam, Yang et al. 1996. *Chinese Ancient Constructions: Potala Palace in Tibet*, vols. 1 and 2. Beijing: Cultural Relics Publishing House.

Namgyal, Phuntsok et al. 1994. *Report on the repairs on the Potala Palace in Tibet*. Beijing: Cultural Relics Publishing House.

Nan, Hui, ed. 1995. *The Potala Palace of Lhasa*. Beijing: China Esperanto Press.

Su, Bai. 1996. *Archaeological studies on the monasteries of Tibetan Buddhism*. Beijing: Cultural Relics Publishing House.

TAR Lhasa City Planning Office. 1982. *Plans for Lhasa City*. Beijing: Cartographic Institute.

Tibetan Administrative Office of the Potala, ed. 1996. *The Potala, holy palace in the snow land*. Beijing: China Travel and Tourism Press.

Zhang, Shishun et al. 1985. *The Jokhang Temple*. Beijing: China Architecture and Industry Publishing House.

Index